A Centaur's Life

18

PRESENTED BY

KEI MURAYAMA

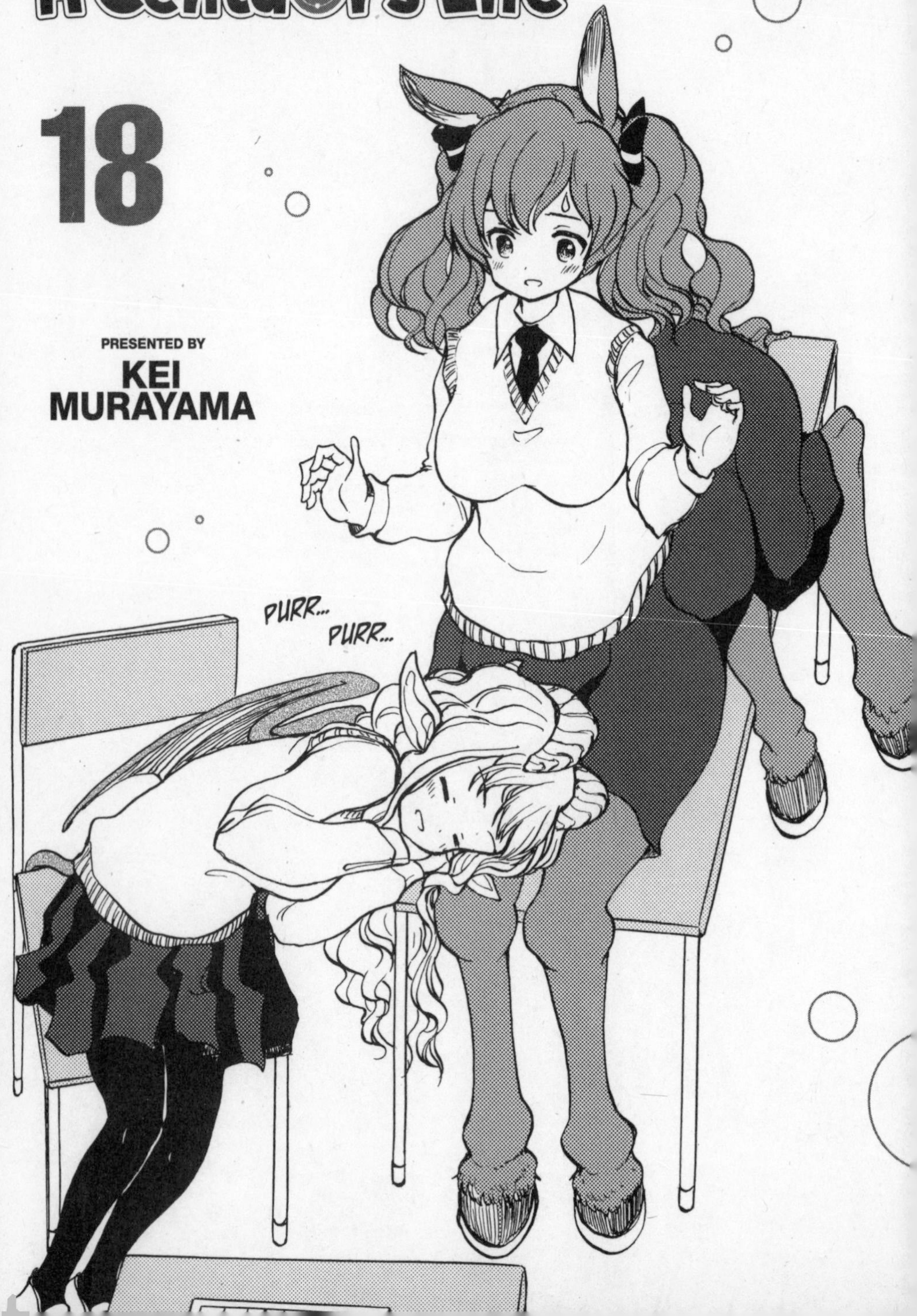
PURR...
PURR...

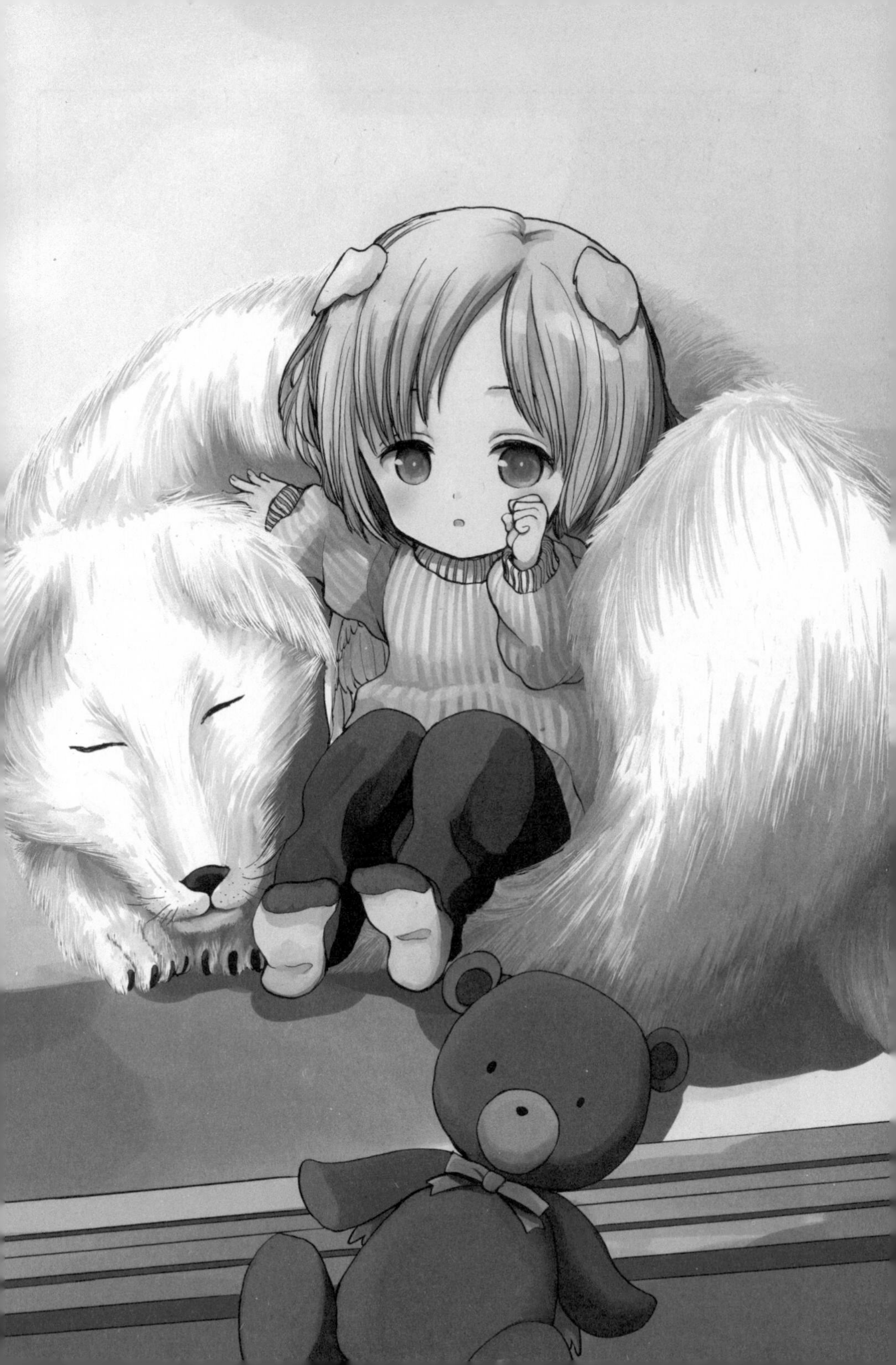

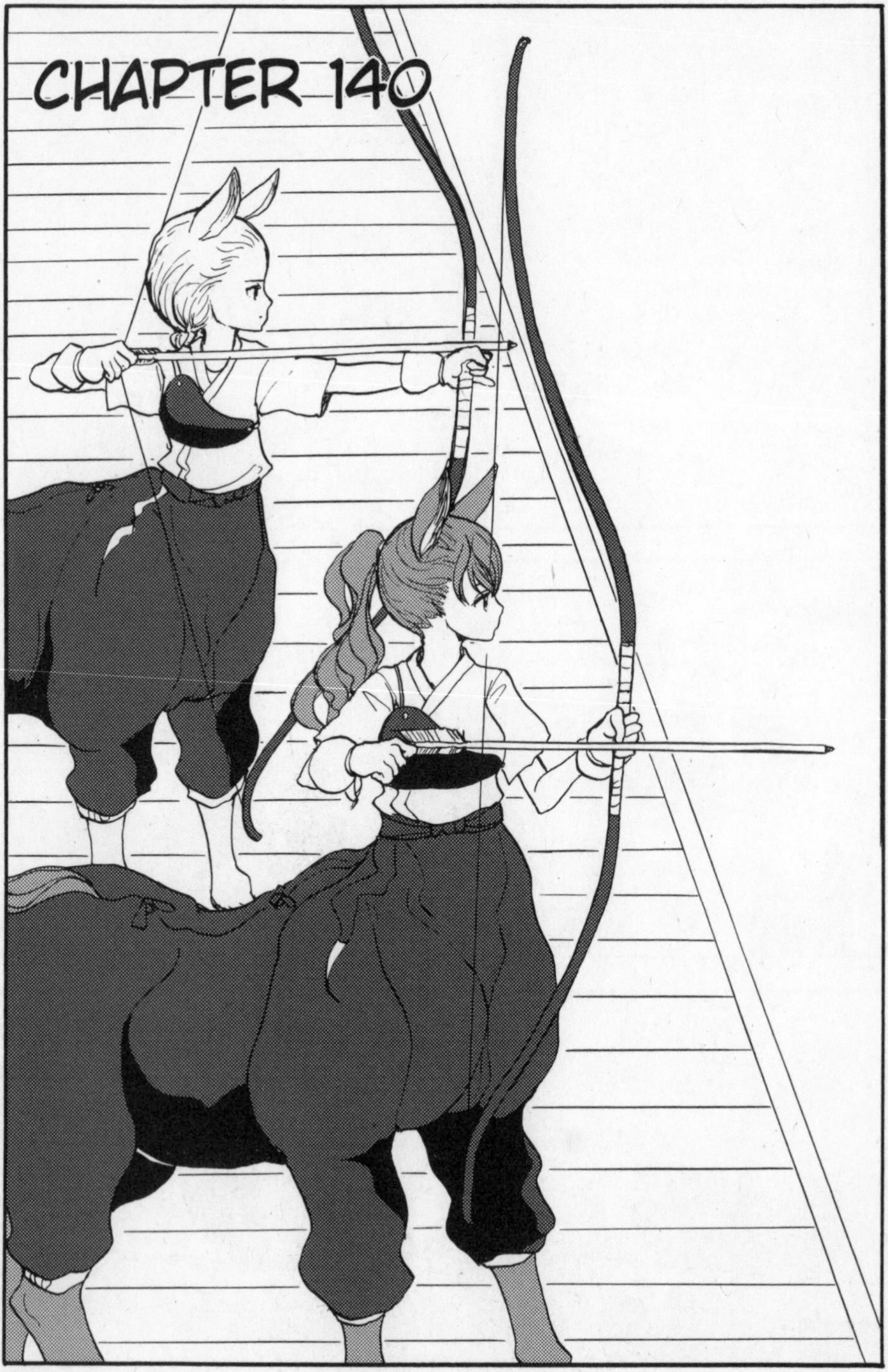
CHAPTER 140

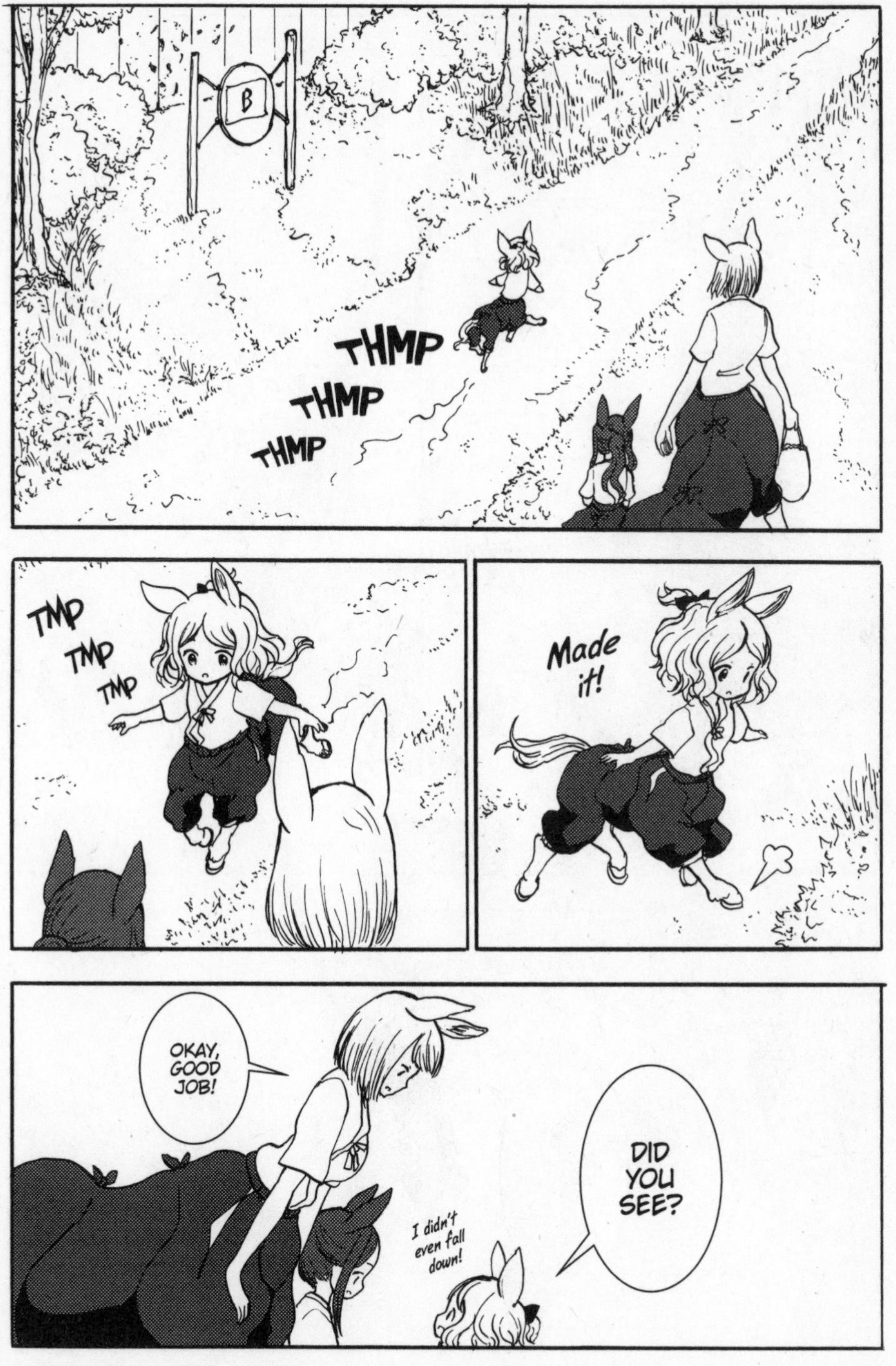
THMP
THMP
THMP
Made it!
TMP
TMP
TMP
DID YOU SEE?
I didn't even fall down!
OKAY, GOOD JOB!

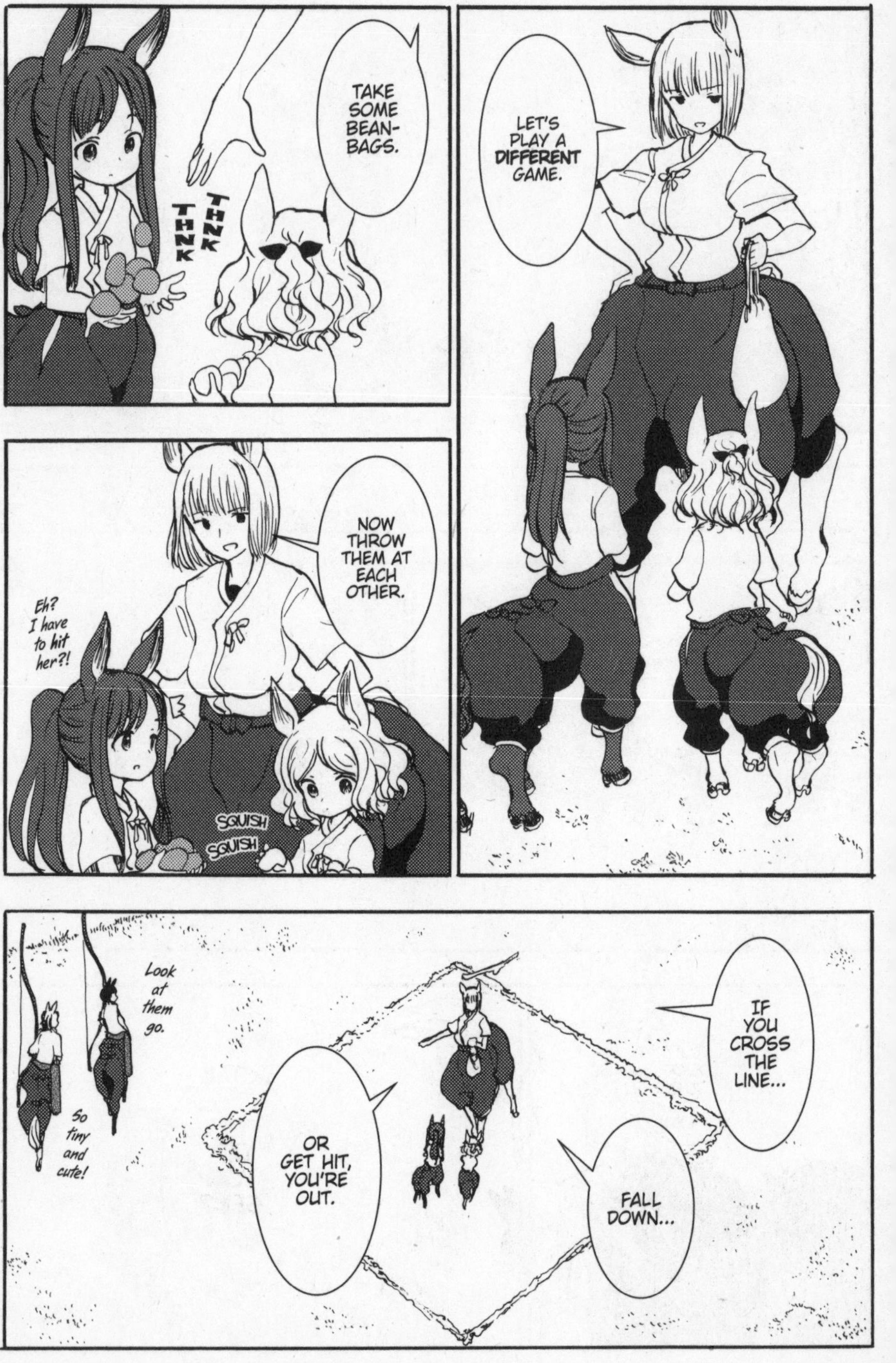
LET'S PLAY A DIFFERENT GAME.
TAKE SOME BEAN-BAGS.
THNK THNK
NOW THROW THEM AT EACH OTHER.
Eh? I have to hit her?!
SQUISH SQUISH
IF YOU CROSS THE LINE...
FALL DOWN...
OR GET HIT, YOU'RE OUT.
Look at them go.
So tiny and cute!

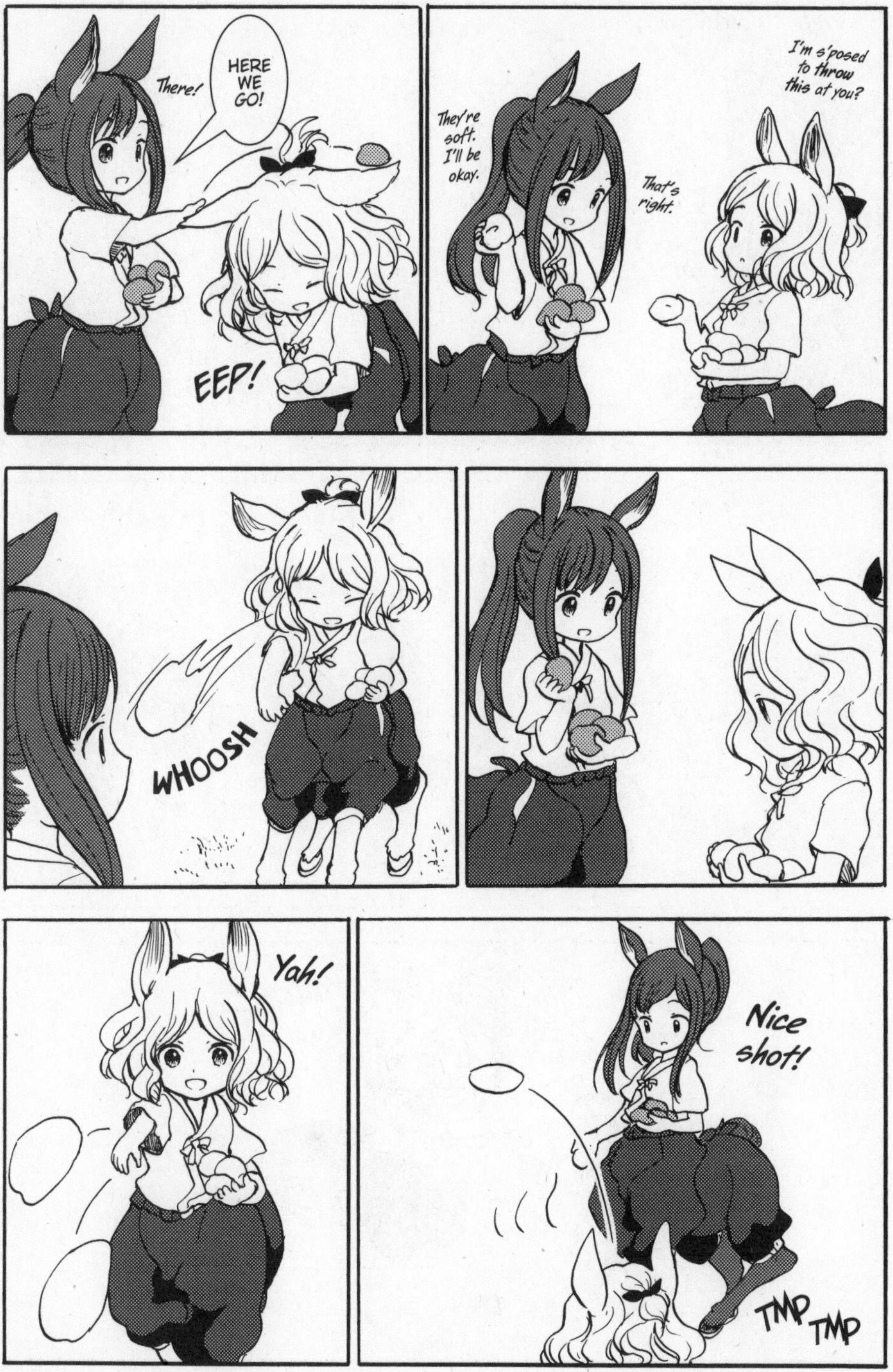
I'm s'posed to throw this at you?
That's right.
They're soft. I'll be okay.
HERE WE GO!
There!
EEP!
WHOOSH
Nice shot!
TMP TMP
Yah!

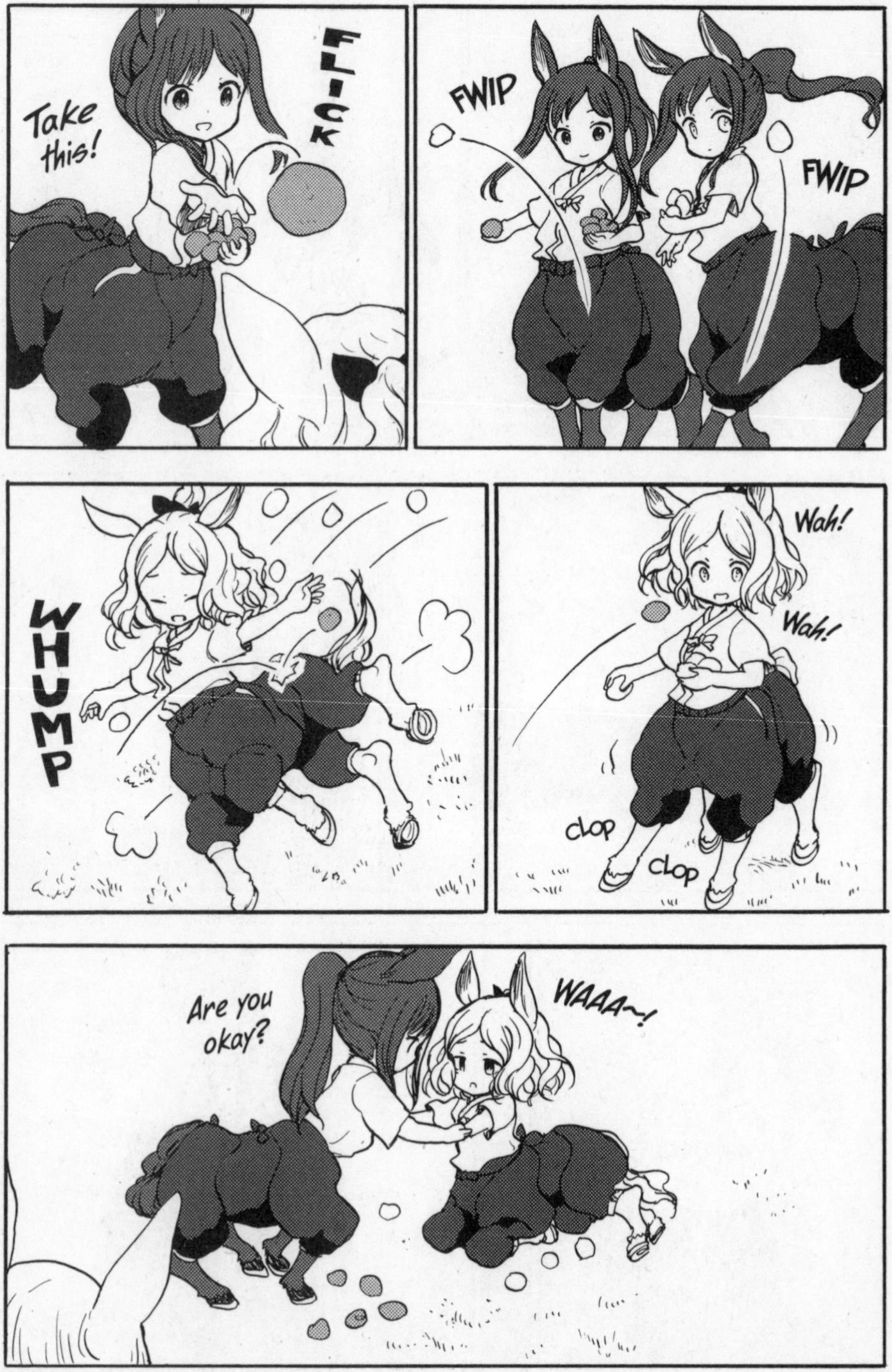
FWIP
FWIP
FLICK
Take this!
Wah!
Wah!
Clop
Clop
WHUMP
WAAA~!
Are you okay?

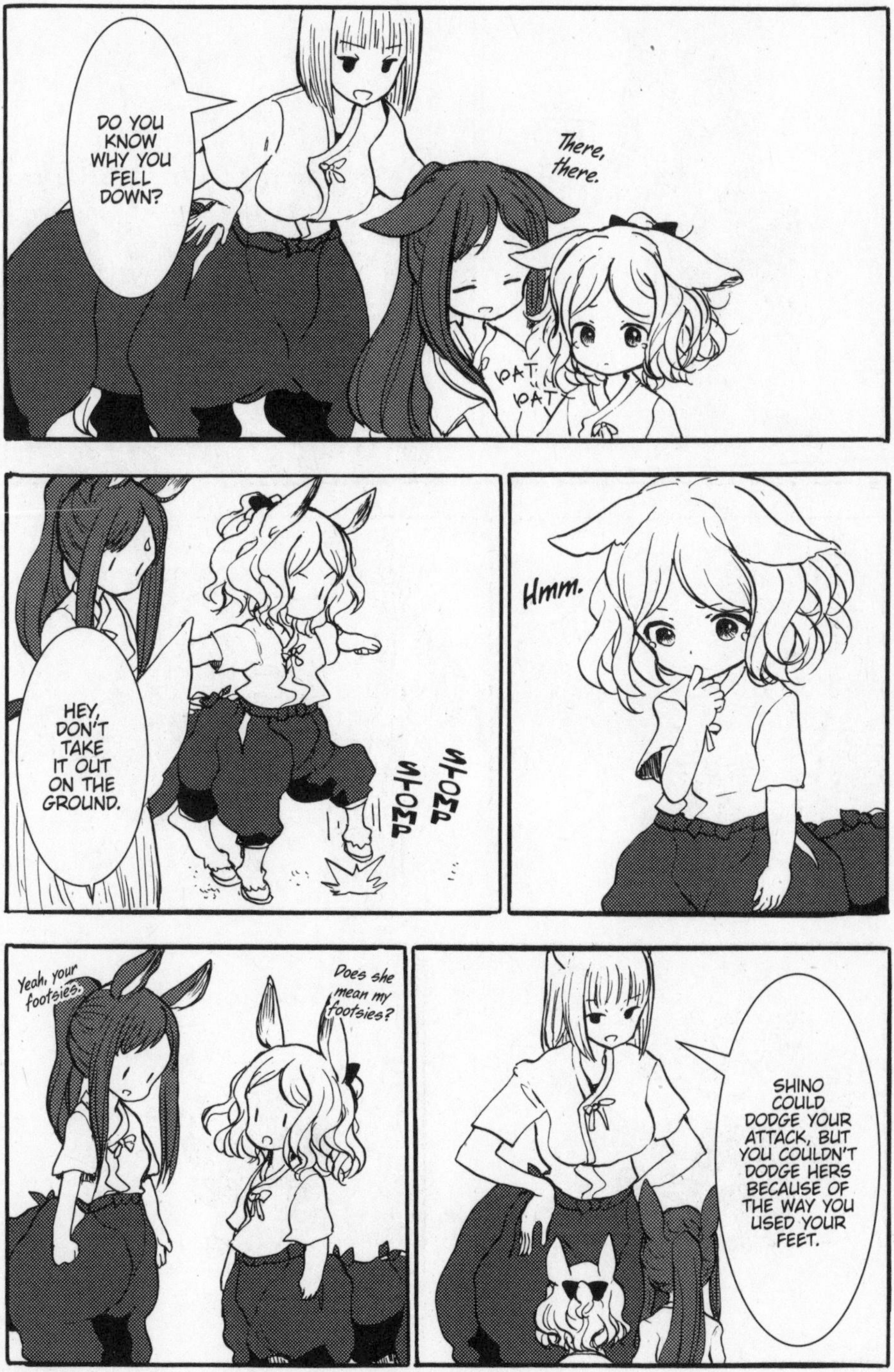
DO YOU KNOW WHY YOU FELL DOWN?
There, there.
PAT PAT
Hmm.
STOMP STOMP
HEY, DON'T TAKE IT OUT ON THE GROUND.
SHINO COULD DODGE YOUR ATTACK, BUT YOU COULDN'T DODGE HERS BECAUSE OF THE WAY YOU USED YOUR FEET.
Does she mean my footsies?
Yeah, your footsies.

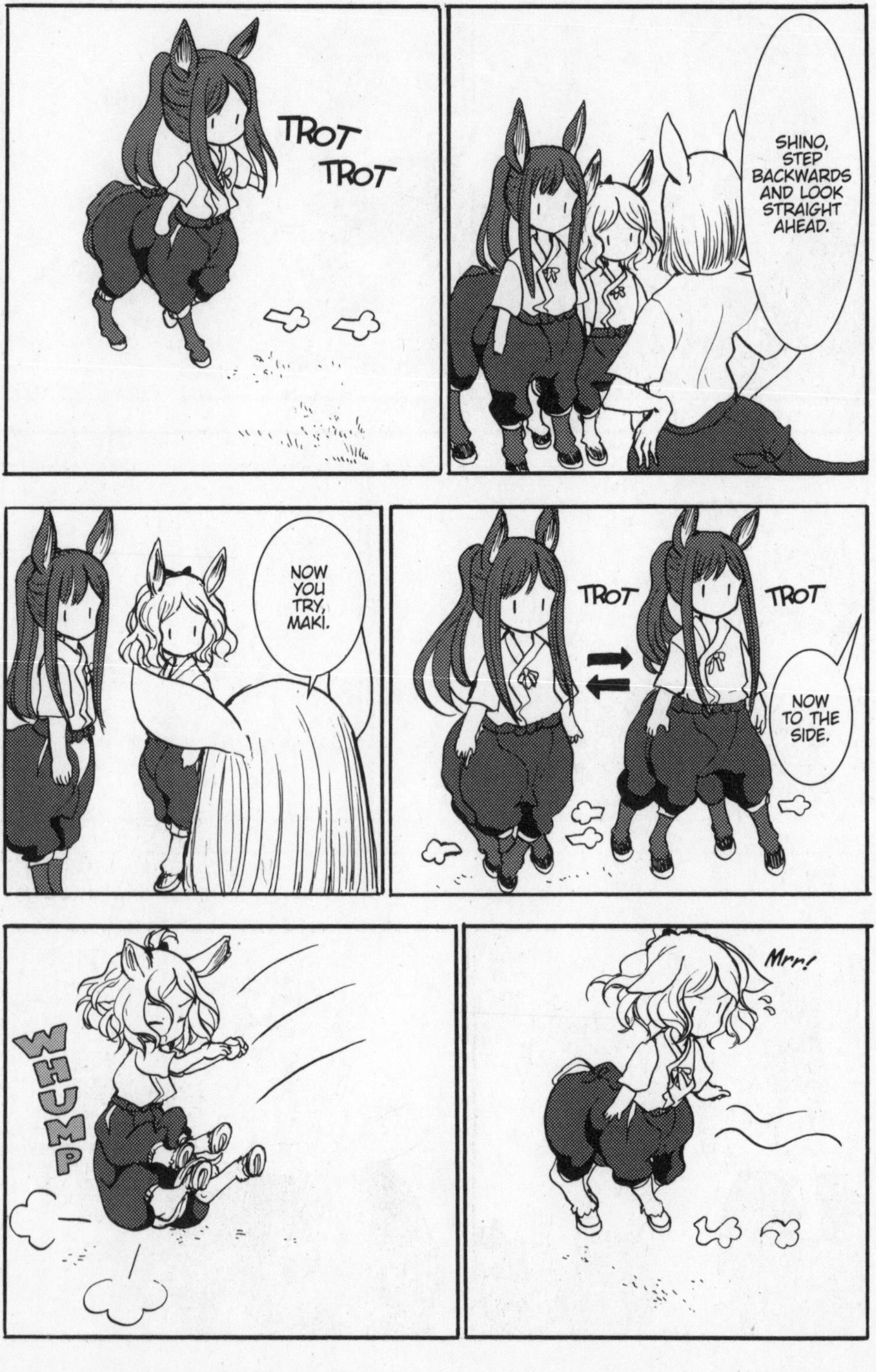
SHINO, STEP BACKWARDS AND LOOK STRAIGHT AHEAD.
TROT TROT
TROT
TROT
NOW TO THE SIDE.
NOW YOU TRY, MAKI.
Mrr!
WHUMP

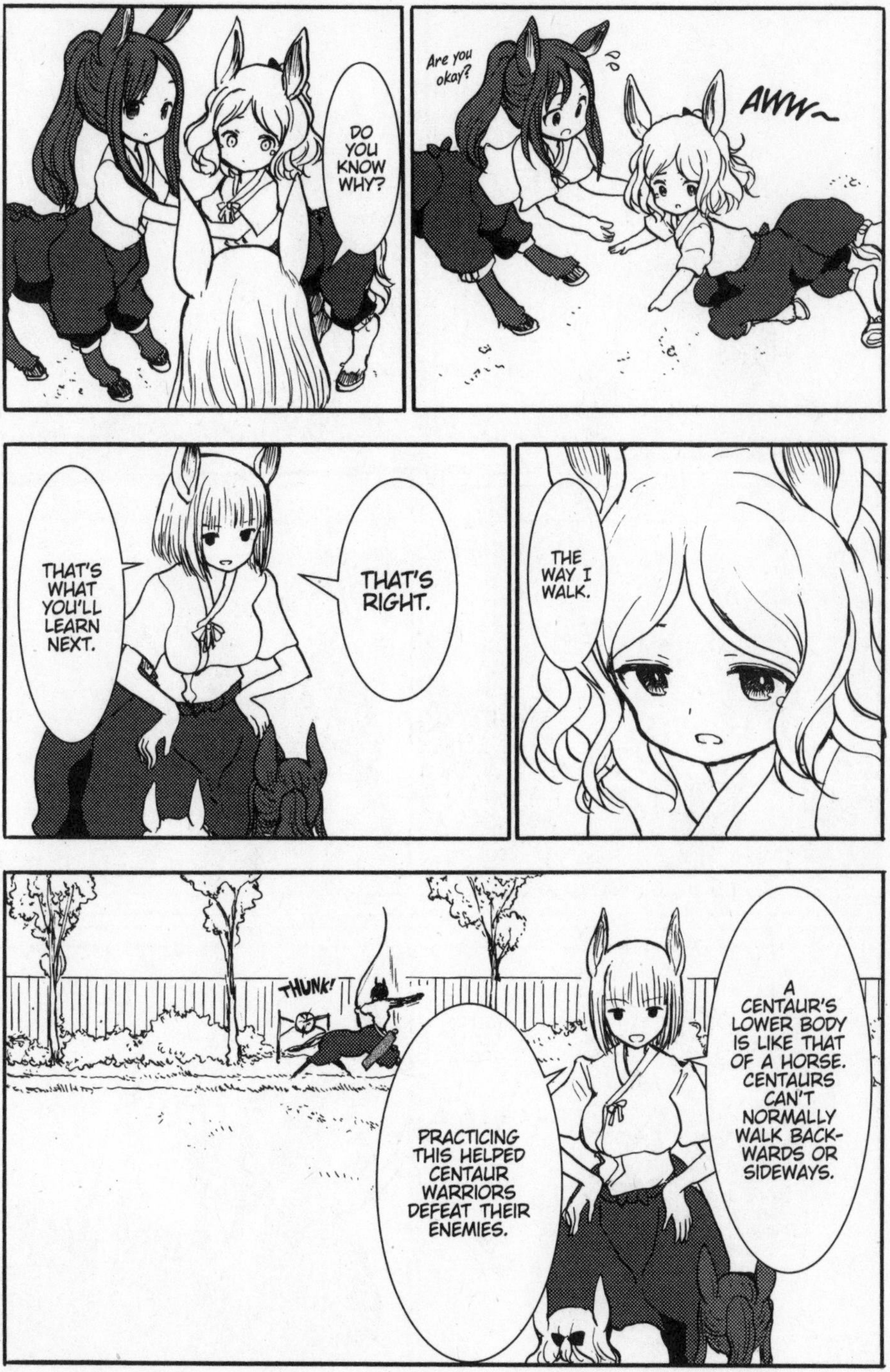
Are you okay?
AWW~
DO YOU KNOW WHY?
THE WAY I WALK.
THAT'S RIGHT.
THAT'S WHAT YOU'LL LEARN NEXT.
A CENTAUR'S LOWER BODY IS LIKE THAT OF A HORSE. CENTAURS CAN'T NORMALLY WALK BACK-WARDS OR SIDEWAYS.
PRACTICING THIS HELPED CENTAUR WARRIORS DEFEAT THEIR ENEMIES.
THUNK!

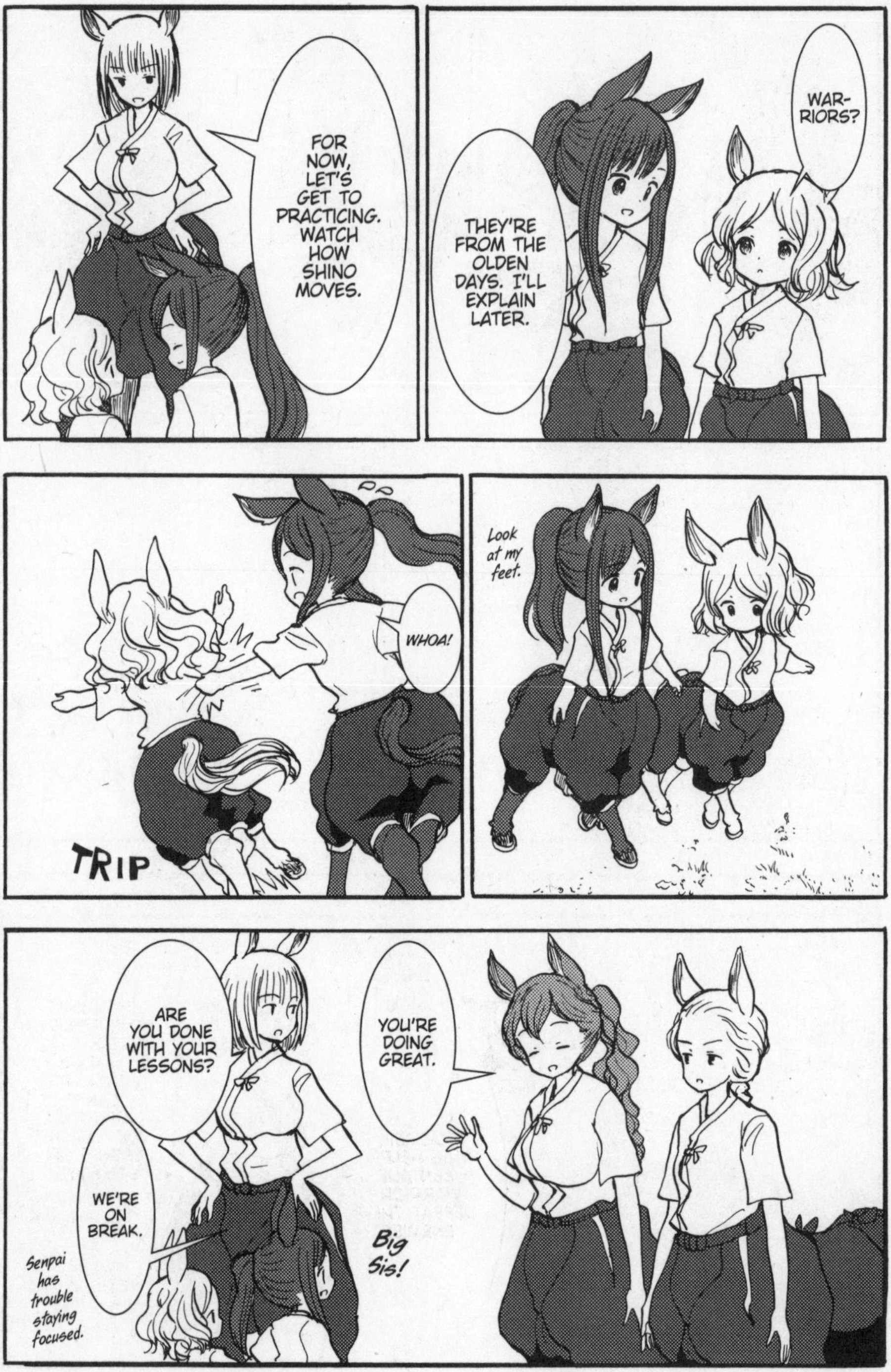
WAR-RIORS?
THEY'RE FROM THE OLDEN DAYS. I'LL EXPLAIN LATER.
FOR NOW, LET'S GET TO PRACTICING. WATCH HOW SHINO MOVES.
Look at my feet.
WHOA!
TRIP
YOU'RE DOING GREAT.
ARE YOU DONE WITH YOUR LESSONS?
Big Sis!
WE'RE ON BREAK.
Senpai has trouble staying focused.

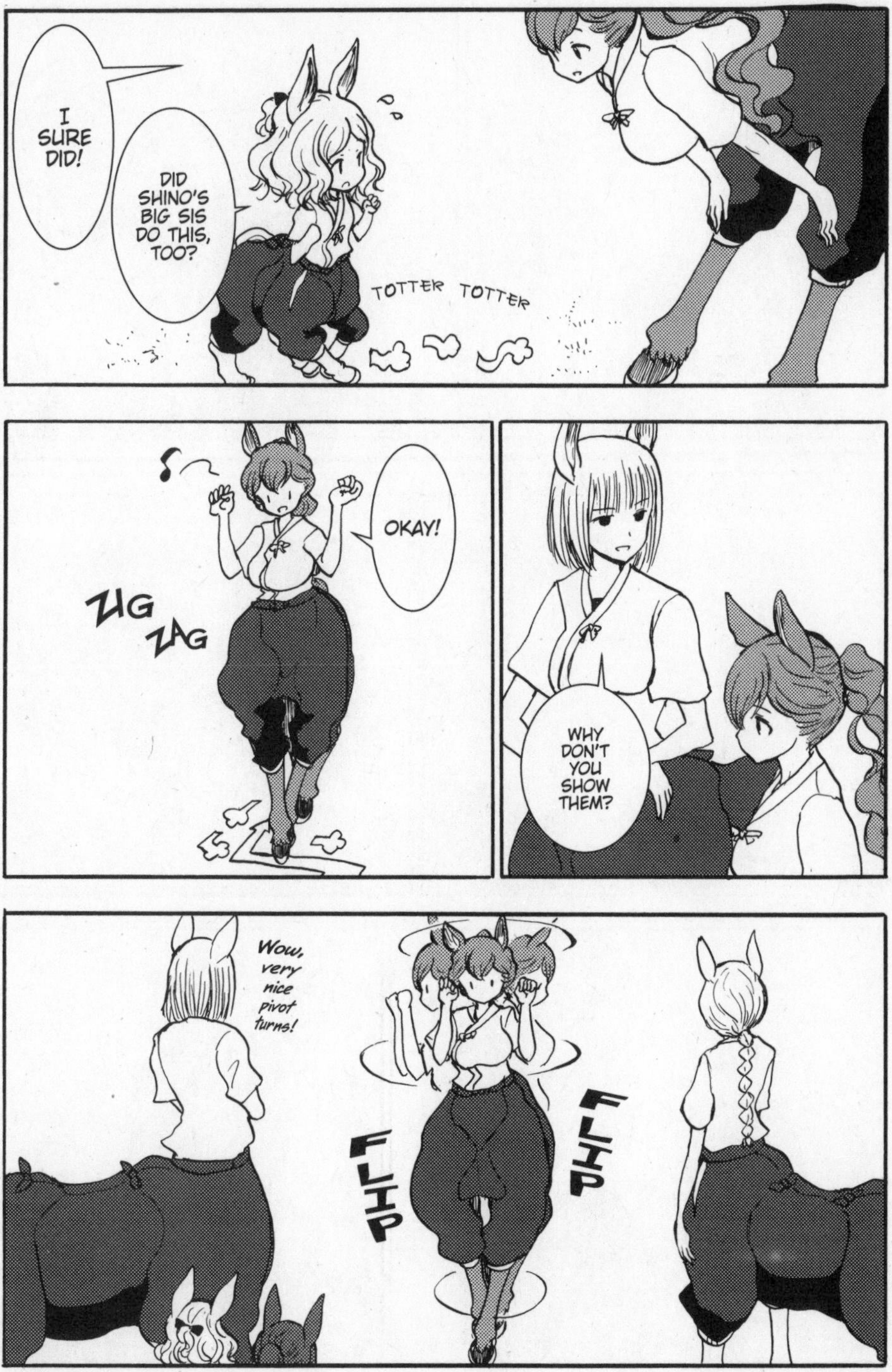
DID SHINO'S BIG SIS DO THIS, TOO?
I SURE DID!
TOTTER TOTTER
WHY DON'T YOU SHOW THEM?
OKAY!
ZIG ZAG
Wow, very nice pivot turns!
FLIP
FLIP

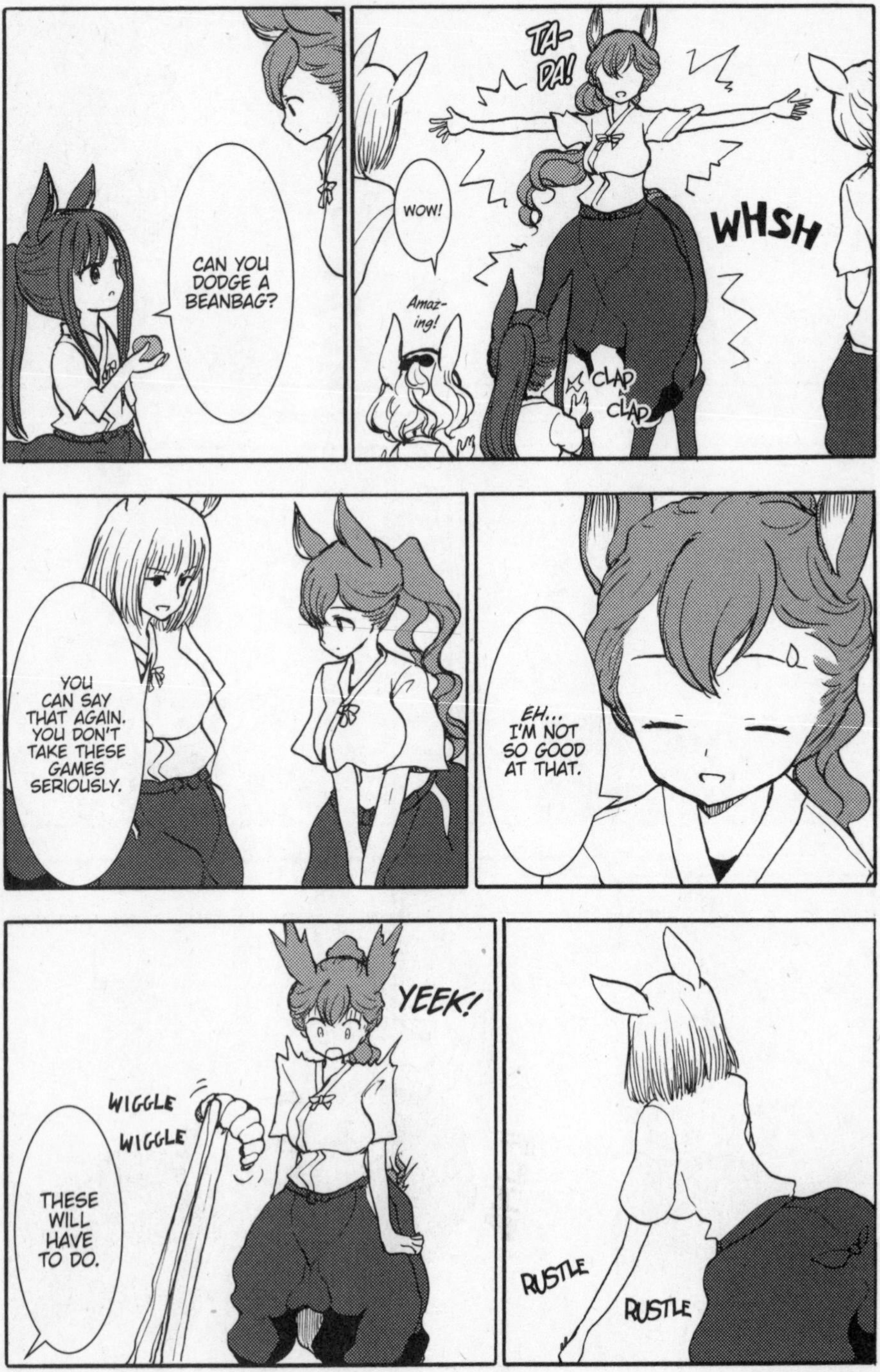
TA-DA!
WHSH
WOW!
Amaz-ing!
CLAP CLAP
CAN YOU DODGE A BEANBAG?
EH... I'M NOT SO GOOD AT THAT.
YOU CAN SAY THAT AGAIN. YOU DON'T TAKE THESE GAMES SERIOUSLY.
RUSTLE
RUSTLE
YEEK!
WIGGLE WIGGLE
THESE WILL HAVE TO DO.

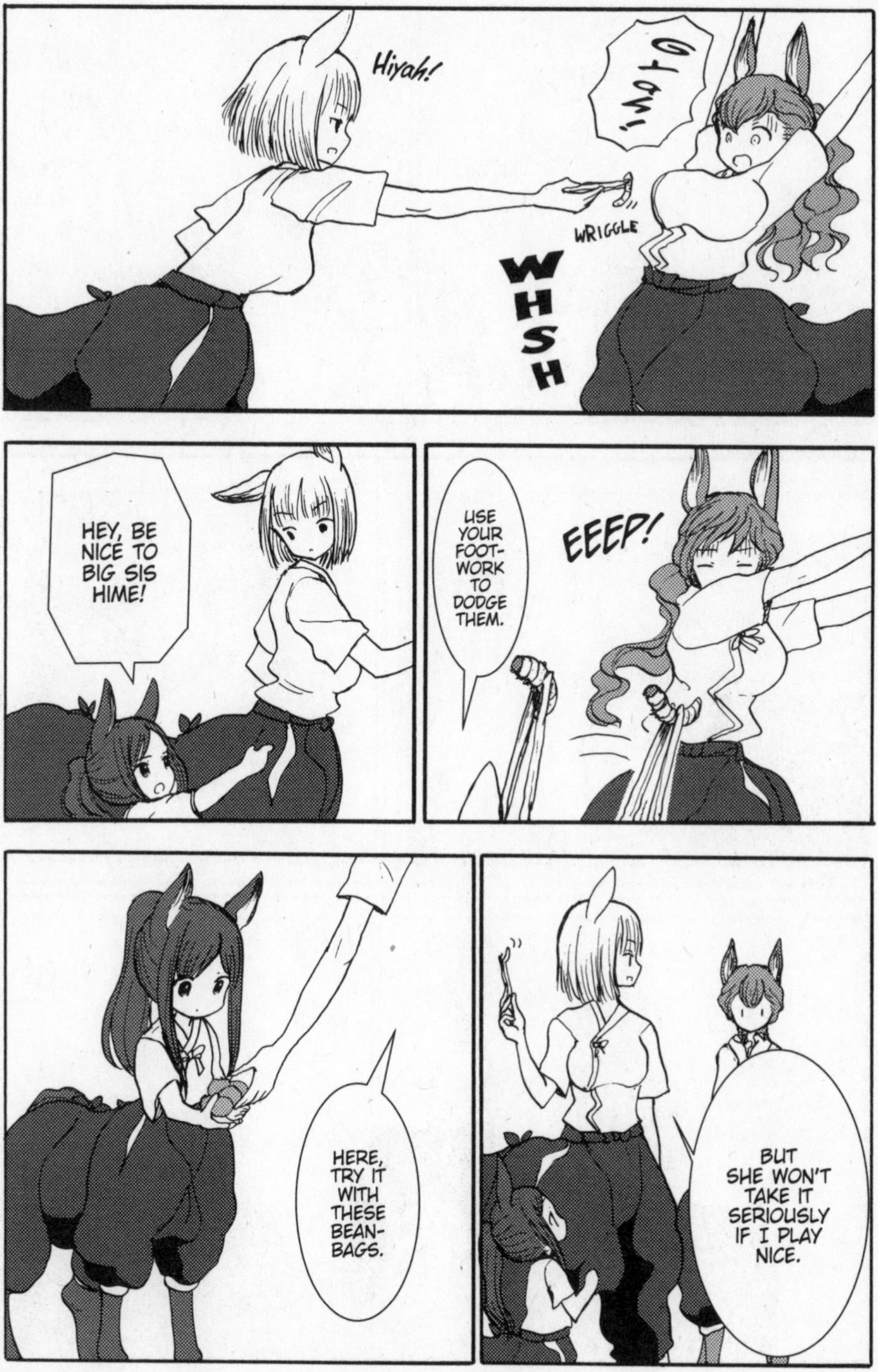
GYAH!
Hiyah!
WRIGGLE
WHSH
EEEP!
USE YOUR FOOT-WORK TO DODGE THEM.
HEY, BE NICE TO BIG SIS HIME!
BUT SHE WON'T TAKE IT SERIOUSLY IF I PLAY NICE.
HERE, TRY IT WITH THESE BEAN-BAGS.

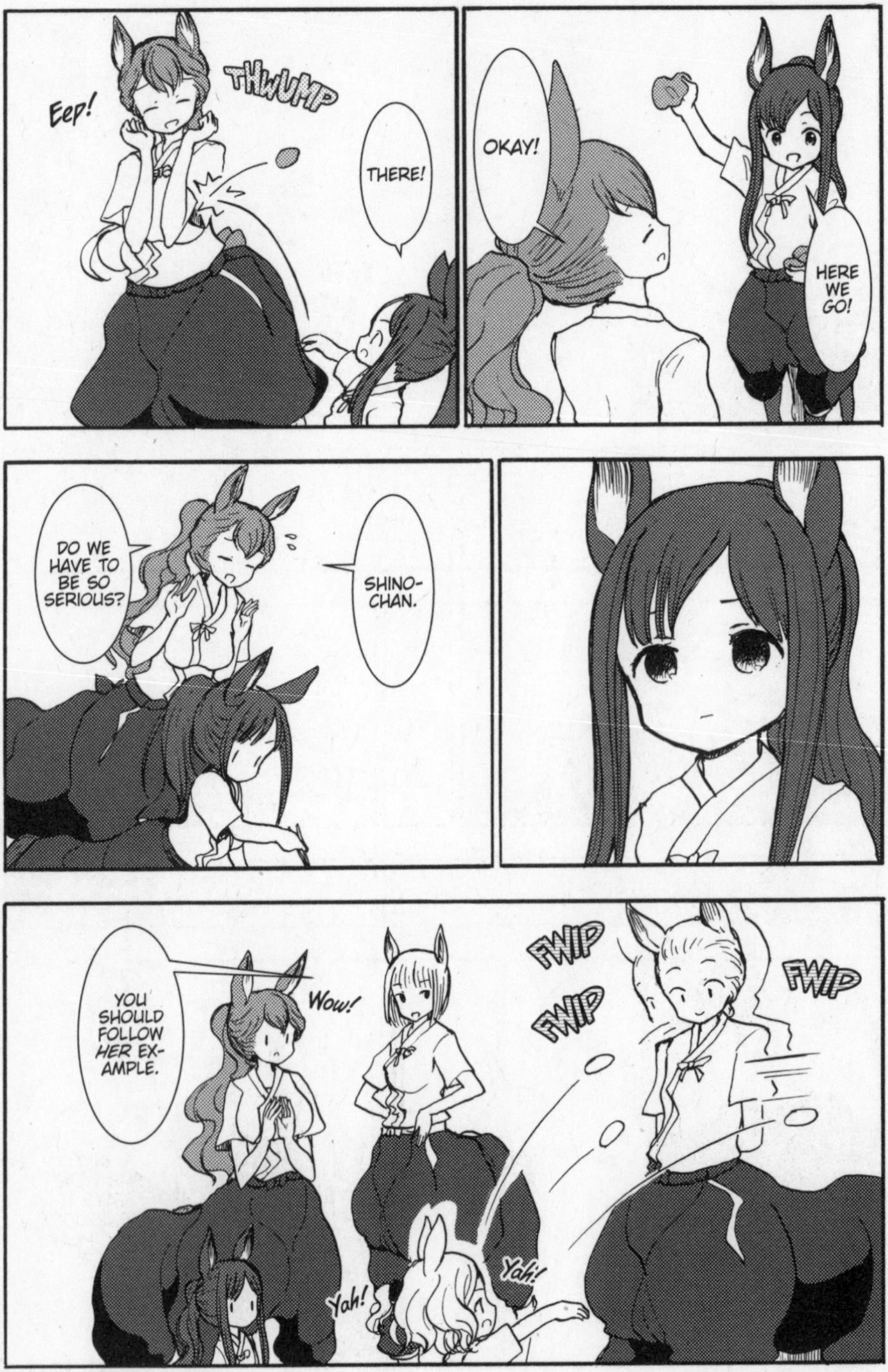
HERE WE GO!
OKAY!
THERE!
THWUMP
Eep!
SHINO-CHAN.
DO WE HAVE TO BE SO SERIOUS?
FWIP
FWIP
FWIP
Wow!
YOU SHOULD FOLLOW *HER* EX-AMPLE.
Yah!
Yah!

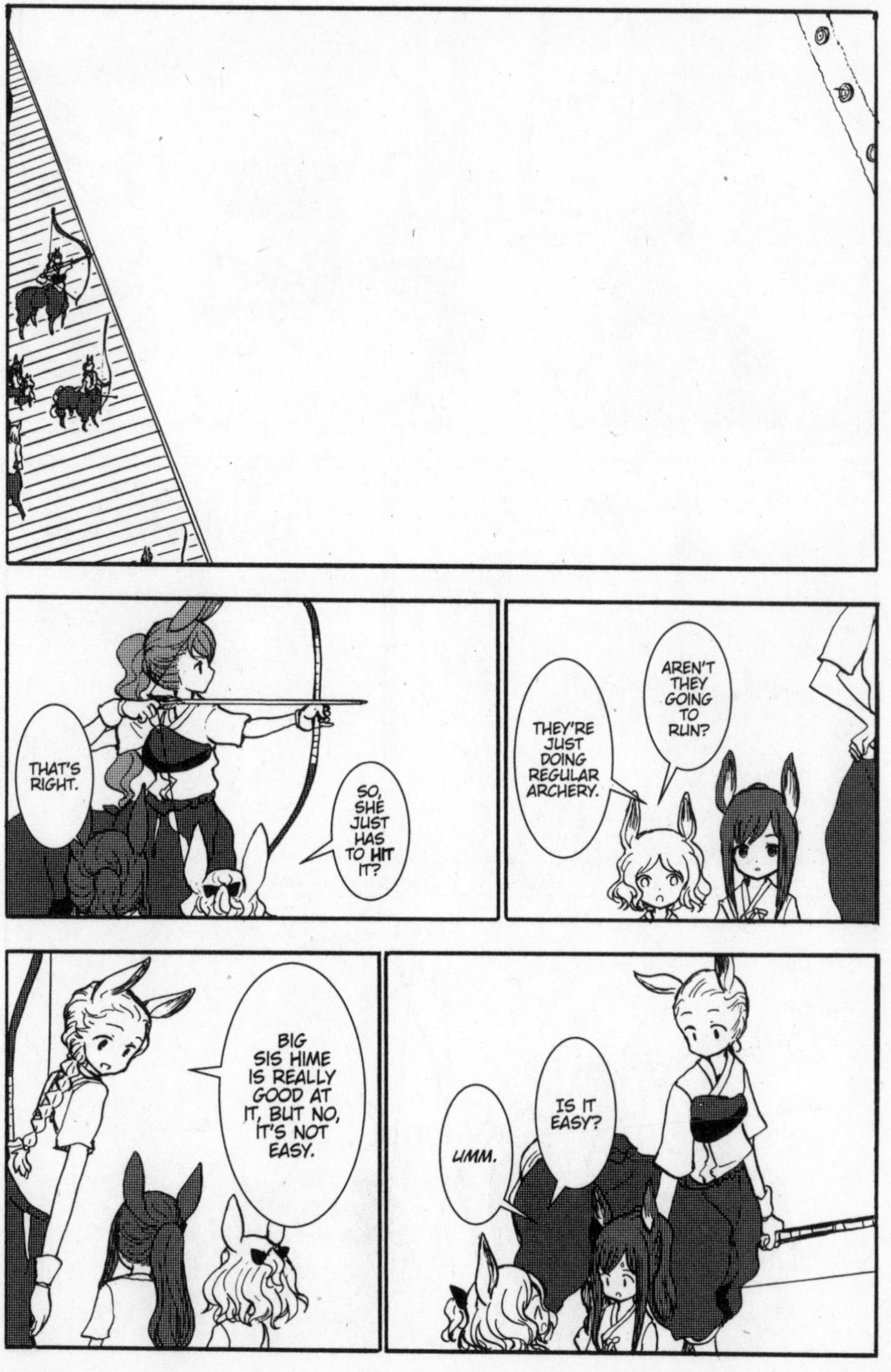
AREN'T THEY GOING TO RUN?
THEY'RE JUST DOING REGULAR ARCHERY.
SO, SHE JUST HAS TO HIT IT?
THAT'S RIGHT.
IS IT EASY?
UMM.
BIG SIS HIME IS REALLY GOOD AT IT, BUT NO, IT'S NOT EASY.

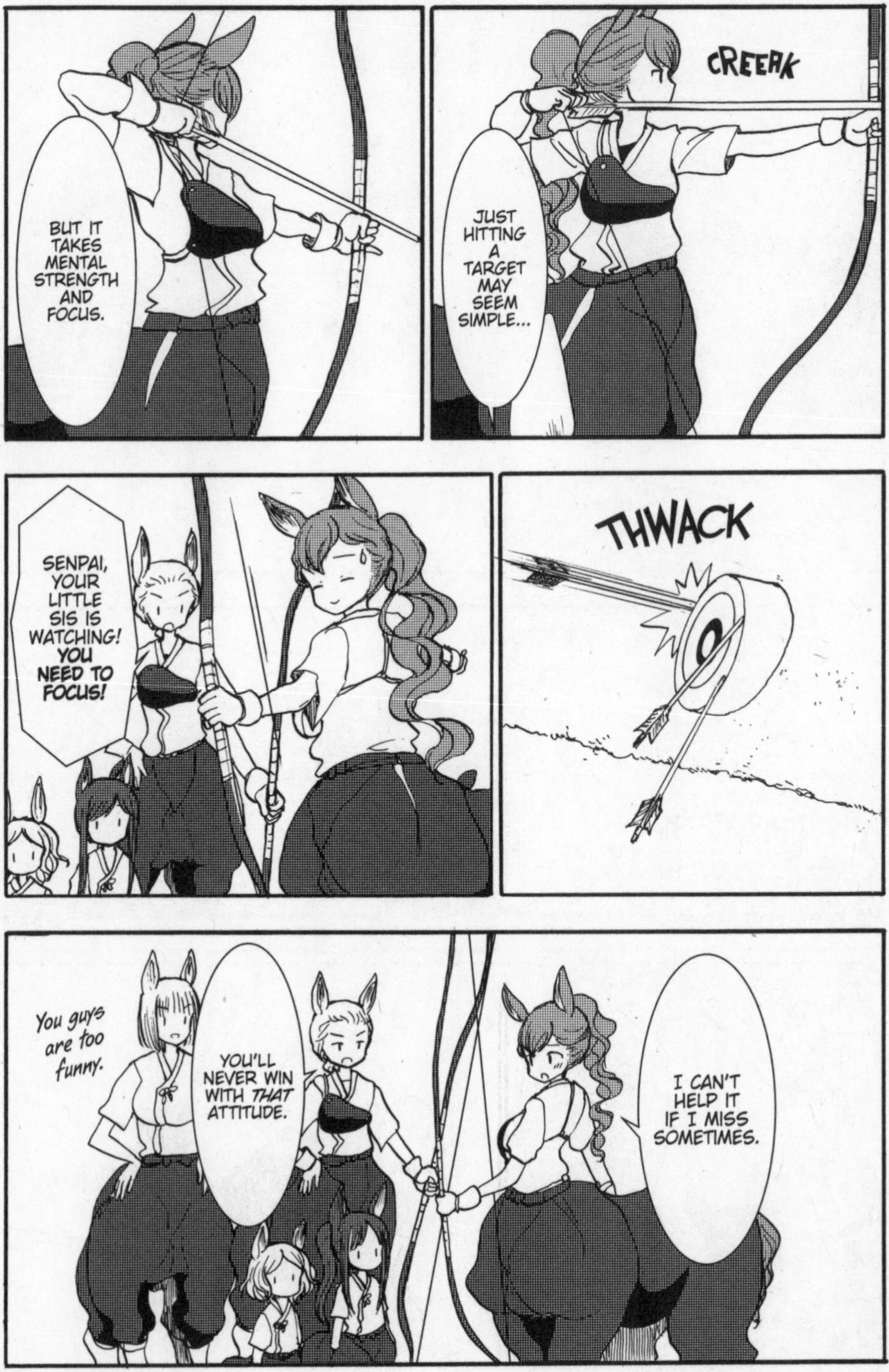
CREEAK
JUST HITTING A TARGET MAY SEEM SIMPLE...
BUT IT TAKES MENTAL STRENGTH AND FOCUS.
THWACK
SENPAI, YOUR LITTLE SIS IS WATCHING! **YOU NEED TO FOCUS!**
I CAN'T HELP IT IF I MISS SOMETIMES.
YOU'LL NEVER WIN WITH *THAT* ATTITUDE.
You guys are too funny.

HEY, BIG SIS.

CREE CREE

SENPAI, REMEMBER TO *FOCUS*.

UMM.

WHAT'S 123,456 PLUS 456,789?

UH-OH!

DON'T WORRY. YOU'LL LEARN ADDITION IN GRADE SCHOOL.

Bulls-eye.

580,245, I THINK.

THUNK

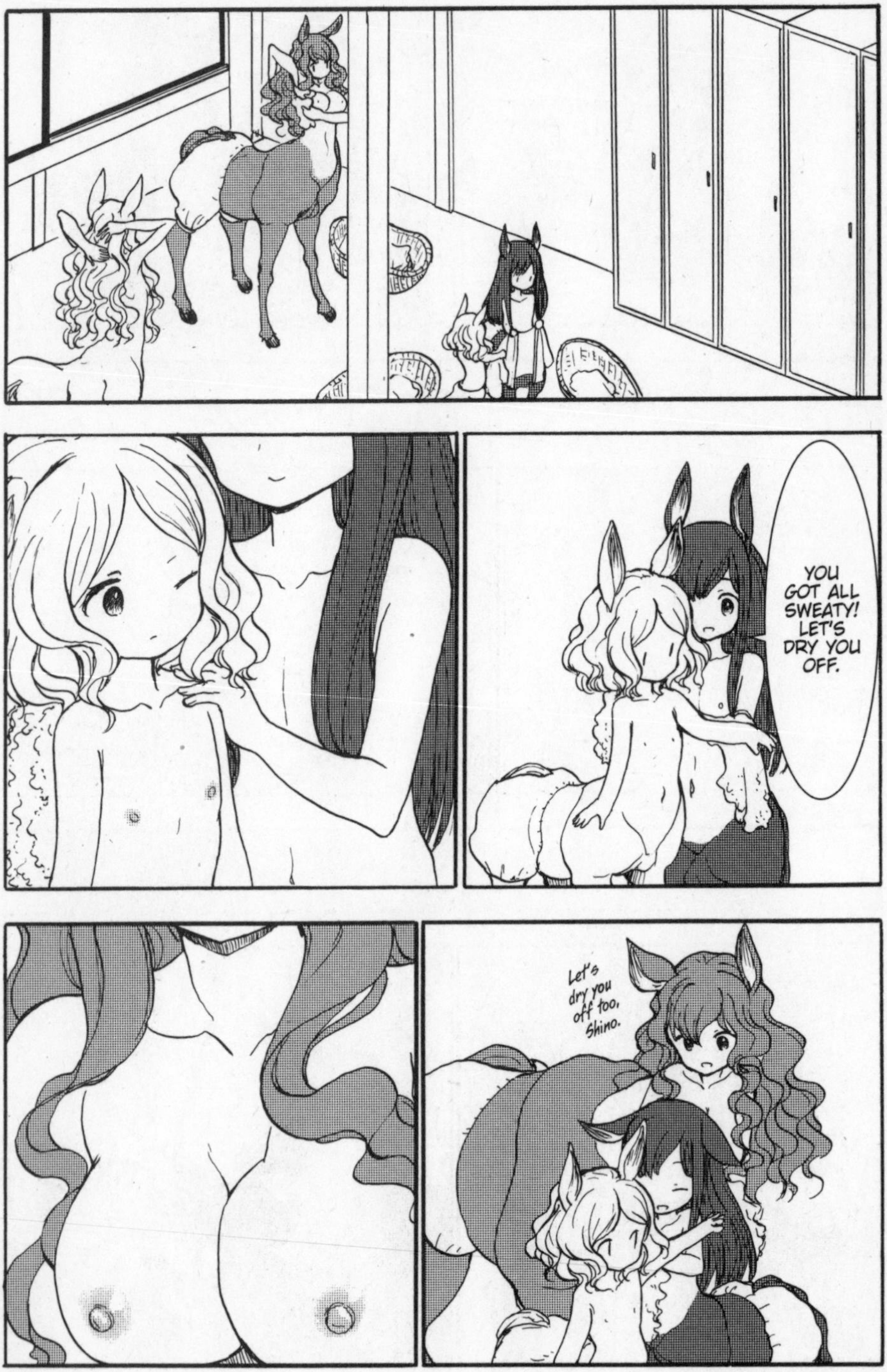
YOU GOT ALL SWEATY! LET'S DRY YOU OFF.
Let's dry you off too, Shino.

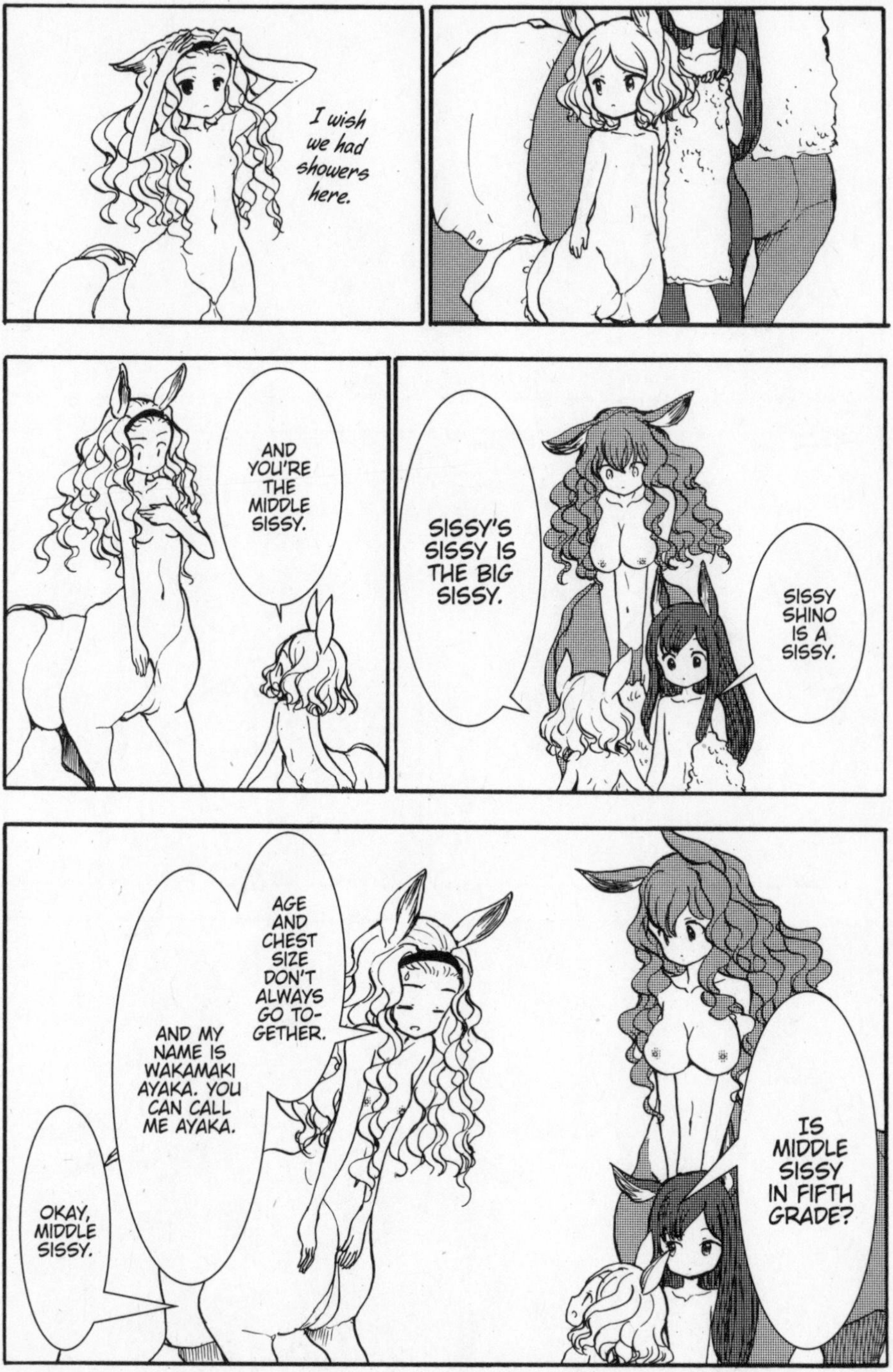
I wish we had showers here.
SISSY SHINO IS A SISSY.
SISSY'S SISSY IS THE BIG SISSY.
AND YOU'RE THE MIDDLE SISSY.
IS MIDDLE SISSY IN FIFTH GRADE?
AGE AND CHEST SIZE DON'T ALWAYS GO TO-GETHER.
AND MY NAME IS WAKAMAKI AYAKA. YOU CAN CALL ME AYAKA.
OKAY, MIDDLE SISSY.

A CentaUr's Life

SPOTLIGHT ON MERFOLK: < 1 > RECAP

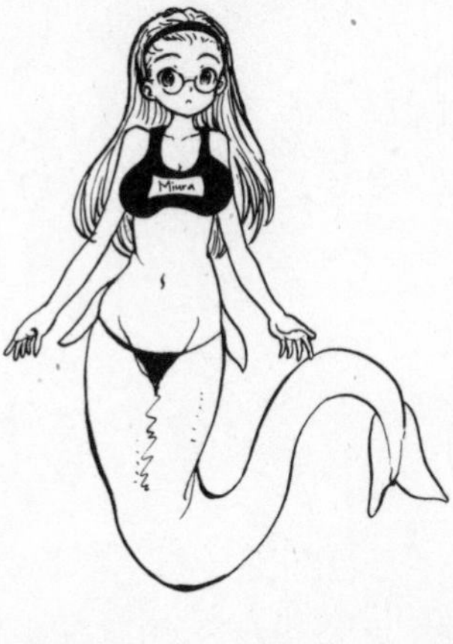
Miura

MERFOLK ARE MAMMALIANS THAT EXCEL AT SWIMMING, JUST AS CENTAURS DO AT RUNNING AND ANGELFOLK DO AT PROJECTING WARMTH. DESPITE WHAT ONE MIGHT THINK, THEIR LEVEL OF ADAPTATION TO THE WATER VARIES BY INDIVIDUAL. SOME MERFOLK CAN REMAIN IN THE WATER ALL DAY, WHILE OTHERS CAN ONLY HANDLE IT AS MUCH AS ANY TERRESTRIAL RACE. THEY ARE NATURALLY FAST SWIMMERS, BUT STILL REQUIRE PRACTICE. WITHOUT TRAINING, MOST MERFOLK ARE UNABLE TO HOLD THEIR BREATH FOR MORE THAN A MINUTE. SOME CAN HOLD THEIR BREATH FOR FIVE MINUTES AT BEST, EVEN WITH TRAINING, WHILE OTHERS CAN HOLD IT FOR UP TO HALF AN HOUR. ADAPTATION TO WATER IS MORE CONSISTENT WITH THOSE WHO LIVE IN MERFOLK COMMUNITIES; BY CONTRAST, THOSE WHO LIVE IN MIXED COMMUNITIES ON LAND DISPLAY A WIDE RANGE OF ADAPTATION. MERFOLK'S ABILITIES AFFECT THEIR SOCIAL STATUS IN THE MERFOLK COMMUNITY. ALTHOUGH THE GENETIC FEATURES OF MERFOLK ARE NOT APPARENT IN JAPANESE PEOPLE, RECESSIVE GENES MAY BE PRESENT IN MANY.

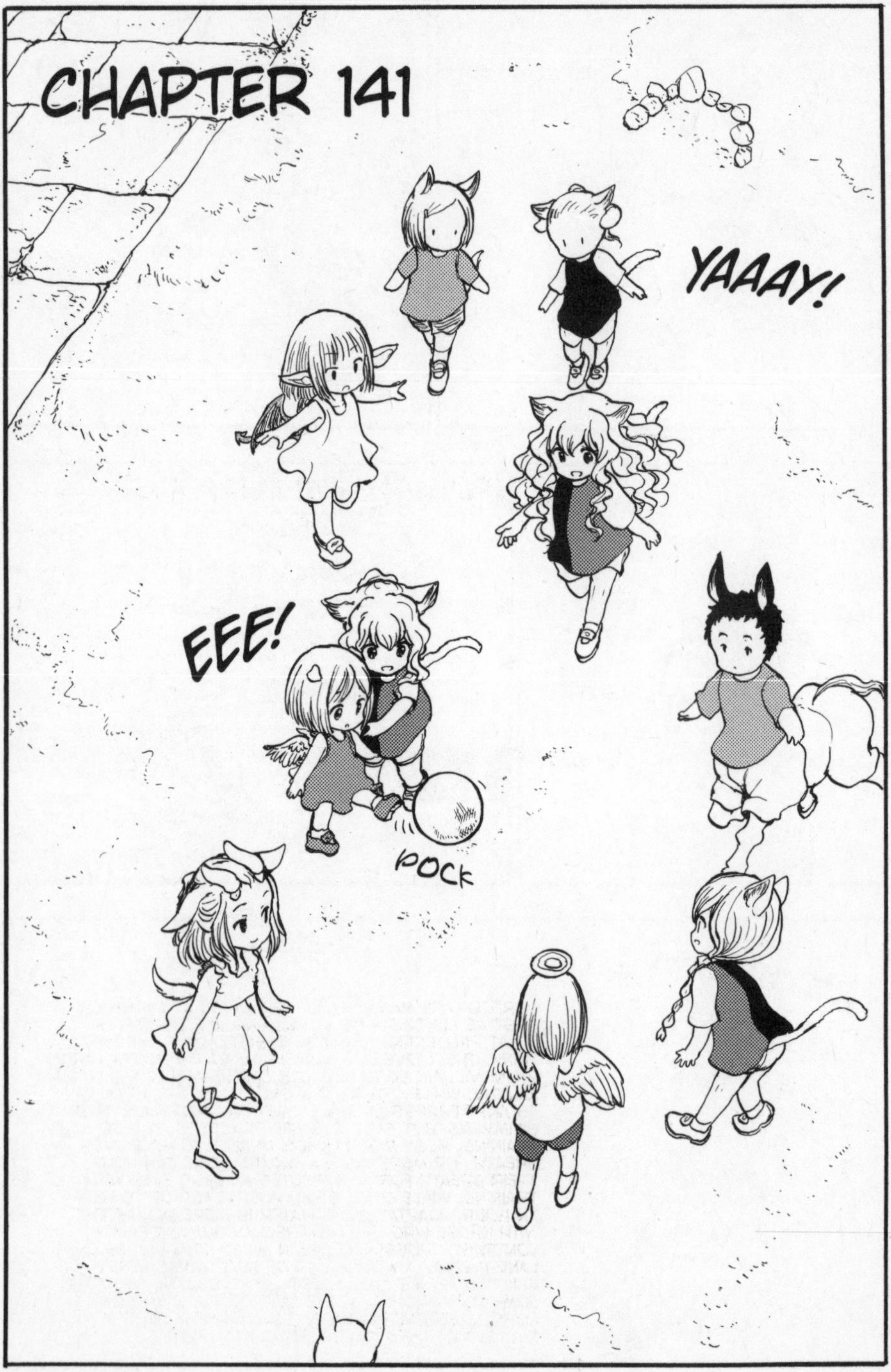
CHAPTER 141
YAAAY!
EEE!
POCK

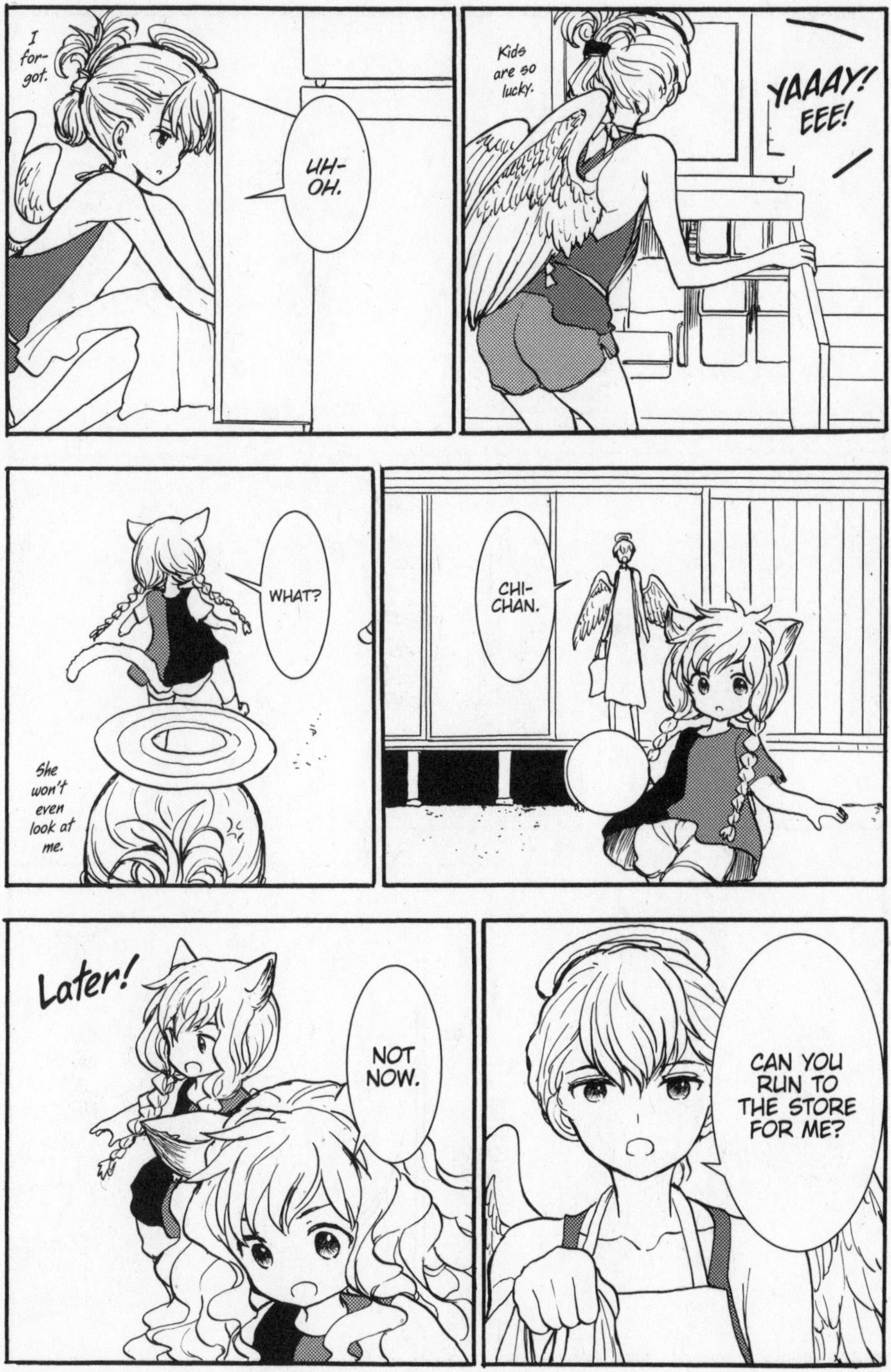
YAAAY! EEE!
Kids are so lucky.
UH-OH.
I for-got.
CHI-CHAN.
WHAT?
She won't even look at me.
CAN YOU RUN TO THE STORE FOR ME?
NOT NOW.
Later!

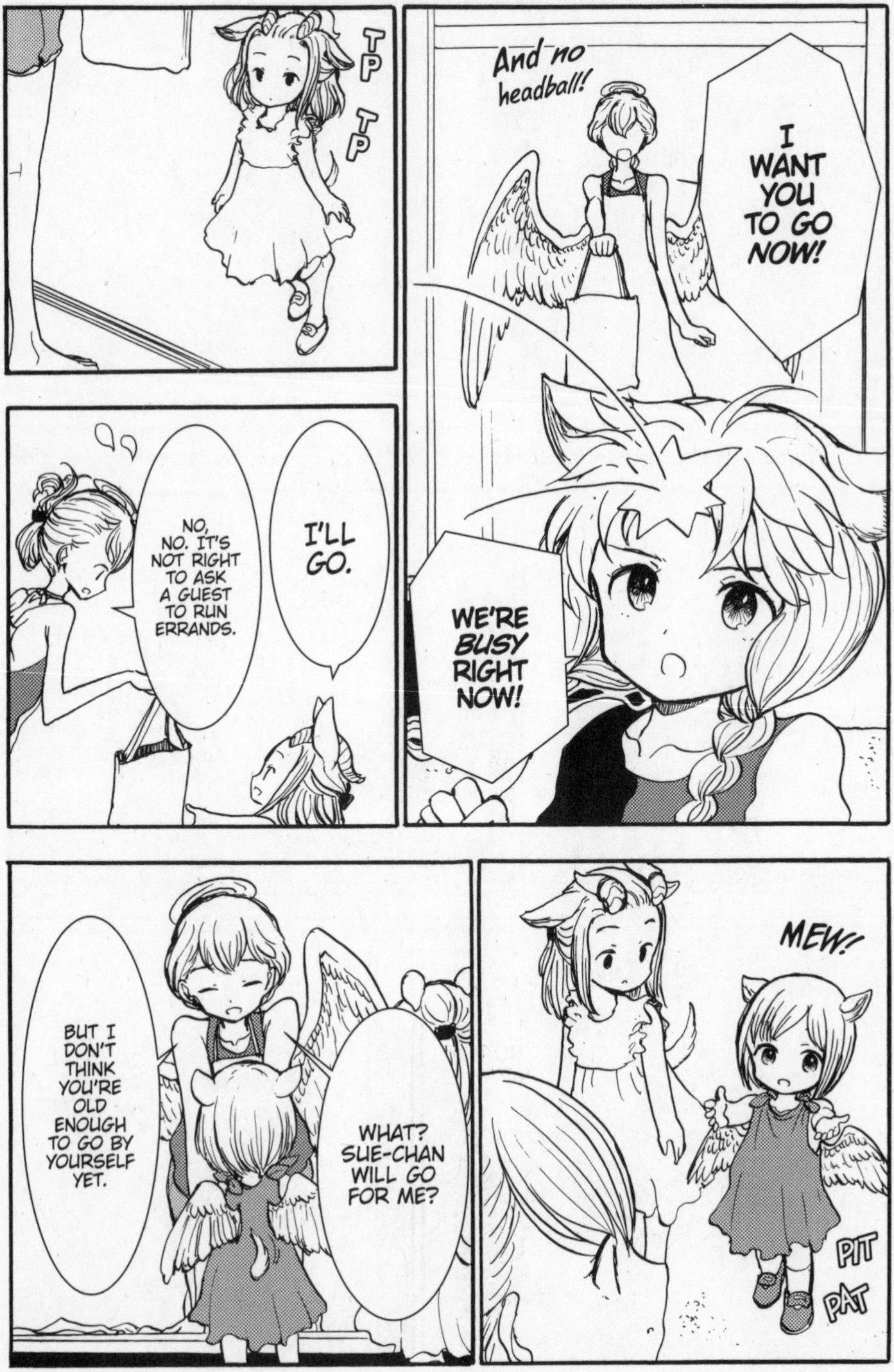
I WANT YOU TO GO NOW!
And no headball!
WE'RE BUSY RIGHT NOW!
TP TP TP
I'LL GO.
NO, NO. IT'S NOT RIGHT TO ASK A GUEST TO RUN ERRANDS.
MEW!
PIT PAT
WHAT? SUE-CHAN WILL GO FOR ME?
BUT I DON'T THINK YOU'RE OLD ENOUGH TO GO BY YOURSELF YET.

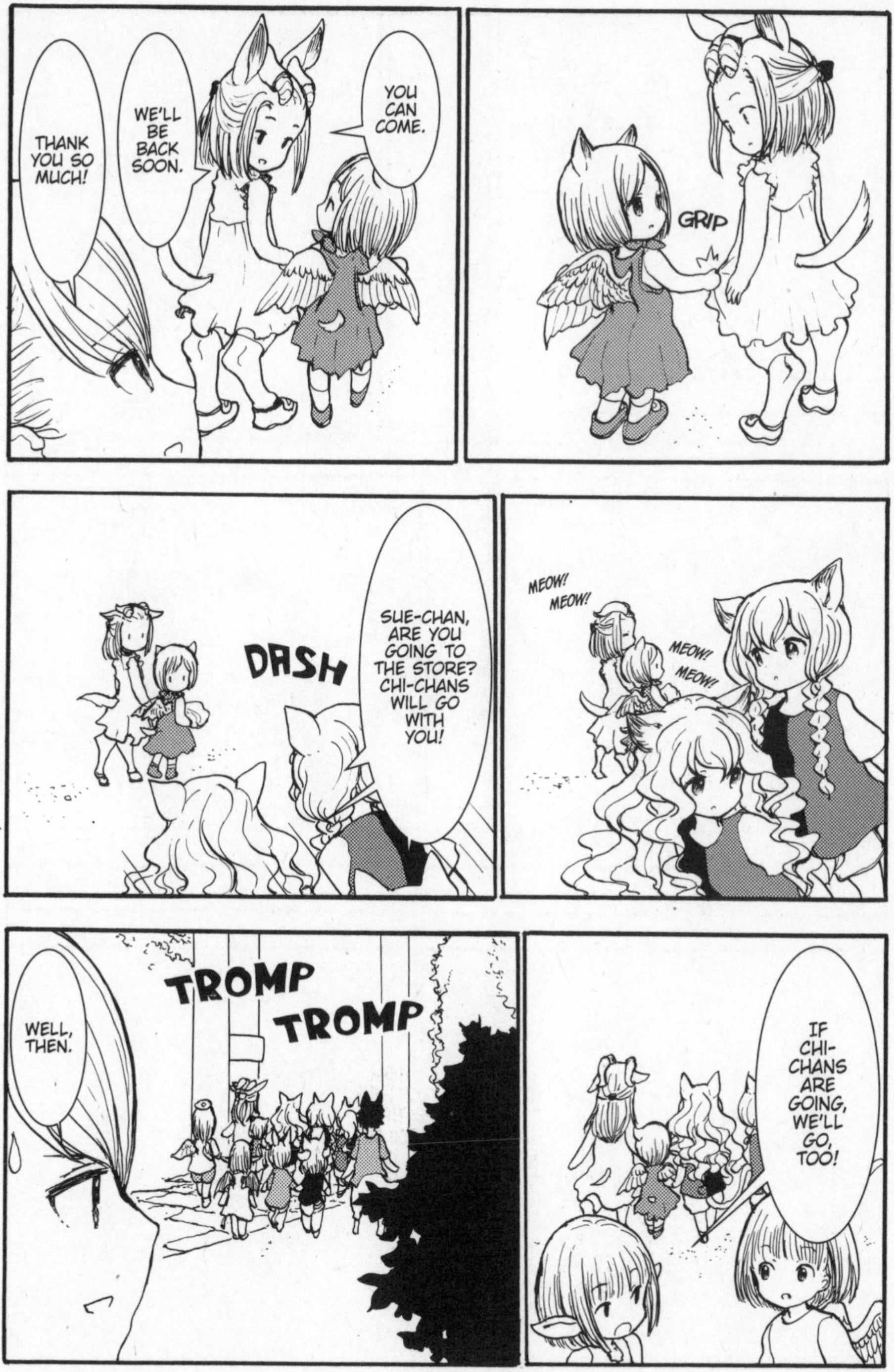
GRIP
YOU CAN COME.
WE'LL BE BACK SOON.
THANK YOU SO MUCH!
MEOW! MEOW!
MEOW! MEOW!
SUE-CHAN, ARE YOU GOING TO THE STORE? CHI-CHANS WILL GO WITH YOU!
DASH
IF CHI-CHANS ARE GOING, WE'LL GO, TOO!
TROMP TROMP
WELL, THEN.

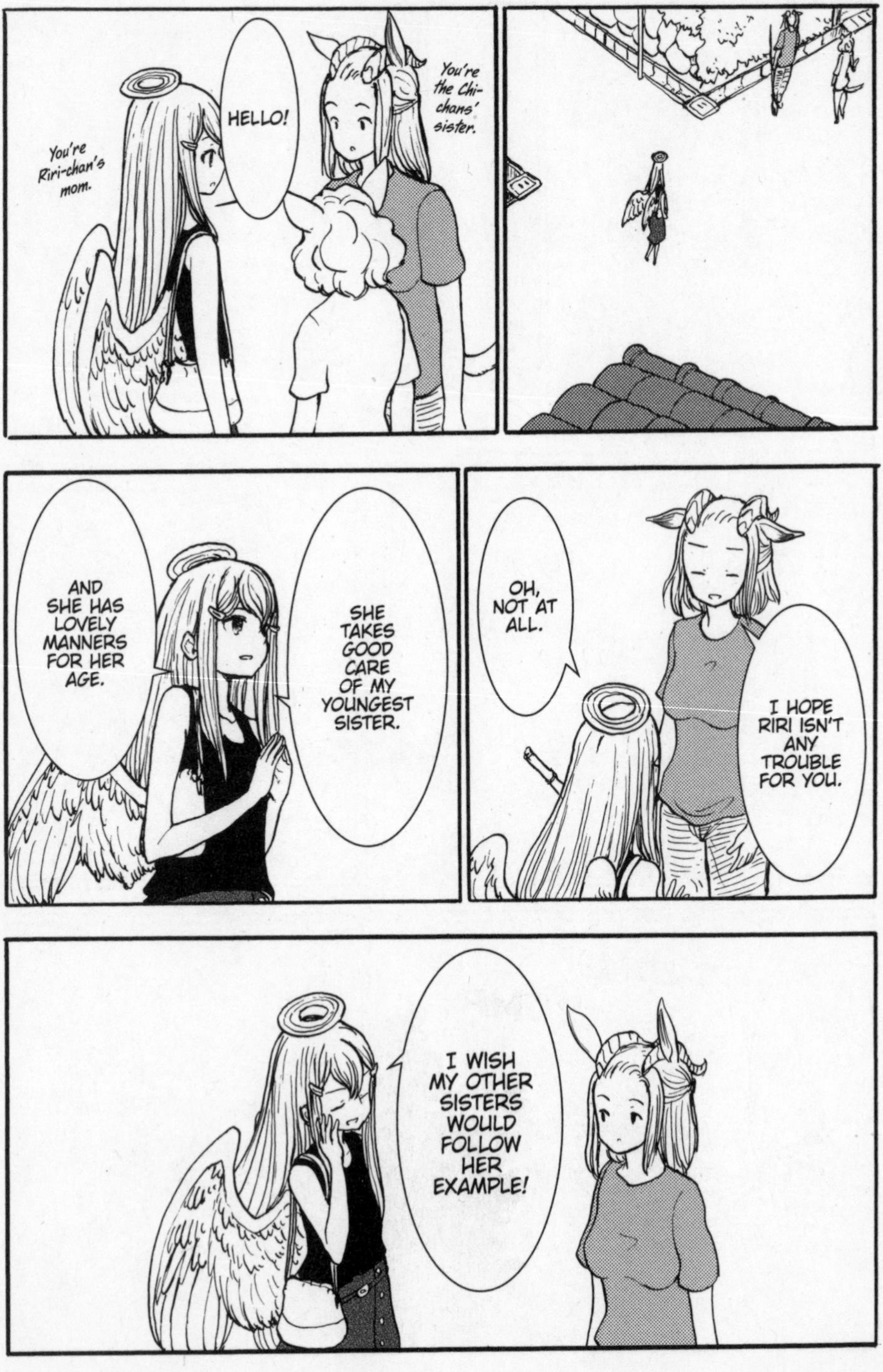
You're the Chi-chans' sister.
HELLO!
You're Riri-chan's mom.
I HOPE RIRI ISN'T ANY TROUBLE FOR YOU.
OH, NOT AT ALL.
SHE TAKES GOOD CARE OF MY YOUNGEST SISTER.
AND SHE HAS LOVELY MANNERS FOR HER AGE.
I WISH MY OTHER SISTERS WOULD FOLLOW HER EXAMPLE!

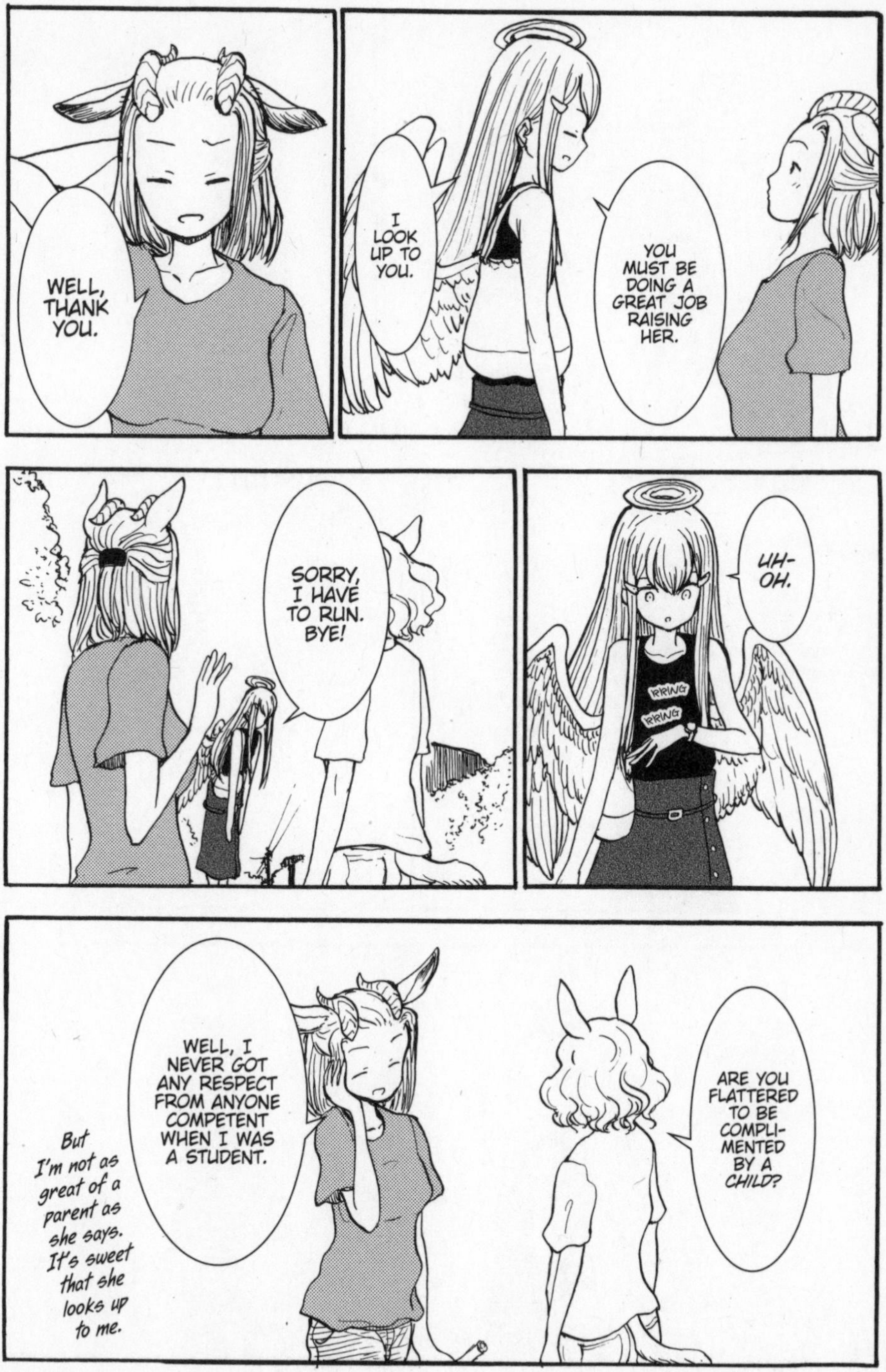
YOU MUST BE DOING A GREAT JOB RAISING HER.
I LOOK UP TO YOU.
WELL, THANK YOU.
UH-OH.
RRING RRING
SORRY, I HAVE TO RUN. BYE!
ARE YOU FLATTERED TO BE COMPLIMENTED BY A CHILD?
WELL, I NEVER GOT ANY RESPECT FROM ANYONE COMPETENT WHEN I WAS A STUDENT.
But I'm not as great of a parent as she says. It's sweet that she looks up to me.

A Centaur's Life

SPOTLIGHT ON MERFOLK:
< 2 > SPECIES AND TRIBES RESEMBLING MERFOLK

SWAMPTHROPUS.

IN GENERAL, MERFOLK CAN SWIM OVERWHELMINGLY FASTER AND FARTHER THAN OTHER MAMMALIANS. THEY CANNOT, HOWEVER, SIGNIFICANTLY SURPASS THE ABILITIES OF A WELL-TRAINED NON-MERFOLK IN DEEP-DIVING OR APNEIC CONDITIONS. THIS IS DUE TO ADAPTATION.

IN THE PAST, THERE WERE SPECIES THAT WERE EVEN BETTER ADAPTED TO WATER THAN MODERN MERFOLK.

KETAPITEX, THOUGH CLASSIFIED AS PRIMATES, HARDLY LOOKED LIKE THEM. THIS EXTINCT SPECIES MORE CLOSELY RESEMBLED MODERN DOLPHINS OR THE ICHTHYOSAURUS, WHICH WAS A MARINE REPTILE OF THE MESOZOIC ERA.

SWAMPTHROPUS LIVED IN RELATIVELY SHALLOW LAKES AND WERE PROBABLY AMPHIBIOUS. THEY HAD LONG DIGITS ON THEIR UPPER LIMBS FOR PREDATION AND UNUSUALLY WELL-DEVELOPED MID-LIMBS. A SKIN MEMBRANE BETWEEN THEIR LONG FINGERS ASSISTED THEIR SWIMMING. THEIR LOWER STERNUMS PROTRUDED SIGNIFICANTLY AND HAD STRONG MUSCLES ATTACHED TO THEM. ON THE OTHER HAND, THEIR LOWER LIMBS WERE SO WEAK THAT THEY COULD BARELY ENDURE WALKING ON LAND. IT WAS ONCE PRESUMED THAT THE TRUE IDENTITY OF THE SWAMP MAN OF URBAN LEGEND WAS THE LAST SURVIVING SWAMPTHROPUS, BUT IN REALITY, THE SPECIES WENT EXTINCT APPROXIMATELY A MILLION YEARS AGO. SWAMPTHROPUS ARE ALSO BELIEVED TO HAVE BEEN INTELLECTUALLY INFERIOR TO EVEN PRIMITIVE HUMANS, SO THEIR CONTINUED HIDDEN EXISTENCE IS LOGICALLY IMPOSSIBLE.

OTHER HUMAN RACES AND SPECIES THAT TRANSITIONED TO AN AQUATIC LIFESTYLE HAVE BEEN FOUND IN FOSSILIZED FORM, BUT NONE OF THEM WERE EVOLUTIONARILY SUCCESSFUL. PERHAPS ADAPTATION TO WATER ALONE WAS NOT ENOUGH TO OCCUPY THE ECONICHE OF LARGE AQUATIC MAMMALS. TODAY, THE MERFOLK RACE IS THE ONLY PRIMATE WITH THE ABILITY TO ADAPT TO AN AQUATIC LIFESTYLE.

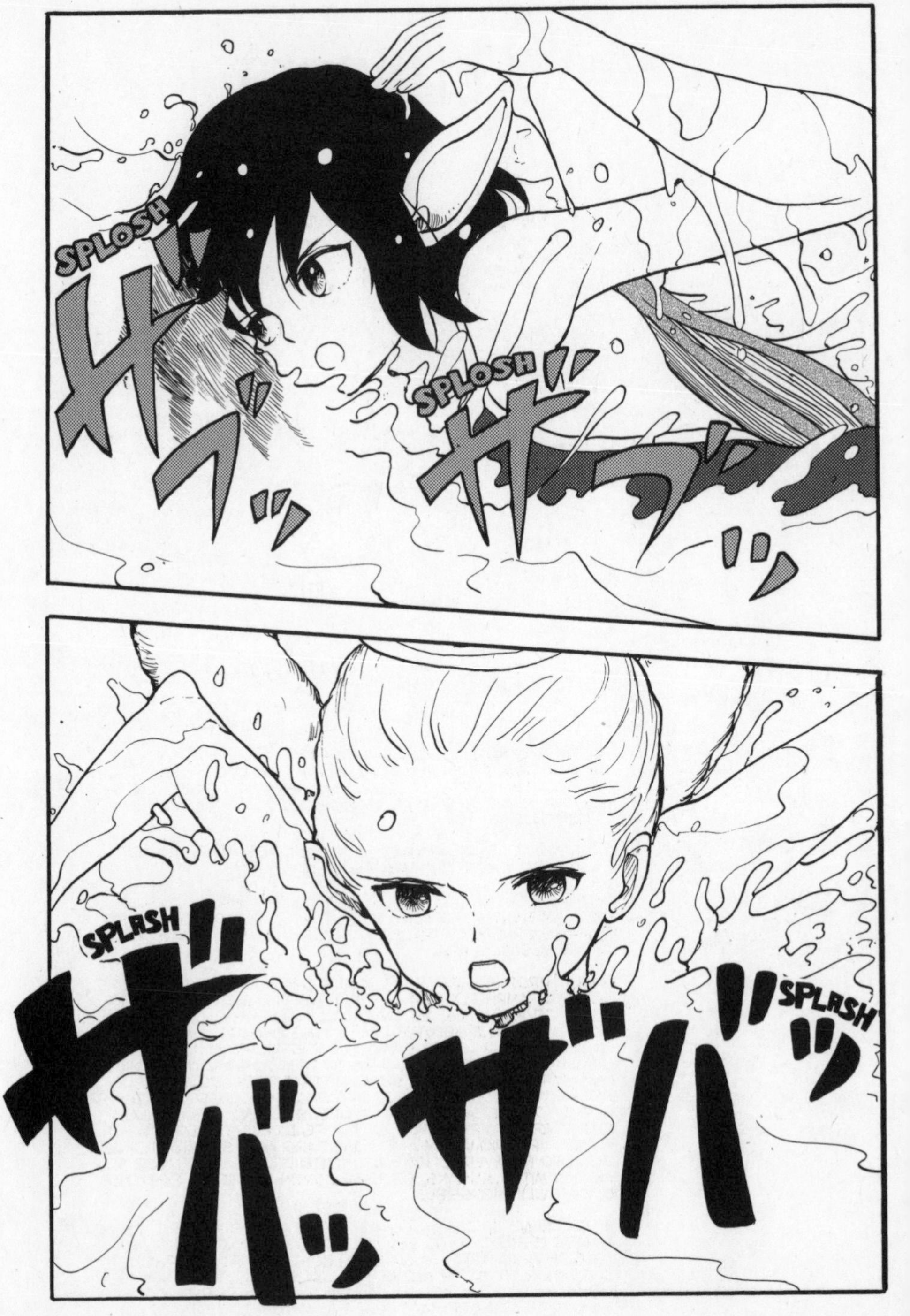
SPLOSH
ザブッ
SPLOSH
ザブッ
SPLASH
ザバッ
SPLASH
ザバッ

CHAPTER 142

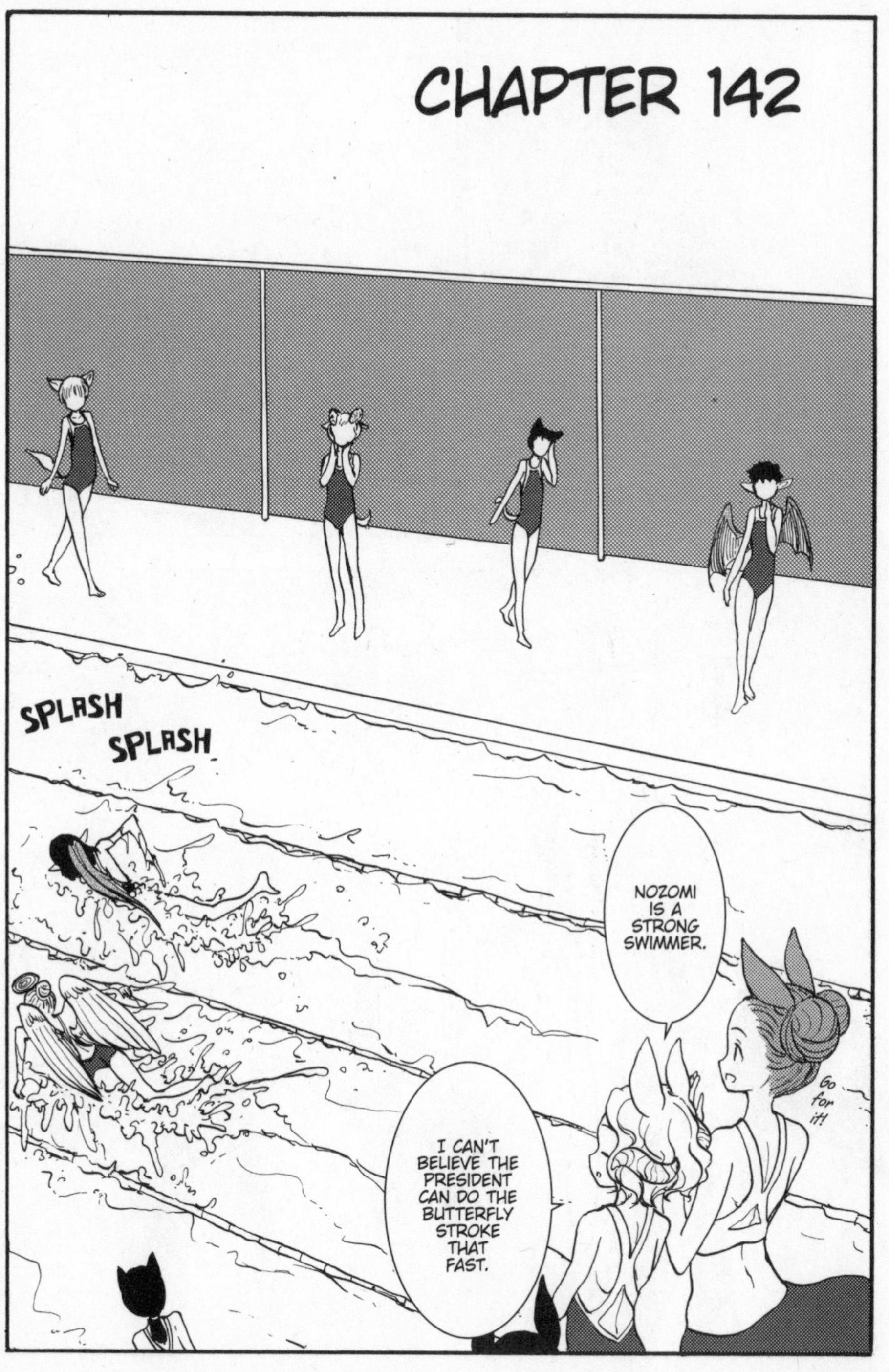
NOZOMI IS A STRONG SWIMMER.
Go for it!
SPLASH
SPLASH
I CAN'T BELIEVE THE PRESIDENT CAN DO THE BUTTERFLY STROKE THAT FAST.

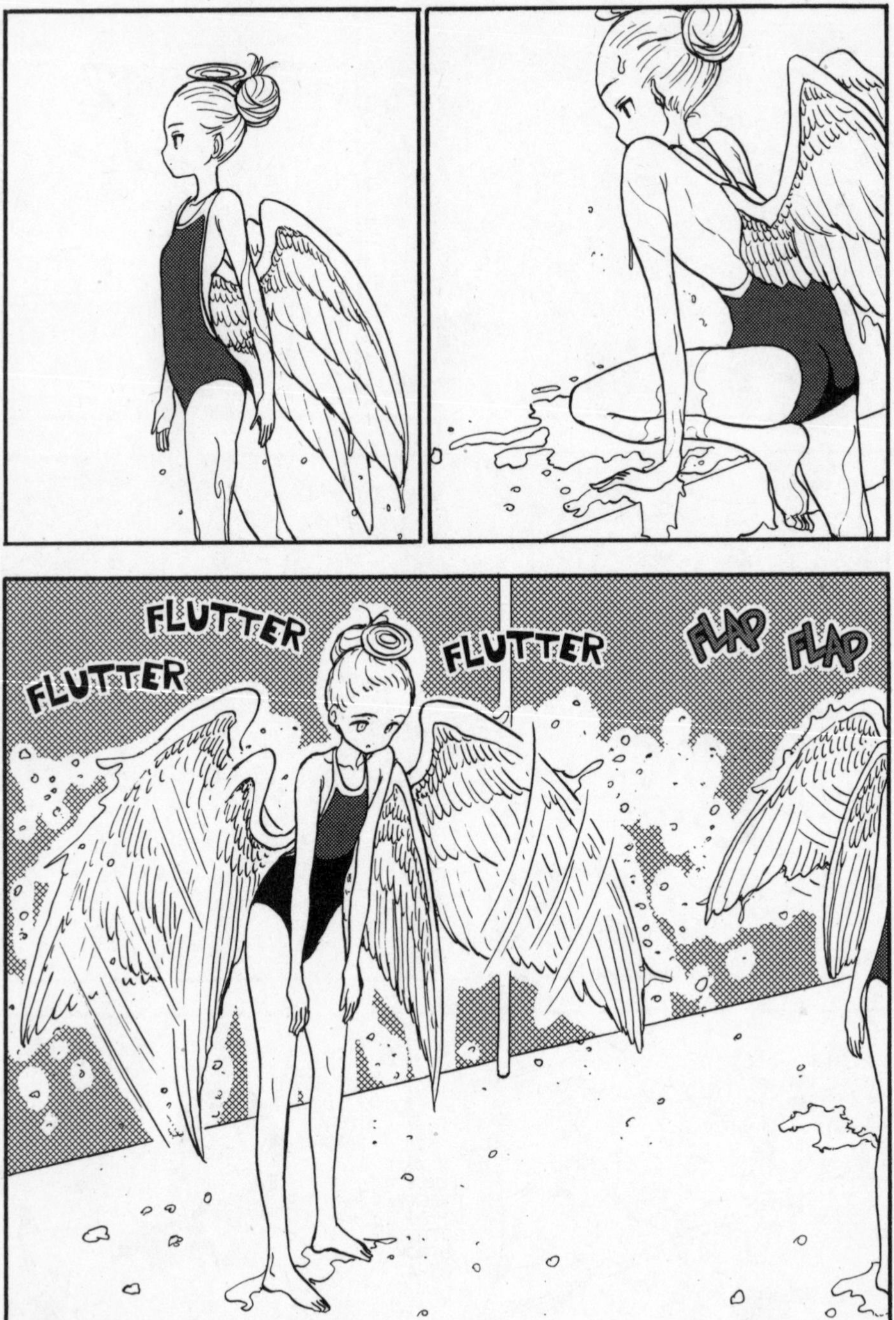
FLAP
FLAP
FLUTTER
FLUTTER
FLUTTER

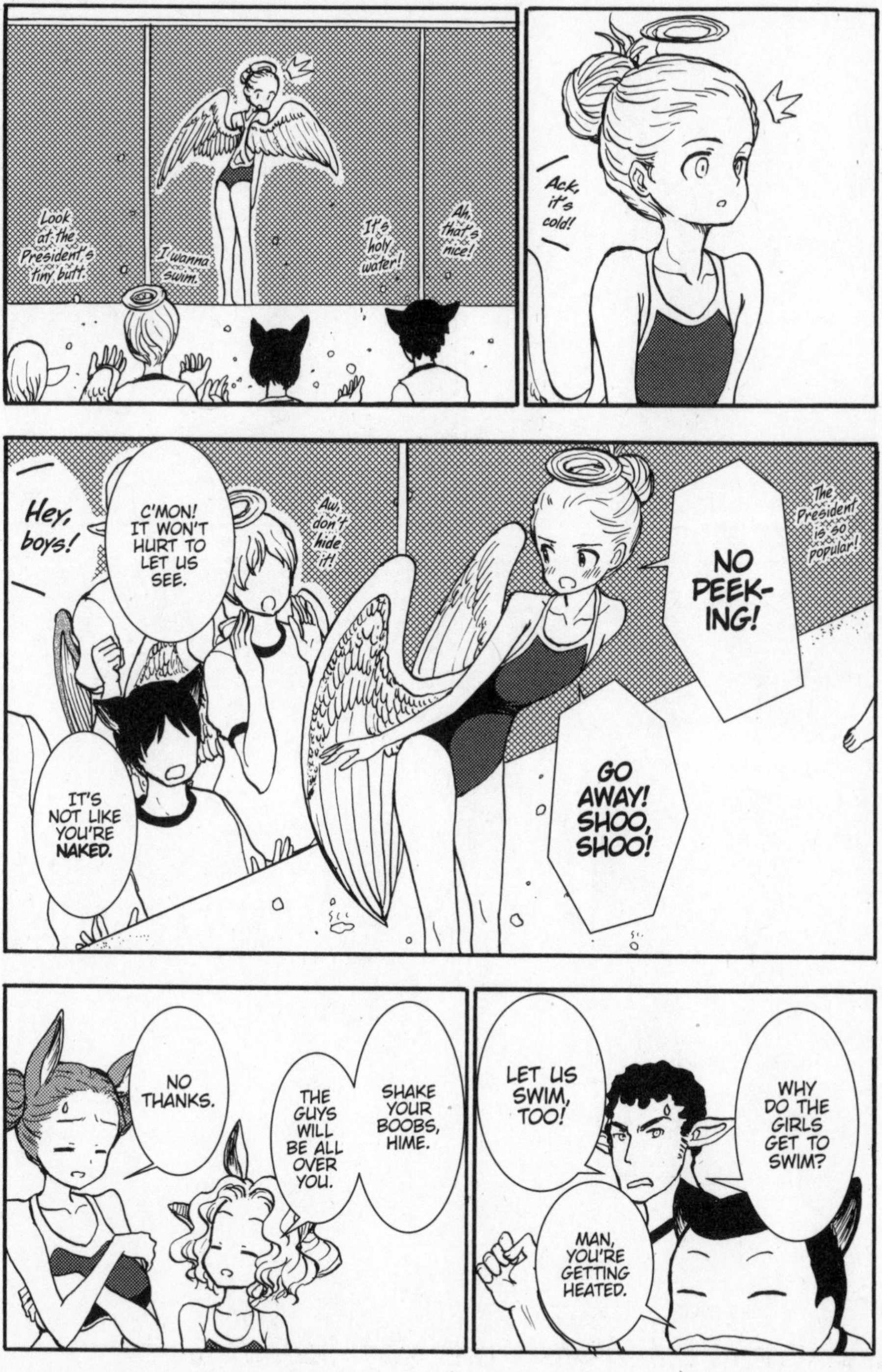
Ack, it's cold!
Ah, that's nice!
It's holy water!
I wanna swim.
Look at the President's tiny butt.
The President is so popular!
NO PEEKING!
GO AWAY! SHOO, SHOO!
Aw, don't hide it!
C'MON! IT WON'T HURT TO LET US SEE.
Hey, boys!
IT'S NOT LIKE YOU'RE NAKED.
WHY DO THE GIRLS GET TO SWIM?
LET US SWIM, TOO!
MAN, YOU'RE GETTING HEATED.
SHAKE YOUR BOOBS, HIME.
THE GUYS WILL BE ALL OVER YOU.
NO THANKS.

A Centaur's Life

SPOTLIGHT ON MERFOLK:
< 3 > MERFOLK COMMUNITIES,
PAST AND PRESENT

IN THE PAST, MERFOLK LIVED IN OCEANS, RIVERS, AND LAKES ALL
OVER THE WORLD, EXCEPT IN POLAR REGIONS AND OTHER AREAS WITH
A SIMILARLY COLD CLIMATE. BUT MERFOLK DID MUCH MORE THAN SIMPLY
INHABIT THESE AREAS; IN THE DAYS BEFORE SHIPPING, ROADS, AND
BRIDGES, MERFOLK PLAYED A MAJOR ROLE IN CONNECTING MAMMALIAN
COMMUNITIES. FOR EXAMPLE, CONSIDER THE DISTRIBUTION OF OBSIDIAN
DURING THE JOMON ERA IN JAPAN. OBSIDIAN FROM KAMINE ISLAND
WAS WIDELY USED IN THE TOKAI AND KANTO REGIONS, BUT KAMINE
ISLAND WAS TWENTY KILOMETERS OUT IN THE PACIFIC OCEAN. GOODS,
PEOPLE, AND THE ORDER OF THE DYNASTY IN THE DYNASTIC PERIOD
WERE TRANSPORTED THROUGH MERFOLK SEA ROUTES, INCLUDING
THE SETO INLAND SEA, UNTIL DIRECT GOVERNMENT ROUTES WERE
DEVELOPED IN THE RITSURYO ERA. THE PHOENICIANS, ANCIENT GREEK
CITY-STATES, AND THE ROMAN EMPIRE ALL FORMED ALLIANCES WITH
THE MERFOLK IN ORDER TO DOMINATE THE SEAS. HOWEVER, MERFOLK
COLONIES WERE THREATENED WHEN OCEANIC EMPIRES COLLAPSED OR
LOST THEIR COASTAL TERRITORY. THE MERFOLK'S ILL-ADVISED WEALTH
LED TO THEIR COLONIES BEING RAIDED AND OCCASIONALLY WIPED
OUT. BY THE MODERN ERA, MERFOLK COMMUNITIES HAD ALL BUT
DISAPPEARED EXCEPT ON SCATTERED ISLANDS.

MOST OF THE MERFOLK COMMUNITIES THAT REMAINED VANISHED
AFTER THE AGE OF DISCOVERY AND THE COLONIAL AGE. THE ONLY
DENSELY-POPULATED MERFOLK COMMUNITIES TODAY ARE IN JAPAN,
WHICH ESCAPED THE UNCIVILIZED PERIOD OF COLONIALIZATION. THE
LARGEST POPULATIONS ARE FOUND IN LAKE KYOU AND LAKE KOUJOU,
ALONG THE PACIFIC COAST OF WESTERN JAPAN. THE MERFOLK MAKE
UP A VERY SMALL PART OF JAPAN'S TOTAL POPULATION--LESS THAN
ONE PERCENT. MANY OF THEM RESIDE ON LAND, INTERMINGLED WITH
OTHER RACES OUTSIDE OF MERFOLK COMMUNITIES.

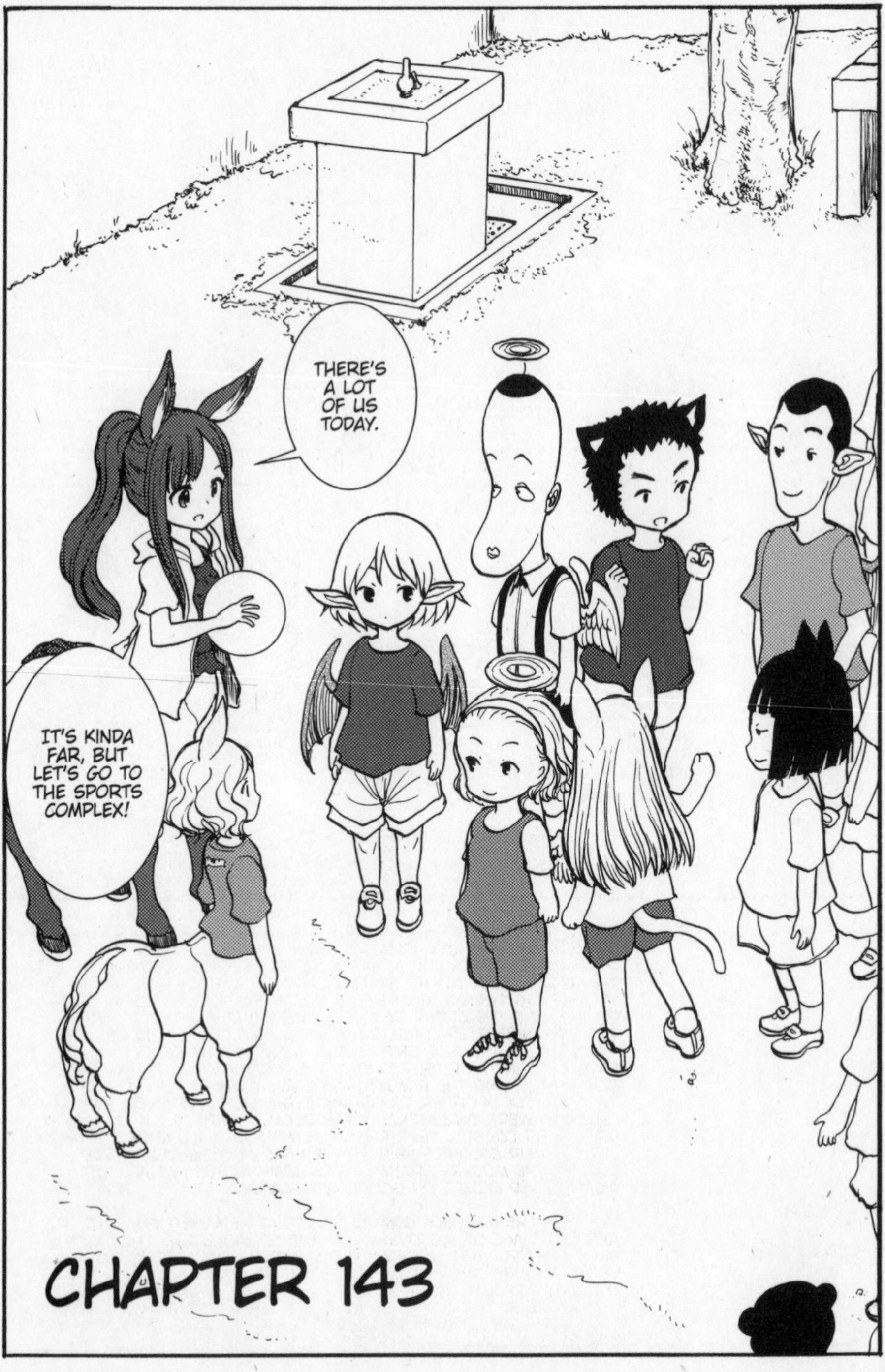
THERE'S A LOT OF US TODAY.
IT'S KINDA FAR, BUT LET'S GO TO THE SPORTS COMPLEX!

CHAPTER 143

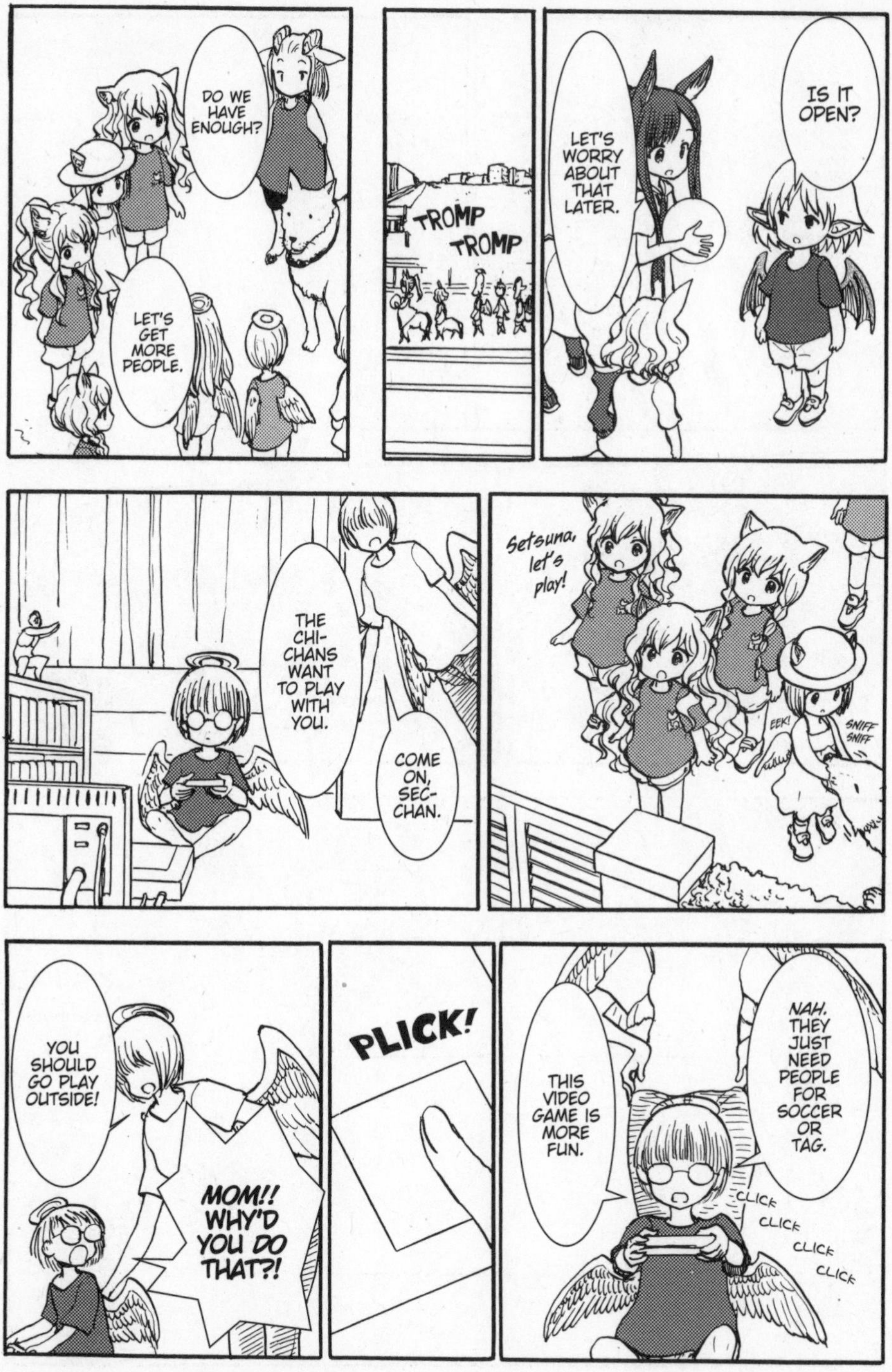
IS IT OPEN?
LET'S WORRY ABOUT THAT LATER.
TROMP TROMP
DO WE HAVE ENOUGH?
LET'S GET MORE PEOPLE.
Setsuna, let's play!
SNIFF SNIFF
EEK!
THE CHI-CHANS WANT TO PLAY WITH YOU.
COME ON, SEC-CHAN.
NAH. THEY JUST NEED PEOPLE FOR SOCCER OR TAG.
THIS VIDEO GAME IS MORE FUN.
CLICK CLICK CLICK CLICK
PLICK!
YOU SHOULD GO PLAY OUTSIDE!
MOM!! WHY'D YOU DO THAT?!

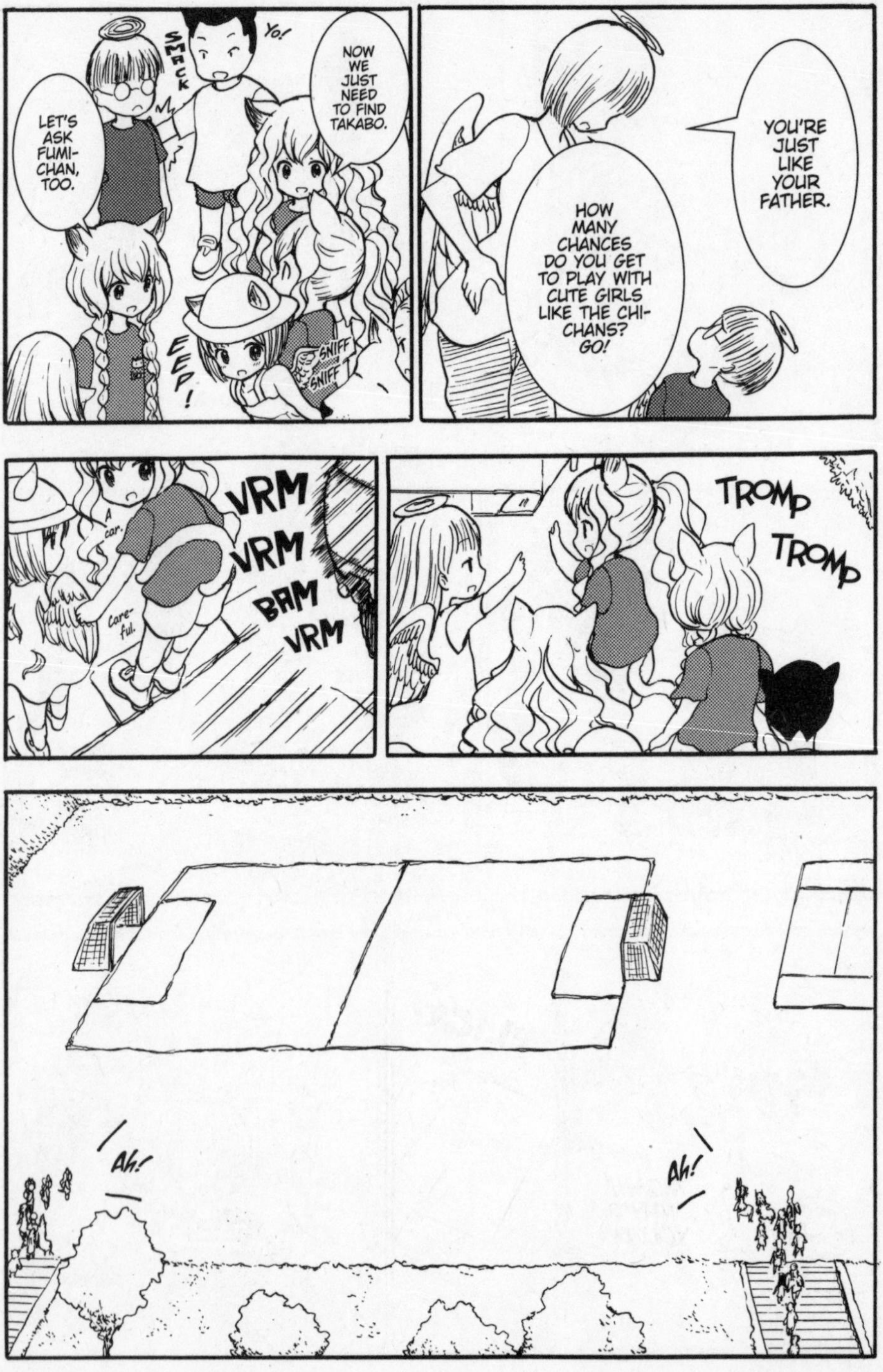
YOU'RE JUST LIKE YOUR FATHER.
HOW MANY CHANCES DO YOU GET TO PLAY WITH CUTE GIRLS LIKE THE CHI-CHANS? GO!
NOW WE JUST NEED TO FIND TAKABO.
Yo!
SMACK
LET'S ASK FUMI-CHAN, TOO.
EEP!
SNIFF SNIFF
TROMP TROMP
VRM VRM BAM VRM
A car.
Care-ful.
Ah!
Ah!

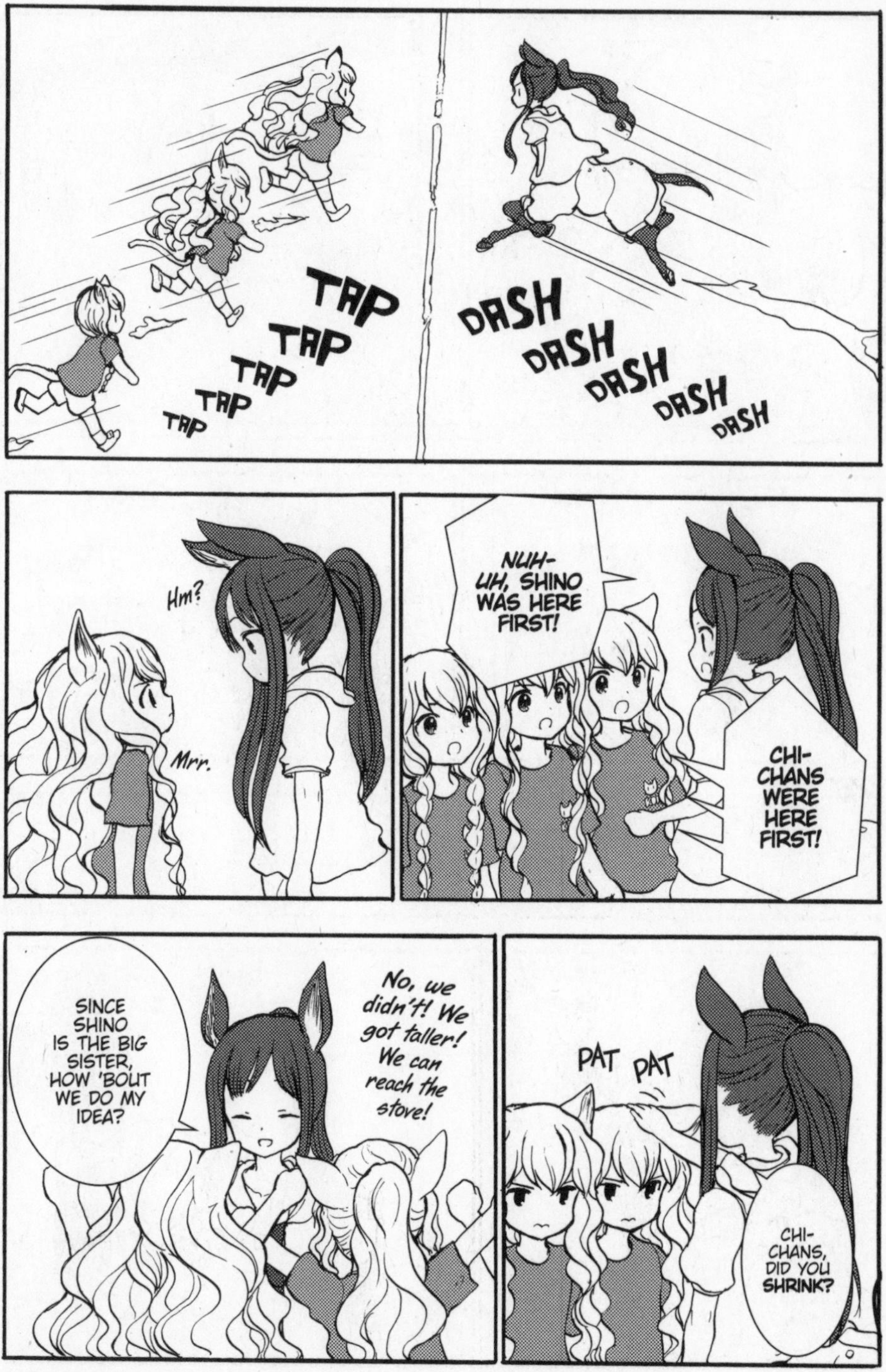
DASH DASH DASH DASH DASH
TAP TAP TAP TAP TAP
CHI-CHANS WERE HERE FIRST!
NUH-UH, SHINO WAS HERE FIRST!
Hm?
Mrr.
PAT PAT
CHI-CHANS, DID YOU SHRINK?
No, we didn't! We got taller! We can reach the stove!
SINCE SHINO IS THE BIG SISTER, HOW 'BOUT WE DO MY IDEA?

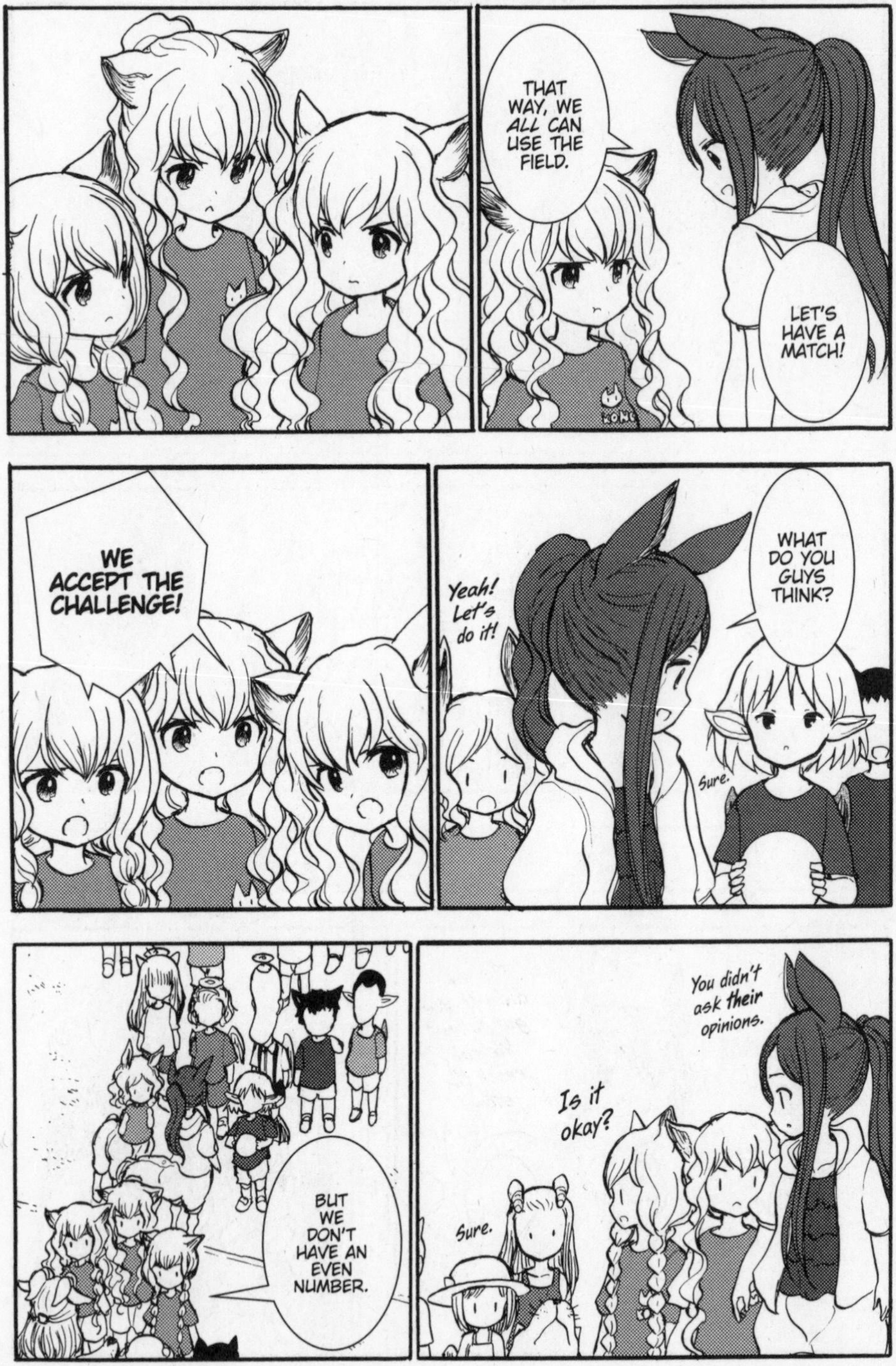
THAT WAY, WE ALL CAN USE THE FIELD.
LET'S HAVE A MATCH!
WHAT DO YOU GUYS THINK?
Yeah! Let's do it!
Sure.
WE ACCEPT THE CHALLENGE!
You didn't ask their opinions.
Is it okay?
Sure.
BUT WE DON'T HAVE AN EVEN NUMBER.

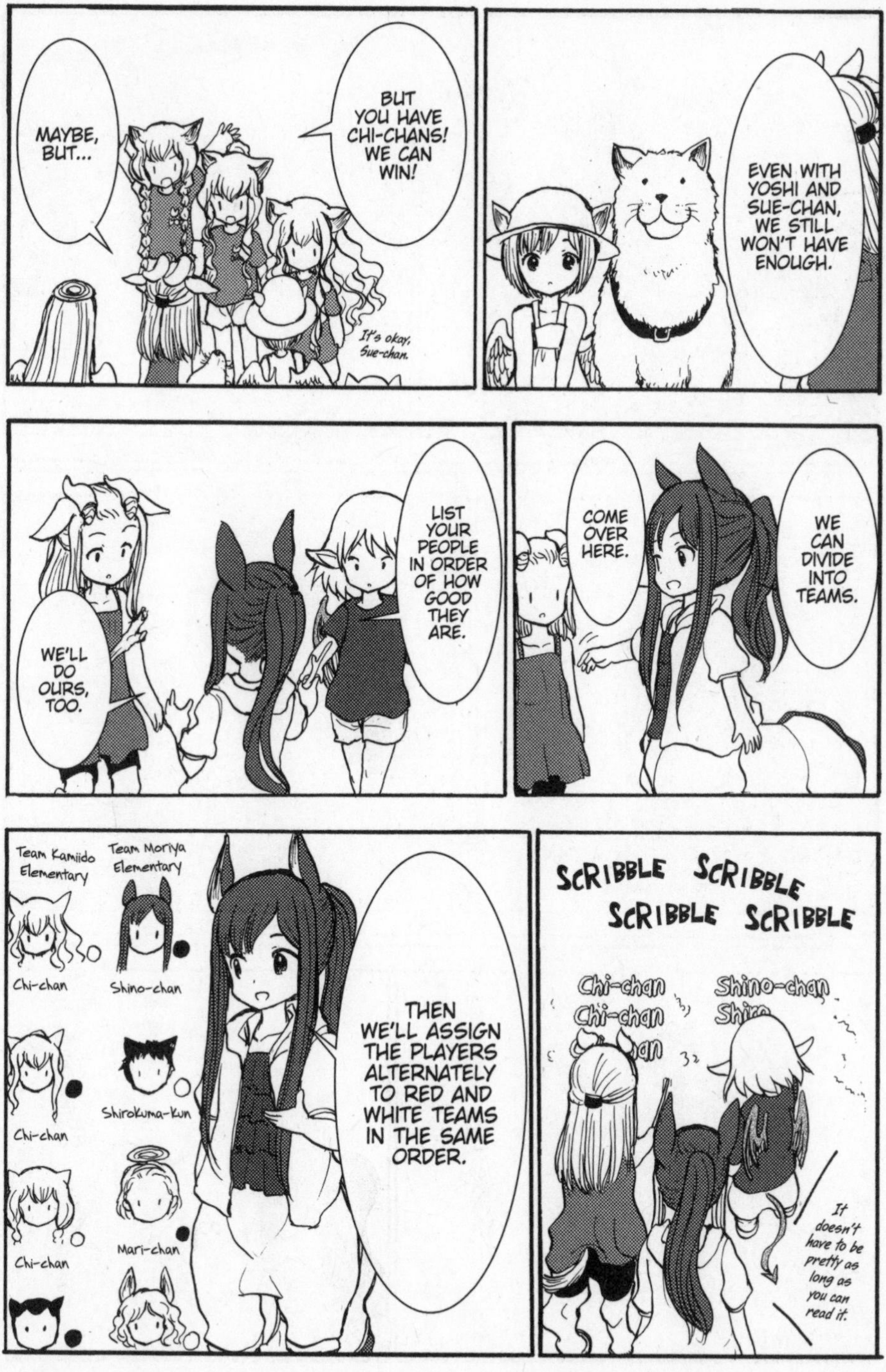
EVEN WITH YOSHI AND SUE-CHAN, WE STILL WON'T HAVE ENOUGH.
BUT YOU HAVE CHI-CHANS! WE CAN WIN!
MAYBE, BUT...
It's okay, Sue-chan.
WE CAN DIVIDE INTO TEAMS.
COME OVER HERE.
LIST YOUR PEOPLE IN ORDER OF HOW GOOD THEY ARE.
WE'LL DO OURS, TOO.
SCRIBBLE SCRIBBLE
SCRIBBLE SCRIBBLE
Shino-chan
Chi-chan
Chi-chan
It doesn't have to be pretty as long as you can read it.
THEN WE'LL ASSIGN THE PLAYERS ALTERNATELY TO RED AND WHITE TEAMS IN THE SAME ORDER.
Team Moriya Elementary
Team Kamiido Elementary
Shino-chan
Chi-chan
Shirokuma-kun
Chi-chan
Mari-chan
Chi-chan

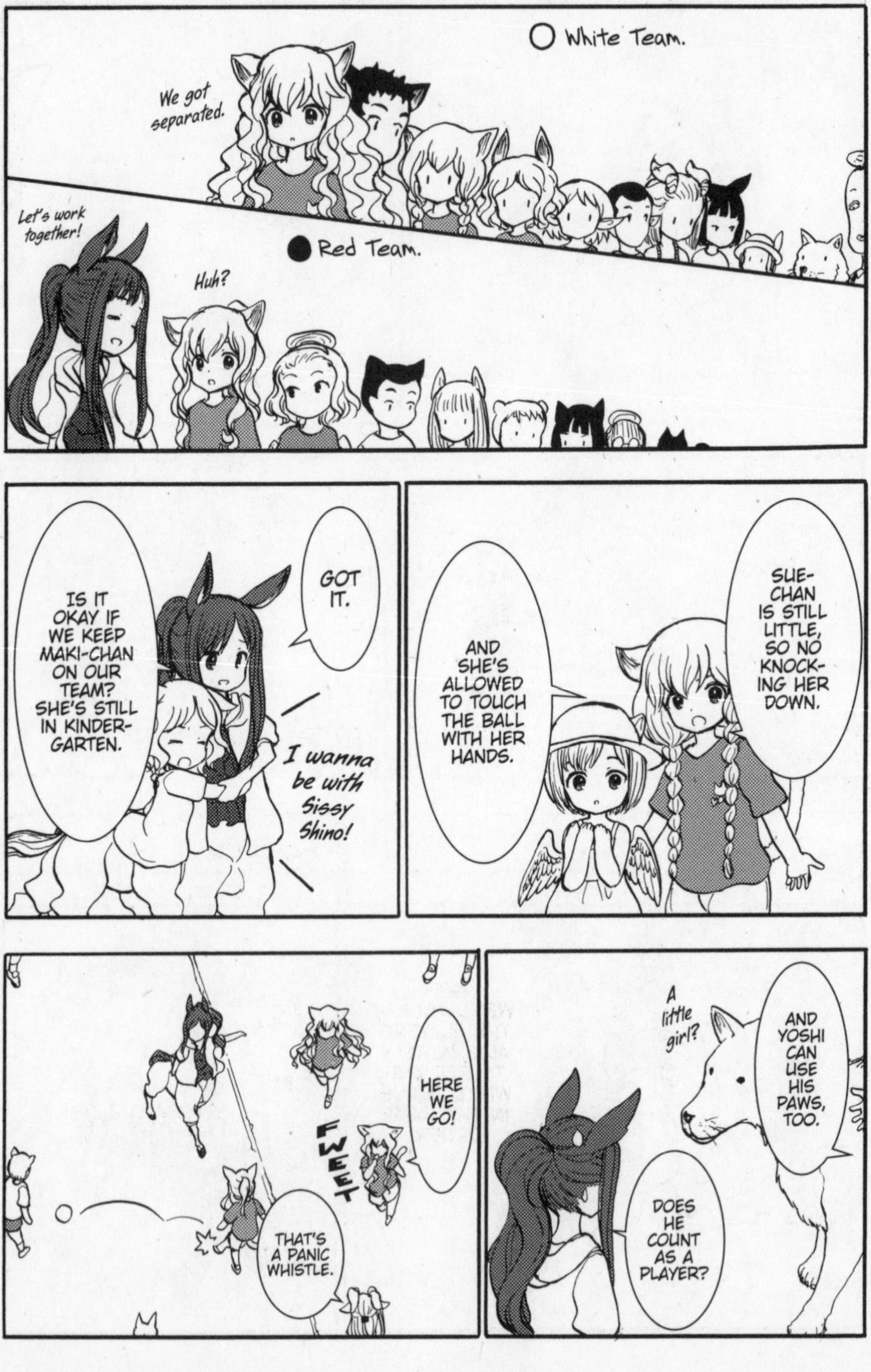
White Team.
We got separated.
Red Team.
Huh?
Let's work together!
SUE-CHAN IS STILL LITTLE, SO NO KNOCKING HER DOWN.
AND SHE'S ALLOWED TO TOUCH THE BALL WITH HER HANDS.
GOT IT.
I wanna be with Sissy Shino!
IS IT OKAY IF WE KEEP MAKI-CHAN ON OUR TEAM? SHE'S STILL IN KINDERGARTEN.
AND YOSHI CAN USE HIS PAWS, TOO.
A little girl?
DOES HE COUNT AS A PLAYER?
HERE WE GO!
FWEET
THAT'S A PANIC WHISTLE.

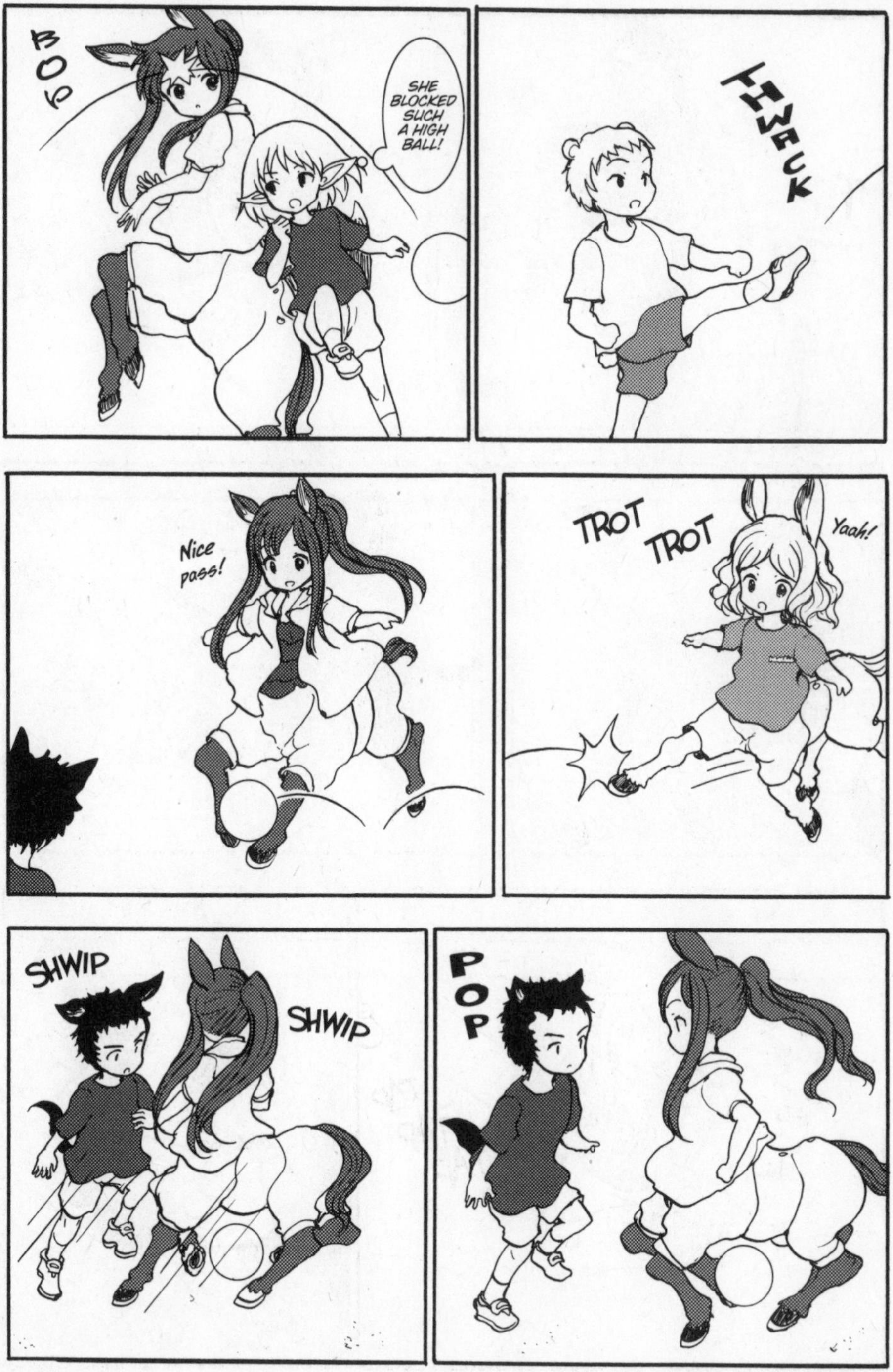
THWACK
BOP
SHE BLOCKED SUCH A HIGH BALL!
TROT TROT
Yaah!
Nice pass!
POP
SHWIP SHWIP

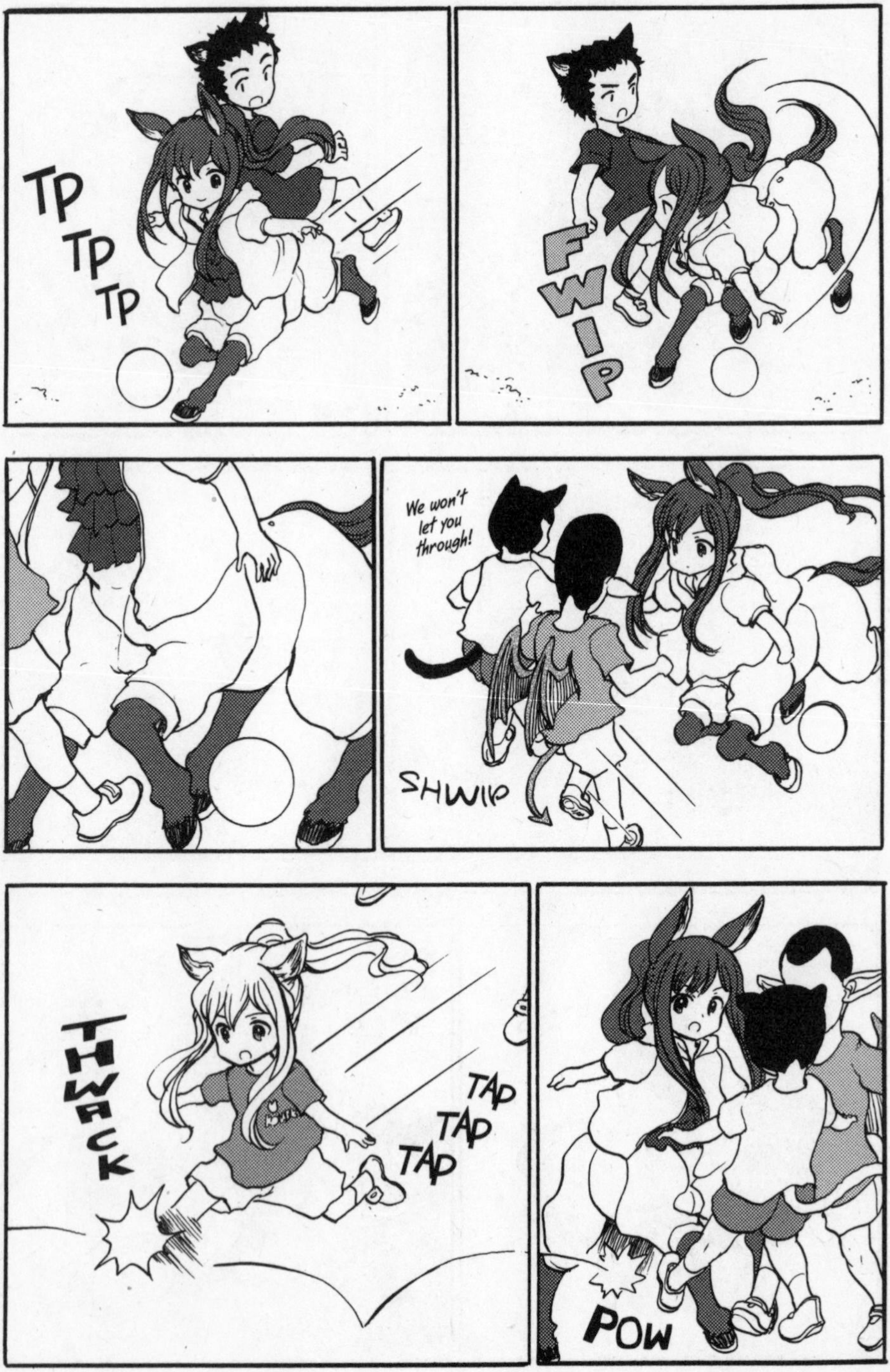
FWIP
TP TP TP
We won't let you through!
SHWIP
POW
THWACK
TAP TAP TAP

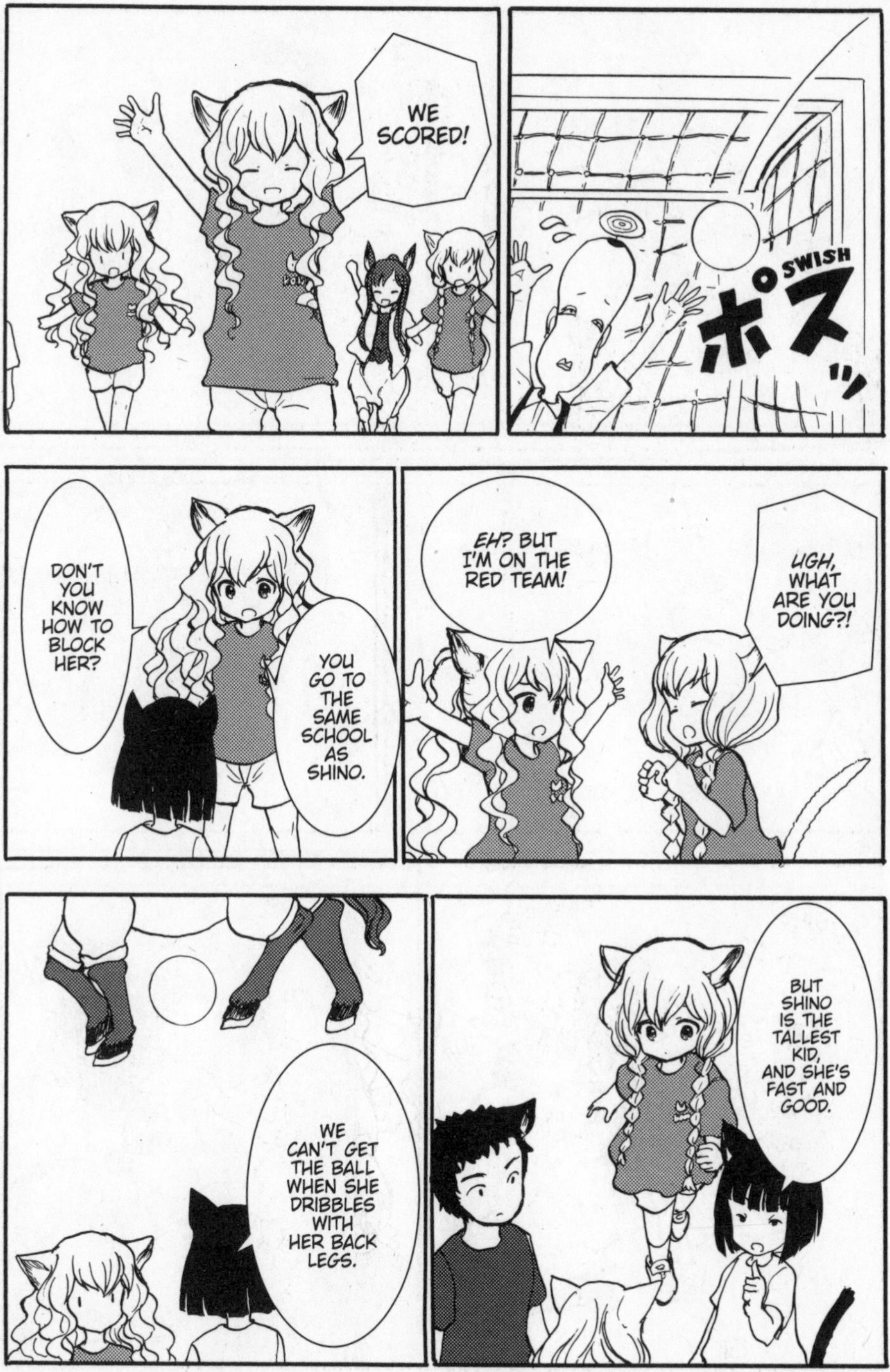
SWISH
ポスッ
WE SCORED!
UGH, WHAT ARE YOU DOING?!
EH? BUT I'M ON THE RED TEAM!
DON'T YOU KNOW HOW TO BLOCK HER?
YOU GO TO THE SAME SCHOOL AS SHINO.
BUT SHINO IS THE TALLEST KID, AND SHE'S FAST AND GOOD.
WE CAN'T GET THE BALL WHEN SHE DRIBBLES WITH HER BACK LEGS.

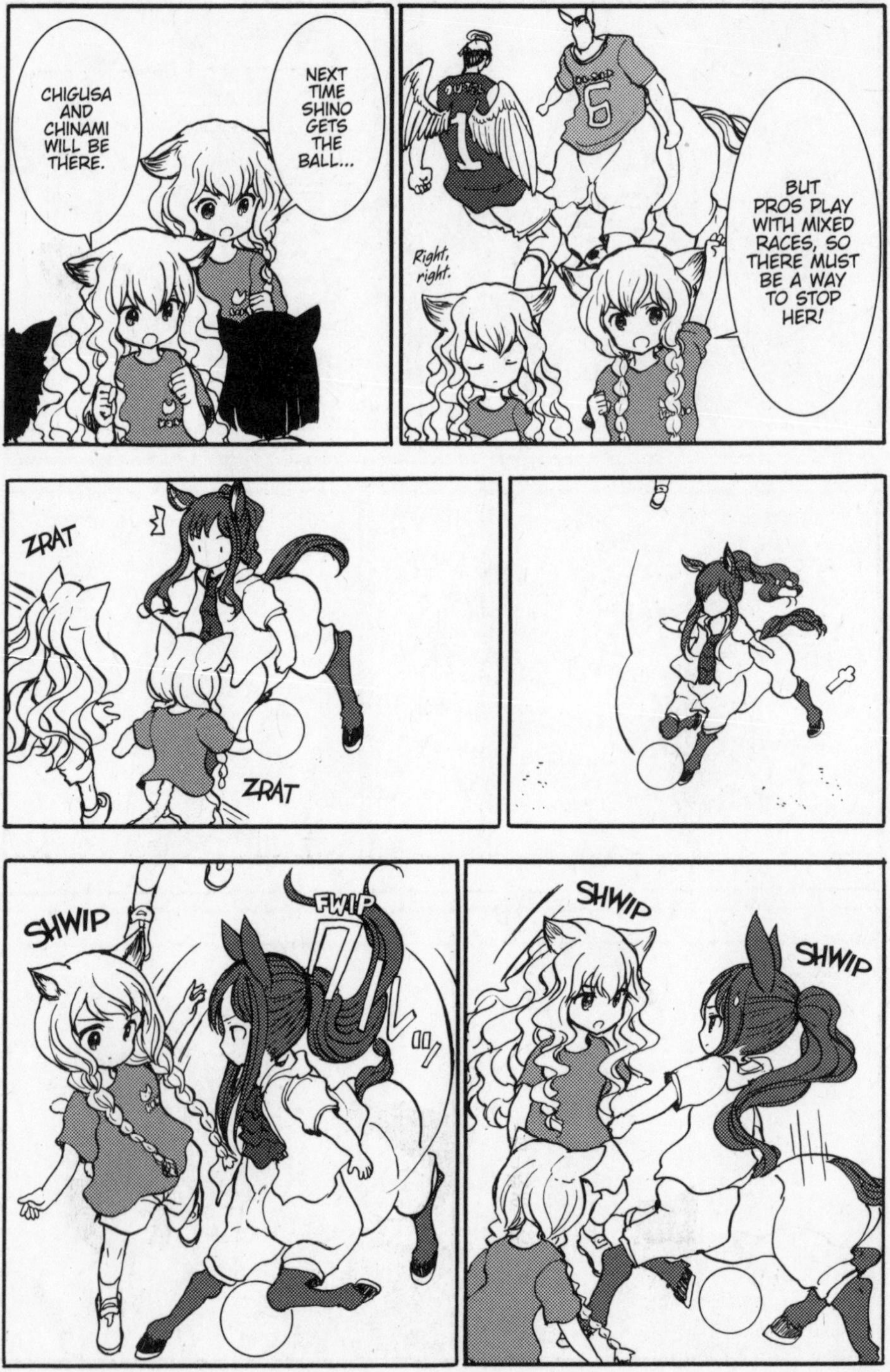
BUT PROS PLAY WITH MIXED RACES, SO THERE MUST BE A WAY TO STOP HER!
Right, right.
NEXT TIME SHINO GETS THE BALL...
CHIGUSA AND CHINAMI WILL BE THERE.
ZRAT
ZRAT
SHWIP
SHWIP
FWIP
SHWIP

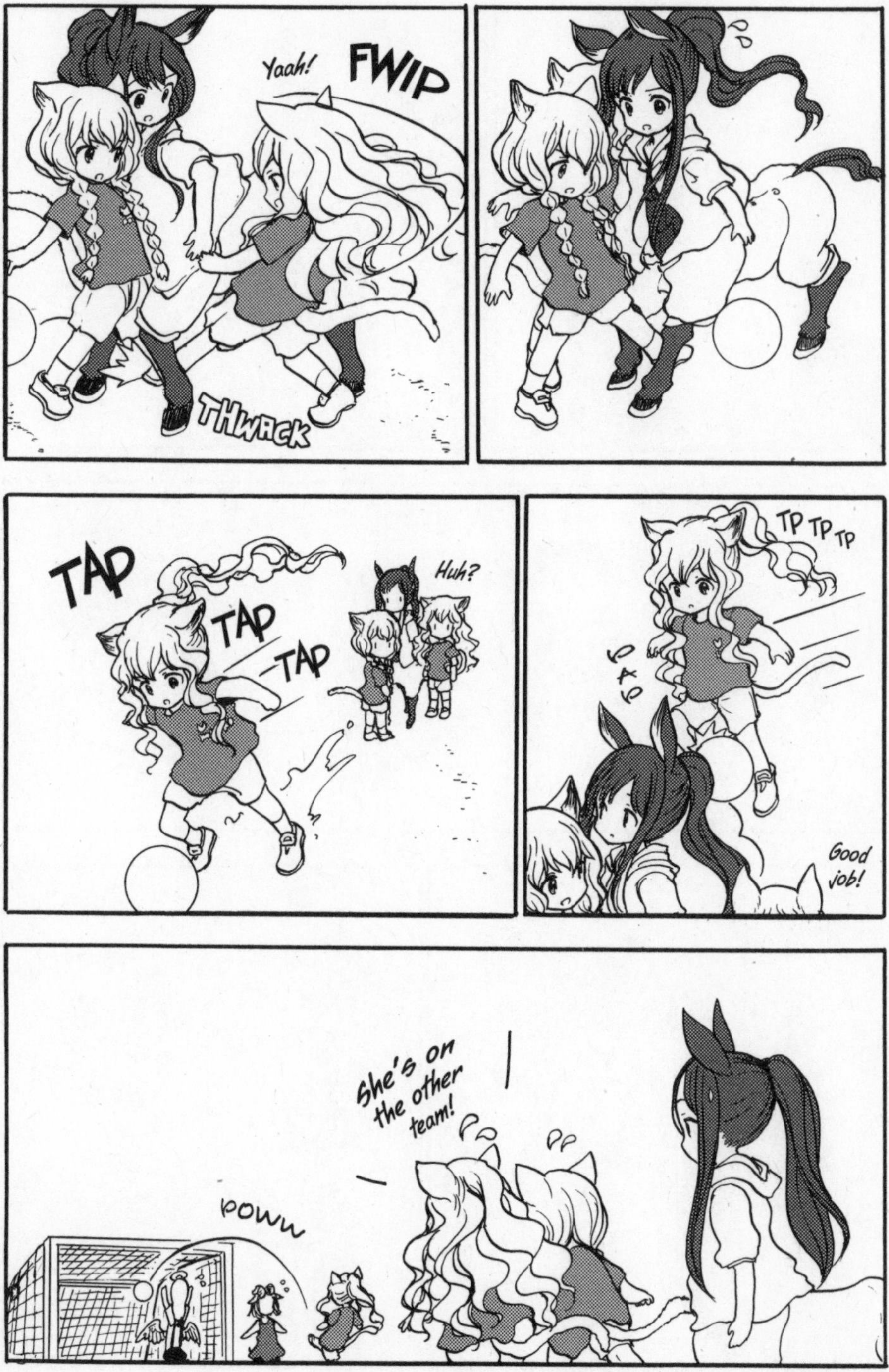
Yaah!
FWIP
THWACK
TP TP TP
Good job!
Huh?
TAP
TAP
TAP
She's on the other team!
POWW

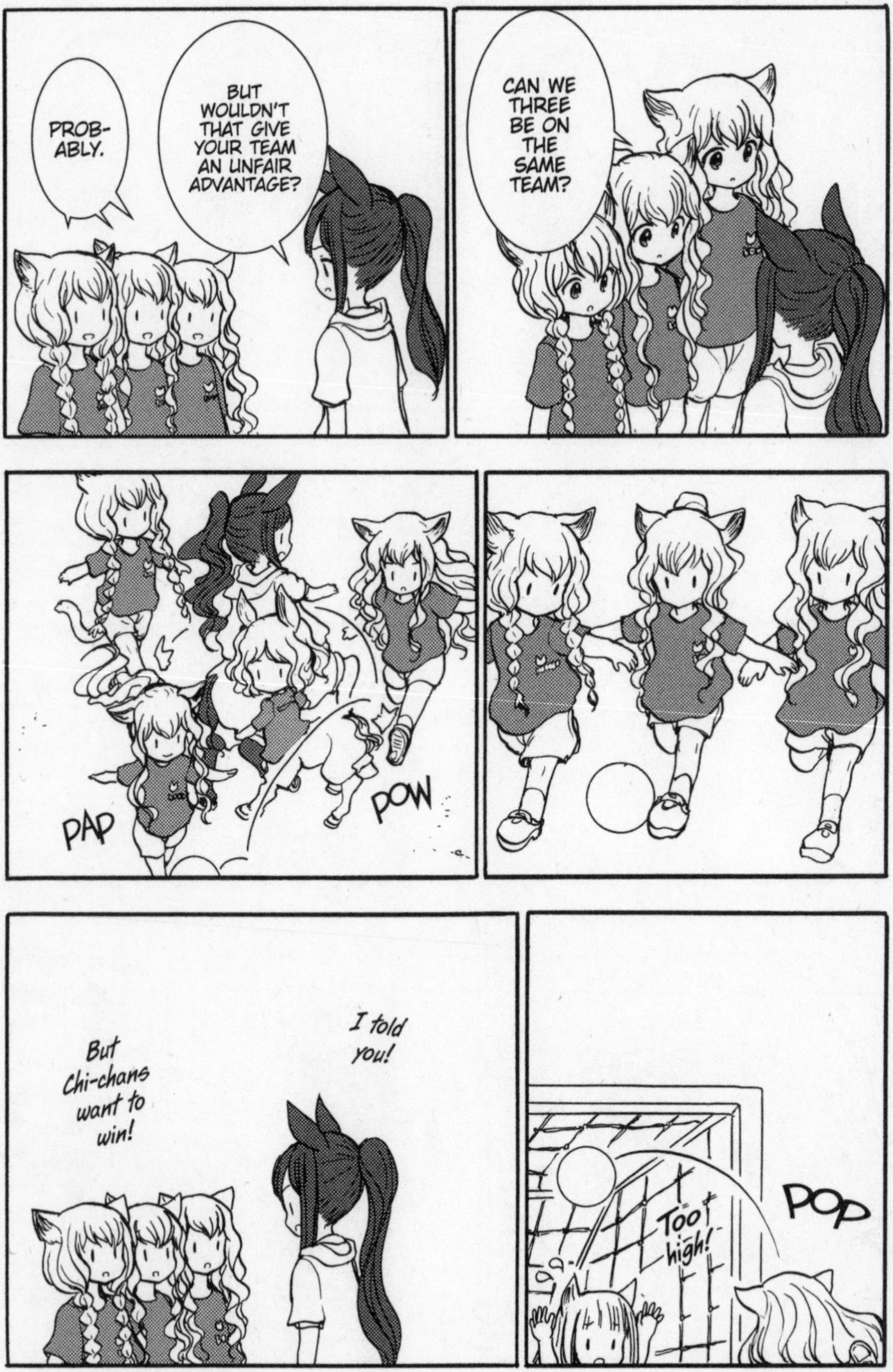
CAN WE THREE BE ON THE SAME TEAM?
BUT WOULDN'T THAT GIVE YOUR TEAM AN UNFAIR ADVANTAGE?
PROB-ABLY.
POW
PAP
POP
Too high!
I told you!
But Chi-chans want to win!

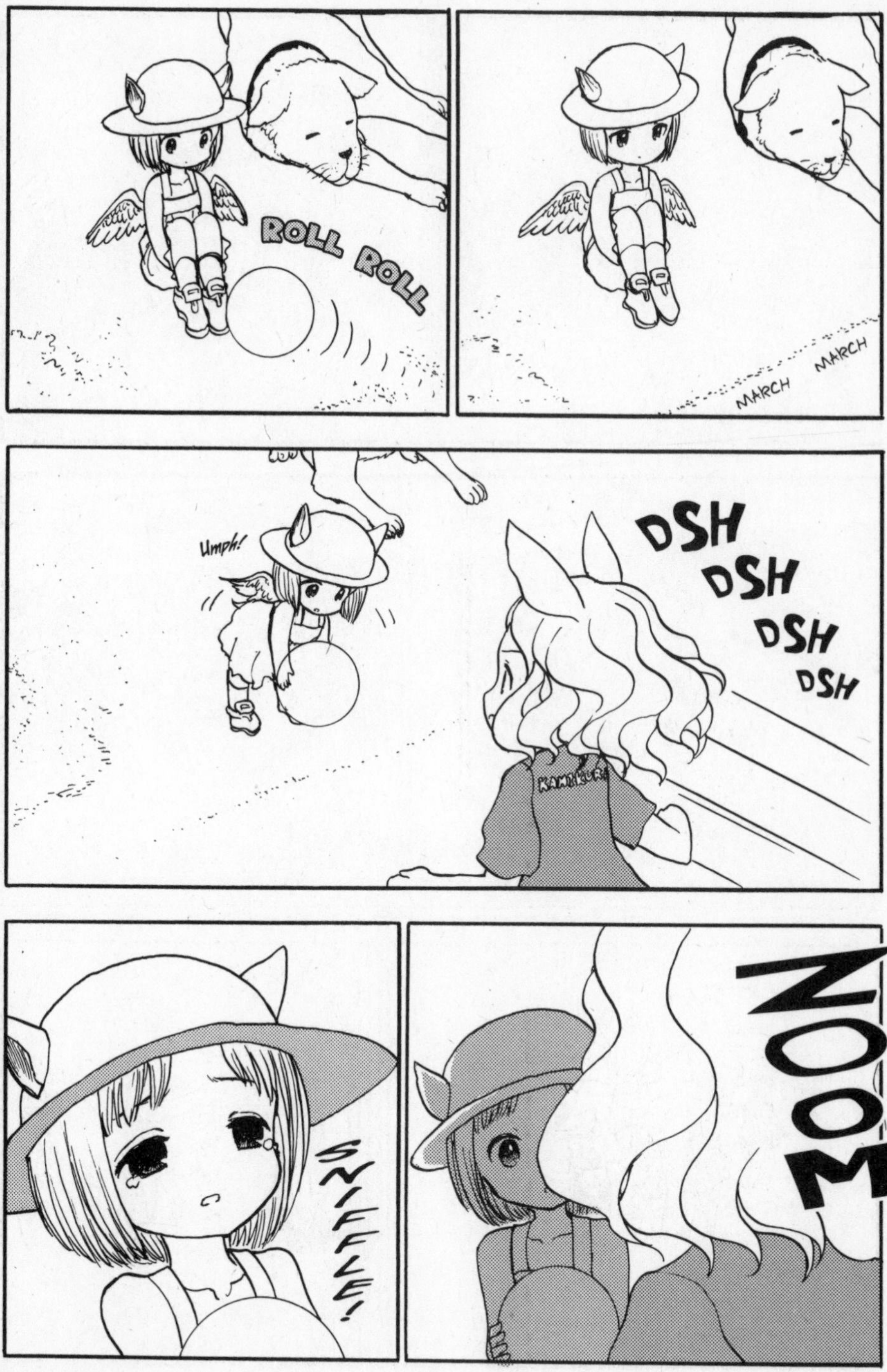
MARCH MARCH
ROLL ROLL
DSH DSH DSH DSH
Umph!
VOOM
SNIFFLE!

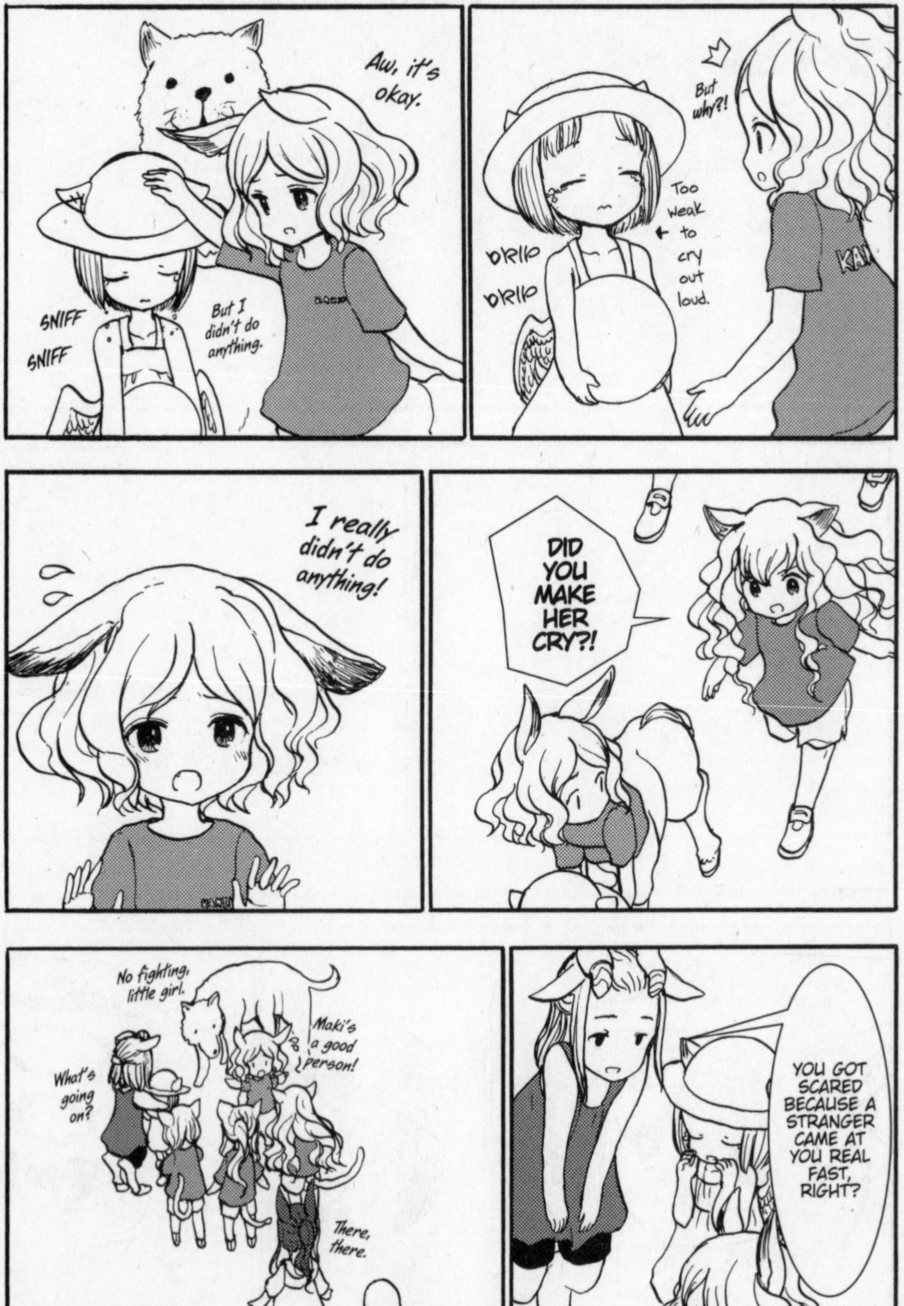

But why?!
Too weak to cry out loud.
DRIP
DRIP
Aw, it's okay.
But I didn't do anything.
SNIFF
SNIFF
DID YOU MAKE HER CRY?!
I really didn't do anything!
YOU GOT SCARED BECAUSE A STRANGER CAME AT YOU REAL FAST, RIGHT?
No fighting, little girl.
Maki's a good person!
What's going on?
There, there.

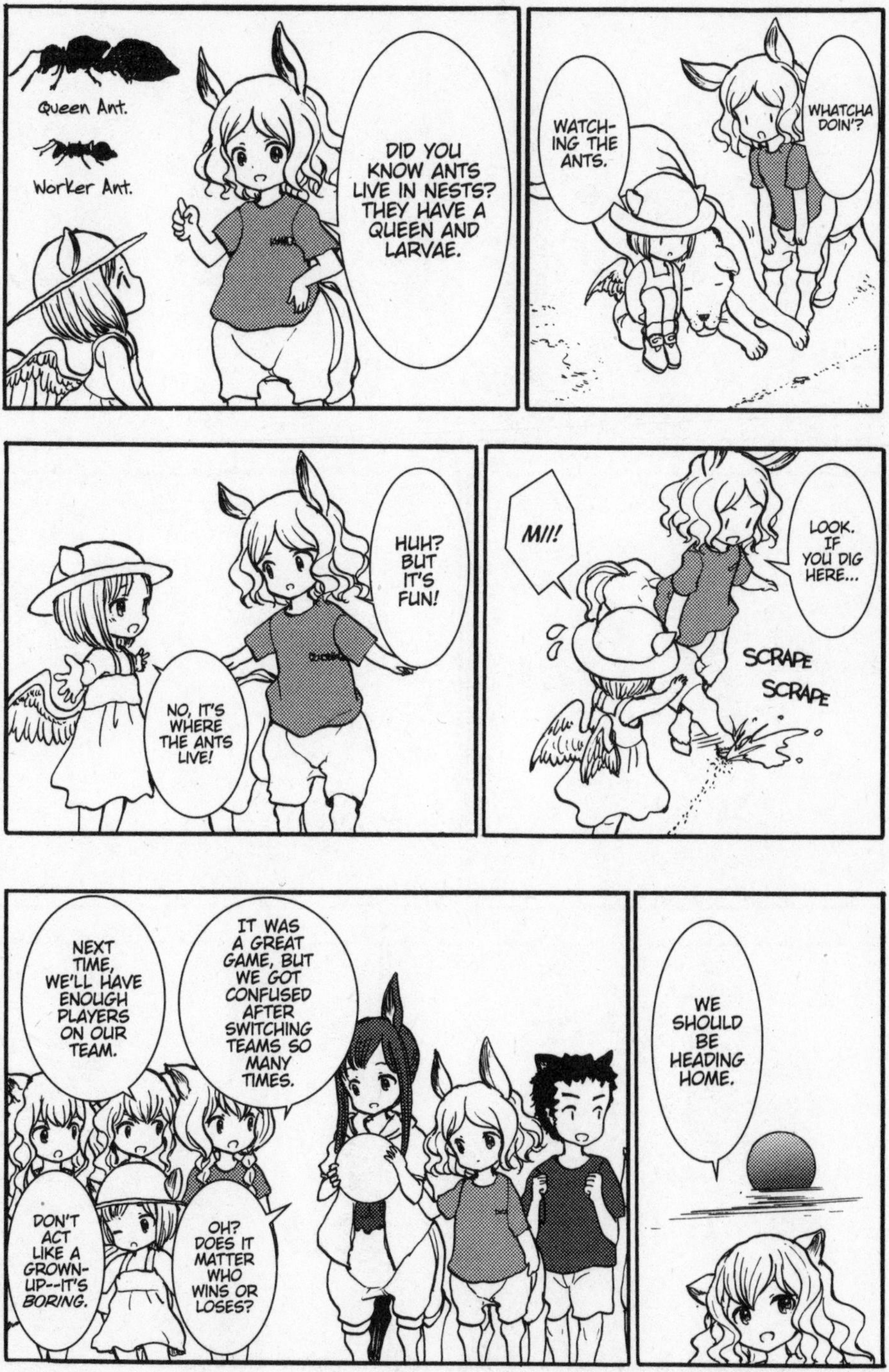
WHATCHA DOIN'?
WATCHING THE ANTS.
DID YOU KNOW ANTS LIVE IN NESTS? THEY HAVE A QUEEN AND LARVAE.
Queen Ant.
Worker Ant.
LOOK. IF YOU DIG HERE...
MII!
SCRAPE
SCRAPE
HUH? BUT IT'S FUN!
NO, IT'S WHERE THE ANTS LIVE!
WE SHOULD BE HEADING HOME.
IT WAS A GREAT GAME, BUT WE GOT CONFUSED AFTER SWITCHING TEAMS SO MANY TIMES.
NEXT TIME, WE'LL HAVE ENOUGH PLAYERS ON OUR TEAM.
OH? DOES IT MATTER WHO WINS OR LOSES?
DON'T ACT LIKE A GROWN-UP--IT'S BORING.

A Centaur's Life

SPOTLIGHT ON MERFOLK:
< 4 > MERFOLK IN ANCIENT JAPAN

IN ANCIENT JAPAN, MERFOLK'S ROLE IN SOCIETY WAS NOT
ONLY WATER TRANSPORTATION, AS IN OTHER PARTS OF THE
WORLD, BUT ALSO RELIGIOUS. THEY WERE ADORED AS BRINGERS
OF NEW CULTURE. RITUAL PONDS FILLED WITH HOLY WATER WERE
ALWAYS FOUND IN THE GARDENS OF NOBLES AND THE POWERFUL
CLANS OF RURAL AREAS. SIMILAR WORSHIP OCCURRED IN ANCIENT
GREECE AS WELL, BUT THE MERFOLK COLONIES AND THE RELIGION
ASSOCIATED WITH THEM VANISHED AS CITY-STATES COLLAPSED.
MERFOLK SURVIVED ON PACIFIC ISLANDS UNTIL A MUCH LATER
ERA, BUT THE INVASION OF WESTERN NATIONS AND SUBSEQUENT
KIDNAPPING, MURDER, AND PANDEMIC DISEASES LED TO THEIR
ANNIHILATION AND THE REWRITING OF THEIR RELIGION DURING THE
MODERN ERA. THEIR BELIEFS, CONSEQUENTLY, ARE FOUND ONLY IN
THE ARCHAEOLOGICAL RECORD. THOUGH THERE HAVE BEEN CLAIMS
OF OPPORTUNITIES FOR RECONSTRUCTION IN RECENT YEARS, IT
PROVED LITTLE MORE THAN A FAD THAT LEANED UNDENIABLY
TOWARD COMMERCIALISM. IT IS TRUE, HOWEVER, THAT THE
DYNASTIES OF JAPAN HAVE CONTINUED TO THIS DAY, RESULTING
IN THE SURVIVAL OF THE MERFOLK COMMUNITY AND ITS RELIGION,
ALBEIT NOT WITHOUT SOME CHANGES. JAPAN'S UNIQUE HIGH MORAL
STANDARDS ARE ALREADY WELL KNOWN, BUT THE MERFOLK'S
SURVIVAL MAY BE DEPENDENT ON THE FATE OF THIS NATION.

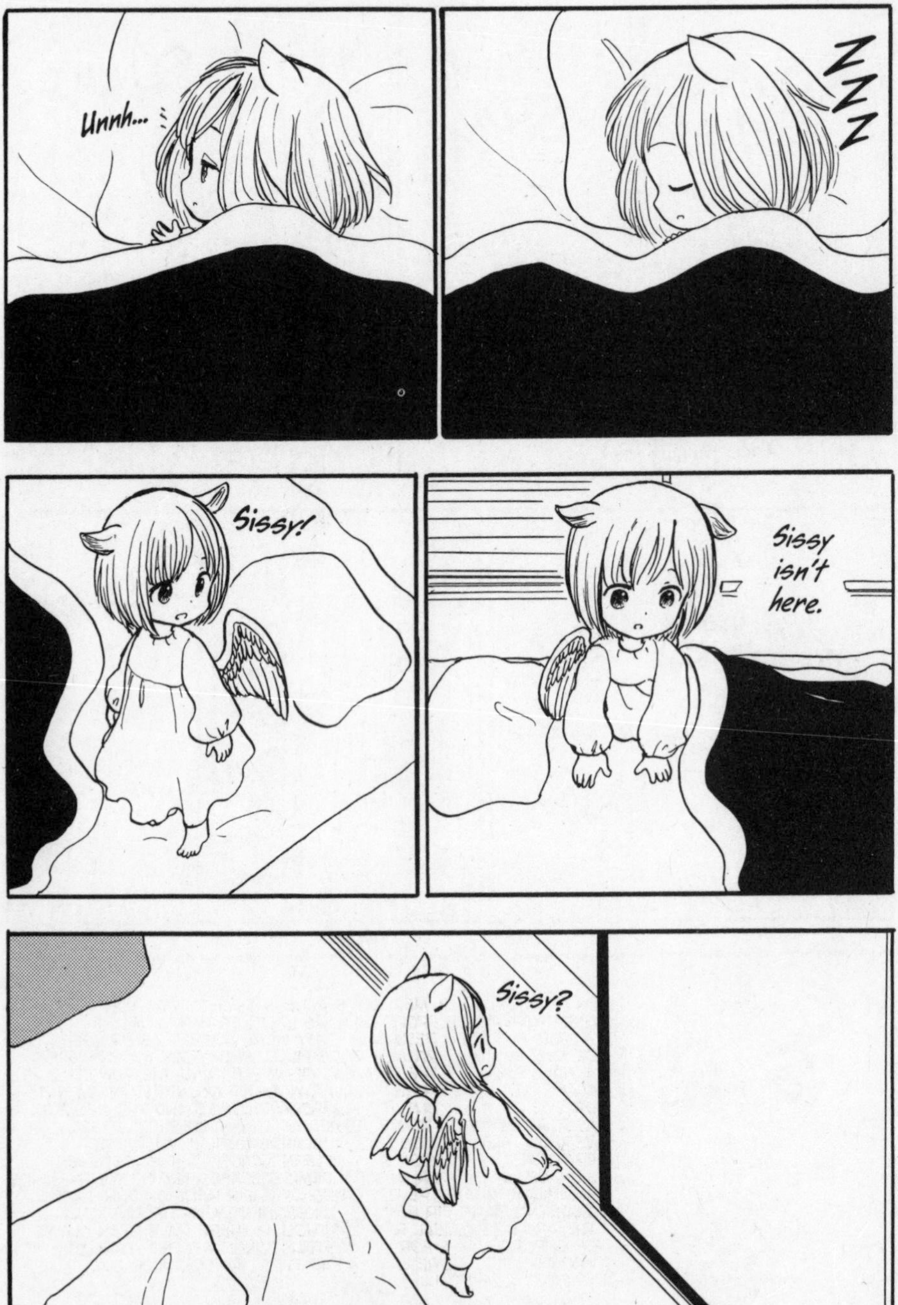
ZZZ
Unnh...
Sissy isn't here.
Sissy!
Sissy?

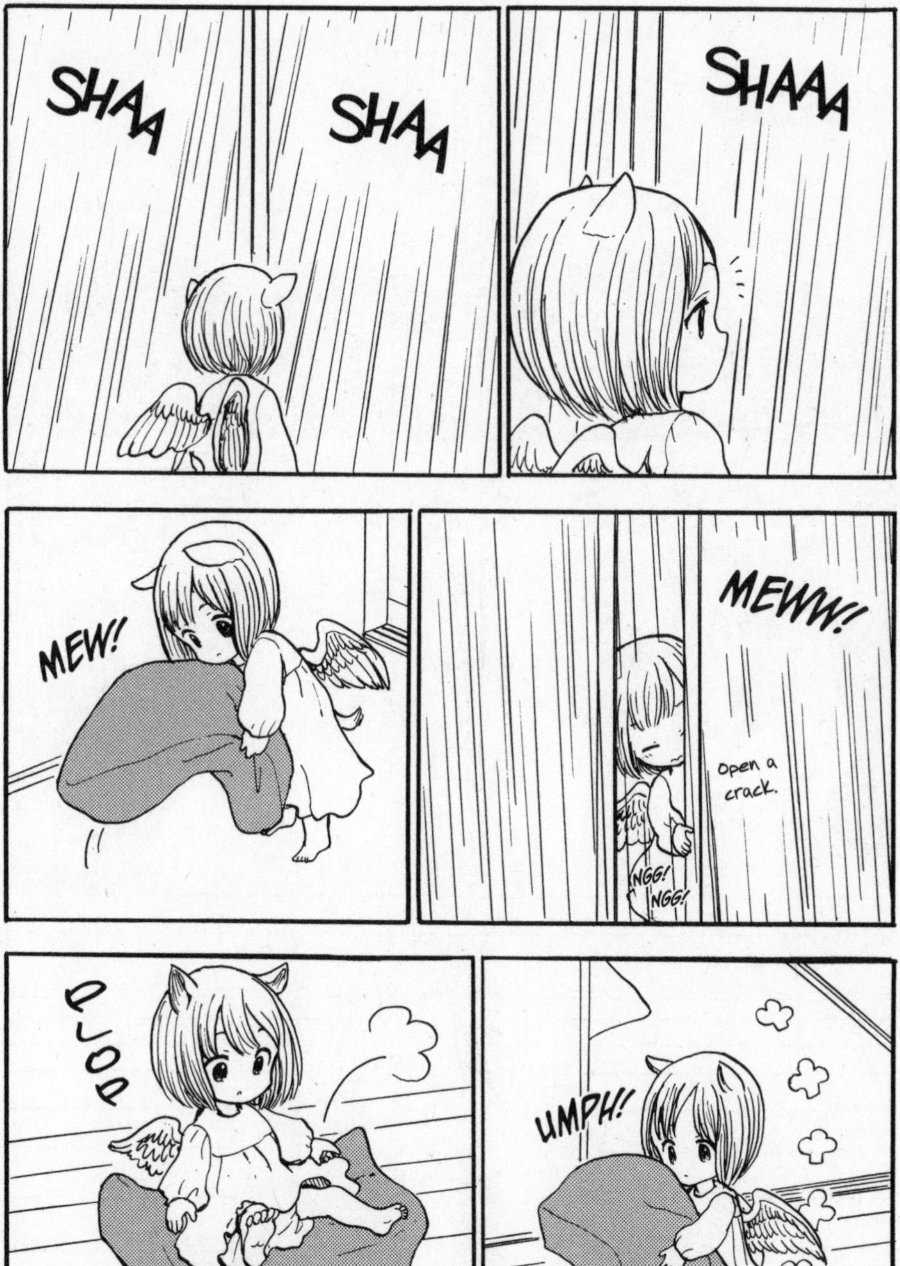
SHAAA
SHAA
SHAA
MEWW!
Open a crack.
NGG!
NGG!
MEW!
UMPH!
PLOP

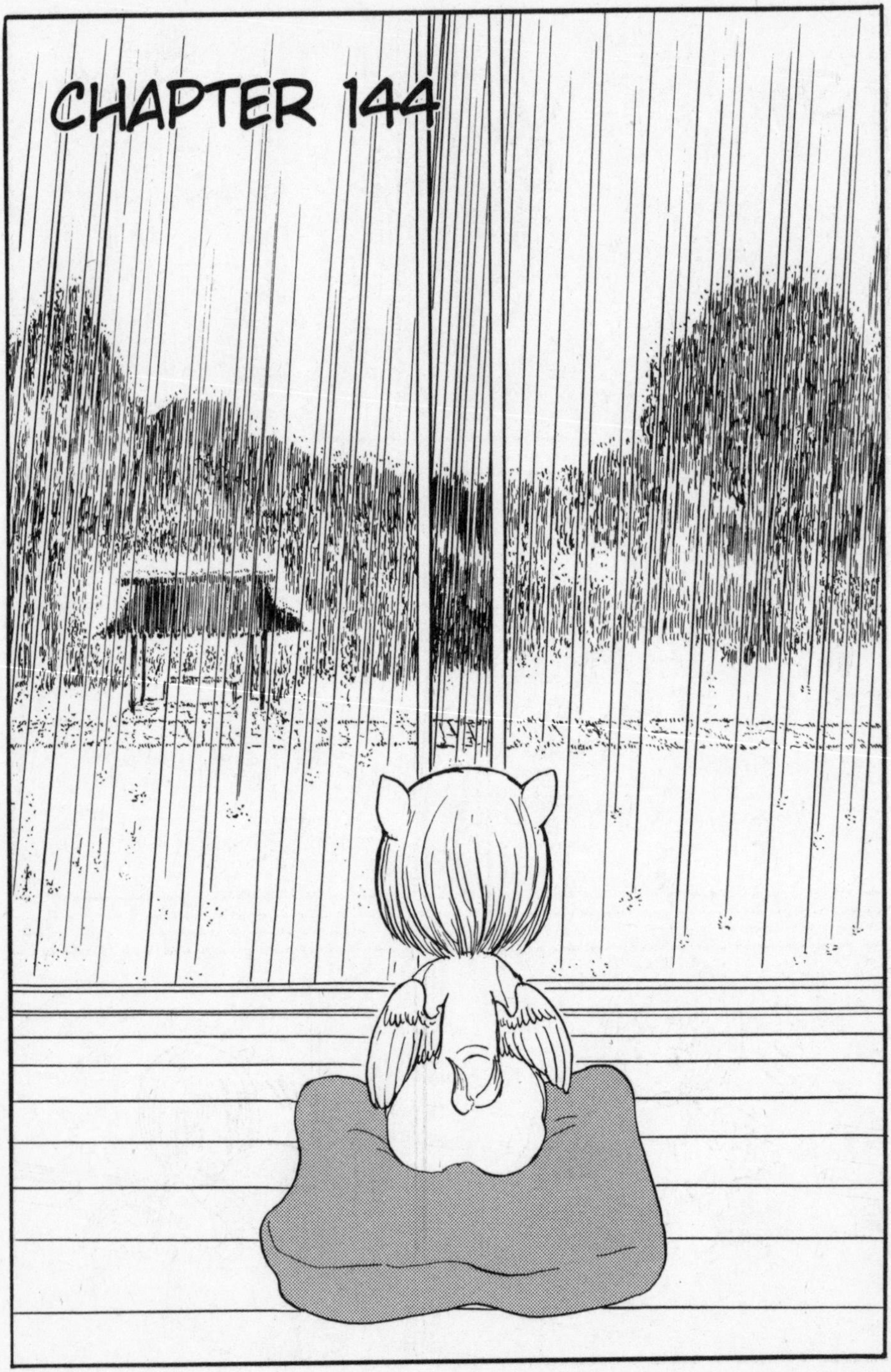
CHAPTER 144

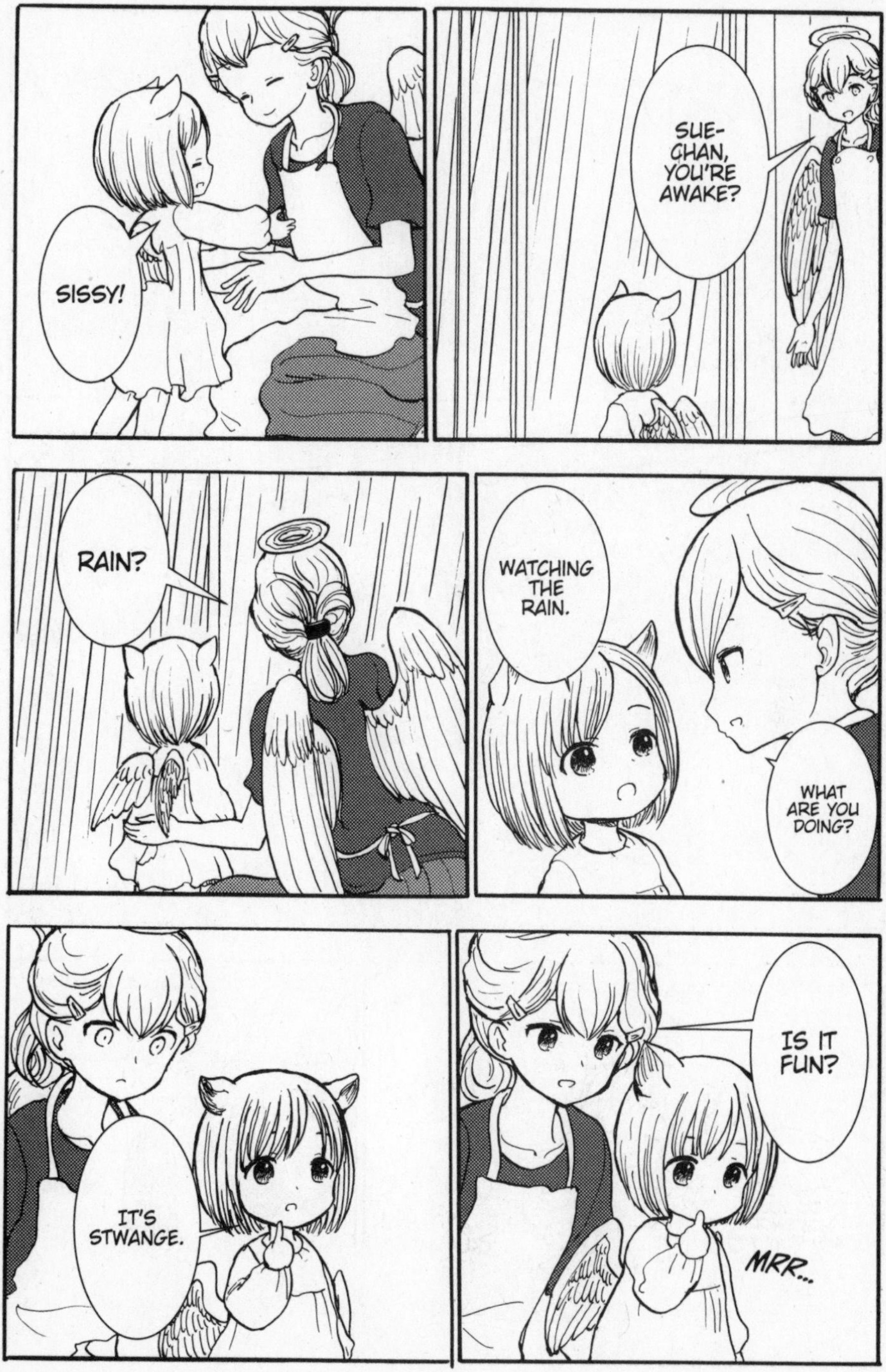
SUE-CHAN, YOU'RE AWAKE?
SISSY!
WHAT ARE YOU DOING?
WATCHING THE RAIN.
RAIN?
IS IT FUN?
MRR...
IT'S STWANGE.

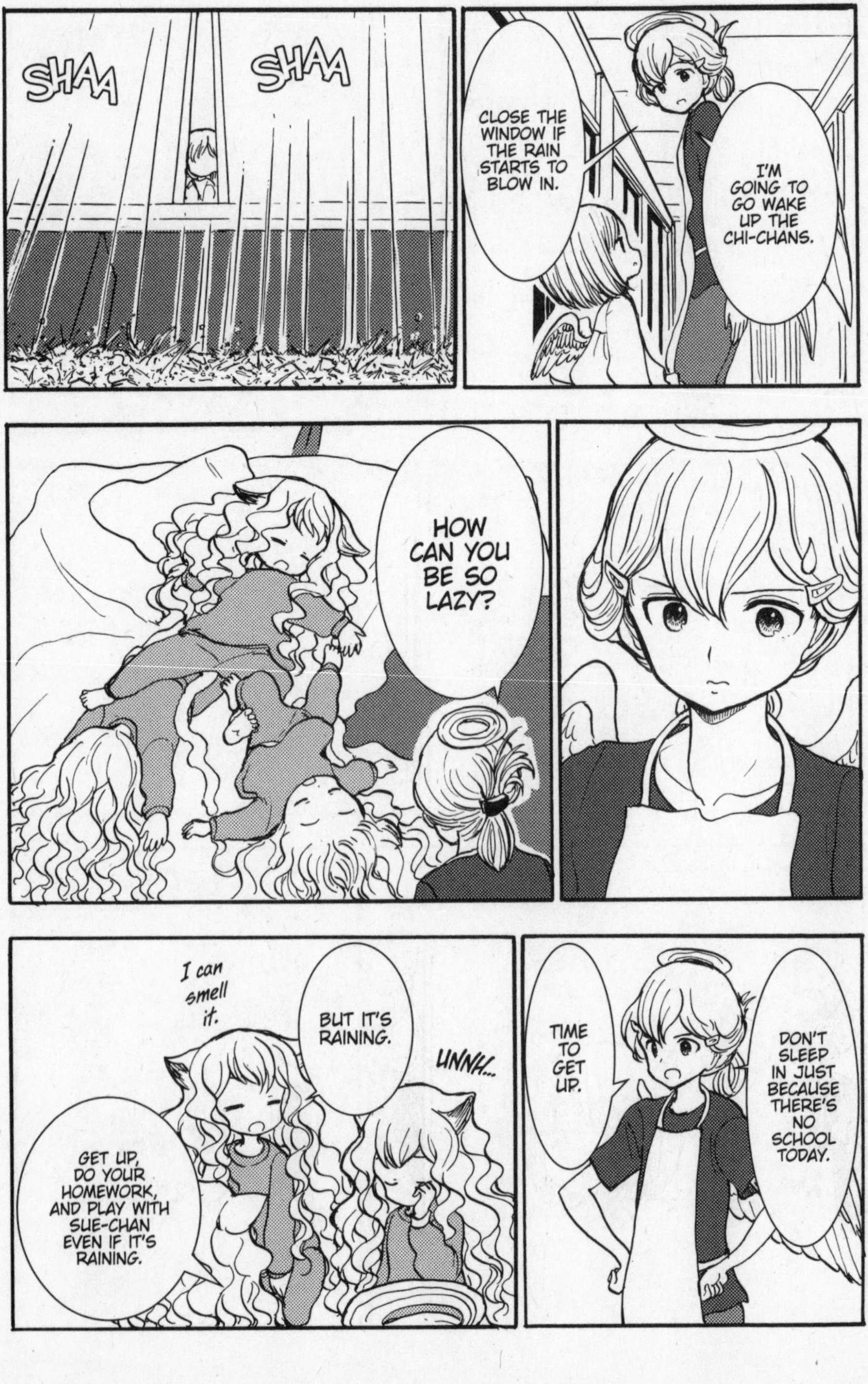
I'M GOING TO GO WAKE UP THE CHI-CHANS.
CLOSE THE WINDOW IF THE RAIN STARTS TO BLOW IN.
SHAA
SHAA
HOW CAN YOU BE SO LAZY?
DON'T SLEEP IN JUST BECAUSE THERE'S NO SCHOOL TODAY.
TIME TO GET UP.
UNNH...
BUT IT'S RAINING.
I can smell it.
GET UP, DO YOUR HOMEWORK, AND PLAY WITH SUE-CHAN EVEN IF IT'S RAINING.

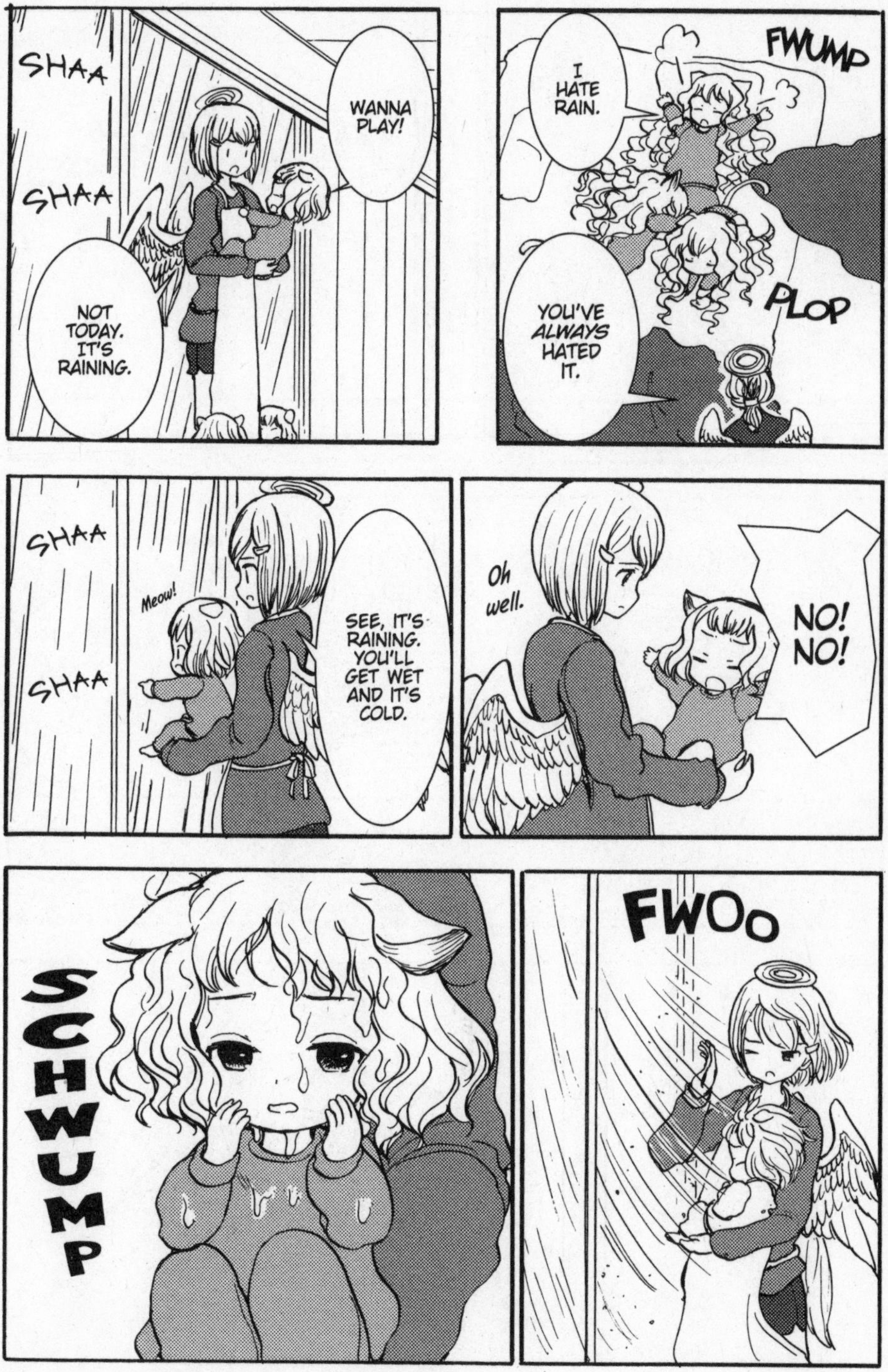
FWUMP
I HATE RAIN.
PLOP
YOU'VE *ALWAYS* HATED IT.
WANNA PLAY!
SHAA
SHAA
NOT TODAY. IT'S RAINING.
NO! NO!
Oh well.
SEE, IT'S RAINING. YOU'LL GET WET AND IT'S COLD.
Meow!
SHAA
SHAA
FWOo
SCHWUMP

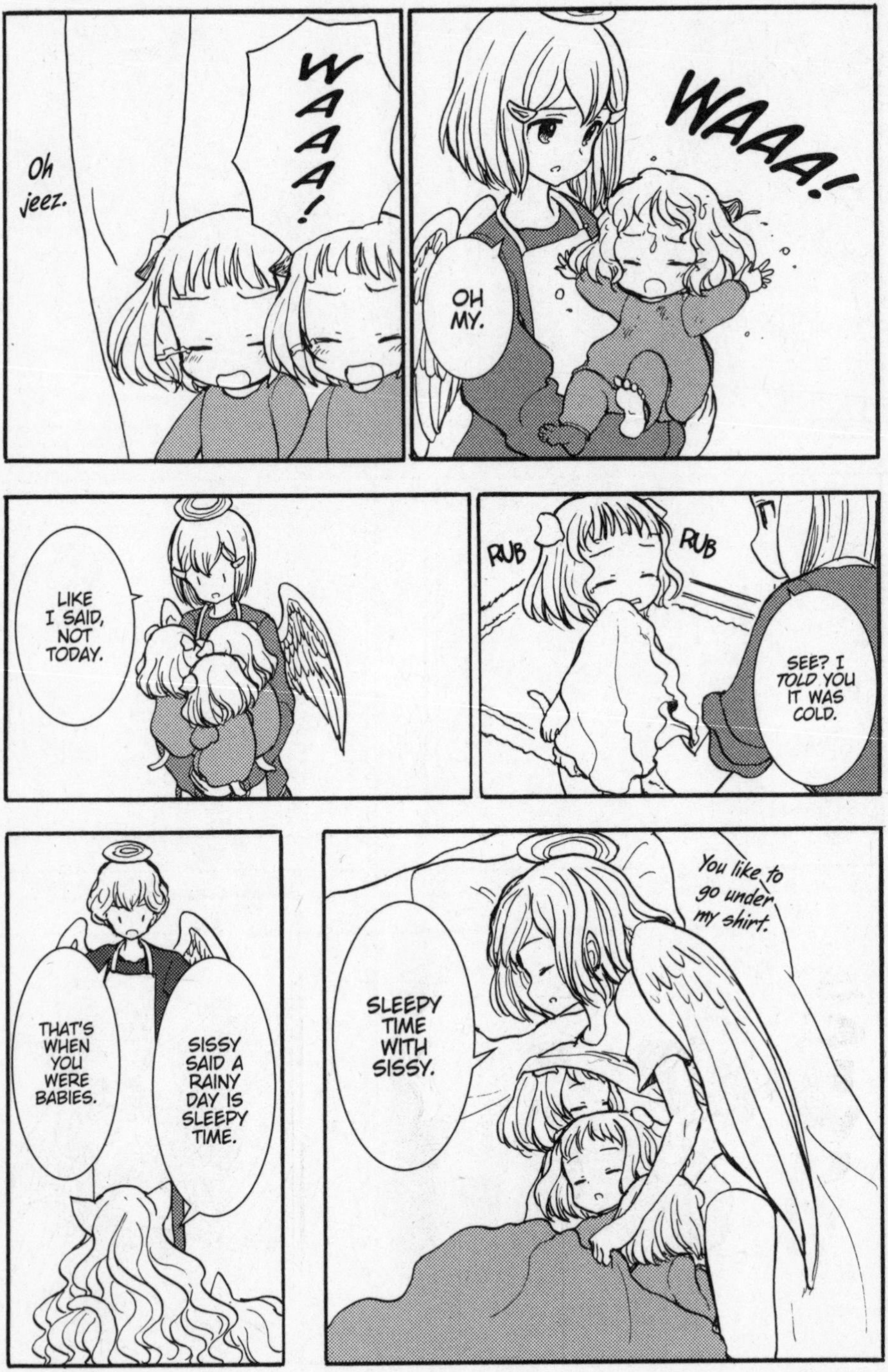
WAAAA!
OH MY.
WAAAA!
Oh jeez.
RUB RUB
SEE? I TOLD YOU IT WAS COLD.
LIKE I SAID, NOT TODAY.
You like to go under my shirt.
SLEEPY TIME WITH SISSY.
SISSY SAID A RAINY DAY IS SLEEPY TIME.
THAT'S WHEN YOU WERE BABIES.

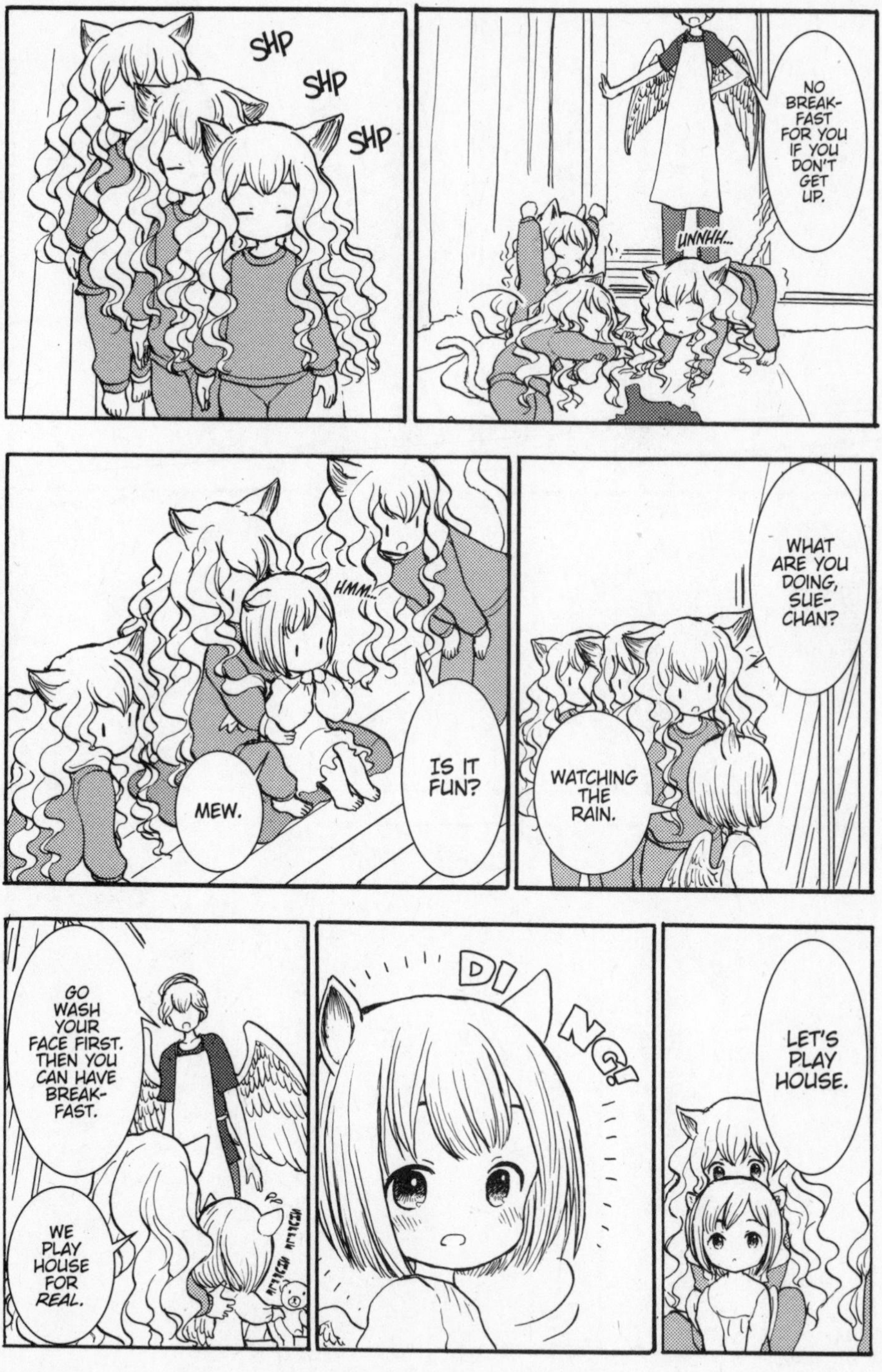
NO BREAK-FAST FOR YOU IF YOU DON'T GET UP.
UNNHH...
SHP
SHP
SHP
WHAT ARE YOU DOING, SUE-CHAN?
WATCHING THE RAIN.
HMM...
IS IT FUN?
MEW.
LET'S PLAY HOUSE.
DING!
GO WASH YOUR FACE FIRST. THEN YOU CAN HAVE BREAK-FAST.
WE PLAY HOUSE FOR *REAL.*

A Centaur's Life

SPOTLIGHT ON MERFOLK:
< 5 > DOMINATION OF THE RIVERS

BEFORE THE WARRING STATES PERIOD, MERFOLK WERE ACTIVE IN THE OCEAN AS
WELL AS IN EVERY BODY OF WATER IN JAPAN. MANY OF THEM ALSO BELONGED TO
SAMURAI GROUPS, WHICH MOST PEOPLE THINK WERE COMPOSED ONLY OF ARMED
CENTAUR WARRIORS, MOUNTED WARRIORS, AND ARMED FOLLOWERS IN MEDIEVAL
JAPAN. HOWEVER, THEY ACTUALLY INCLUDED MANY CIVILIANS, SUCH AS FALCONERS,
DOG TRAINERS, COOKS, LACQUER CRAFTSMEN, INDIGO-DYE CRAFTSMEN, SWORD-
SMITHS, WOODCUTTERS, MARKET SUPERVISORS, AND EVEN *KAWARAMONO*--LOW-
CLASS OUTCASTS WHO PERFORMED THE MOST DESPISED LABOR. IN OTHER WORDS,
SAMURAI GROUPS IN MEDIEVAL JAPAN WERE SELF-SUSTAINING COMMUNITIES THAT
GATHERED MATERIALS, PROCESSED AND MANUFACTURED THEM INTO PRODUCTS,
TRANSPORTED THE PRODUCTS BETWEEN TERRITORIES, AND SOLD THEM AT MARKETS.
NEEDLESS TO SAY, MERFOLK WERE KEY TO THE PHYSICAL AND SPIRITUAL SUPPORT
OF THE GROUPS AND THEIR DOMINANCE OVER THE WATERS. ALL MERFOLK WERE TIED
TO THE IMPERIAL COURT IN SOME WAY AND ESTABLISHED A UNIQUE POSITION IN THE
DISTRIBUTION OF INFORMATION (IN ADDITION TO GOODS), WHERE EACH TERRITORY
WAS UNOFFICIALLY ABSORBED IN THE SHADOW OF THE RITSURYO CODES.

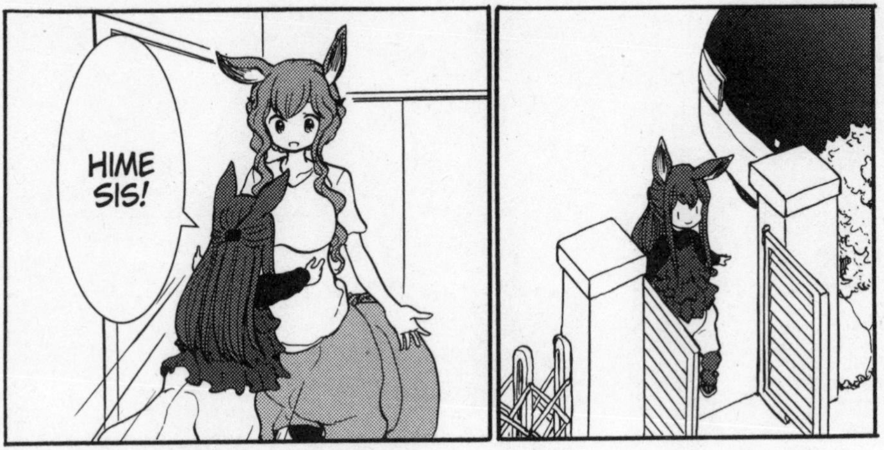
HIME SIS!

CHAPTER 145

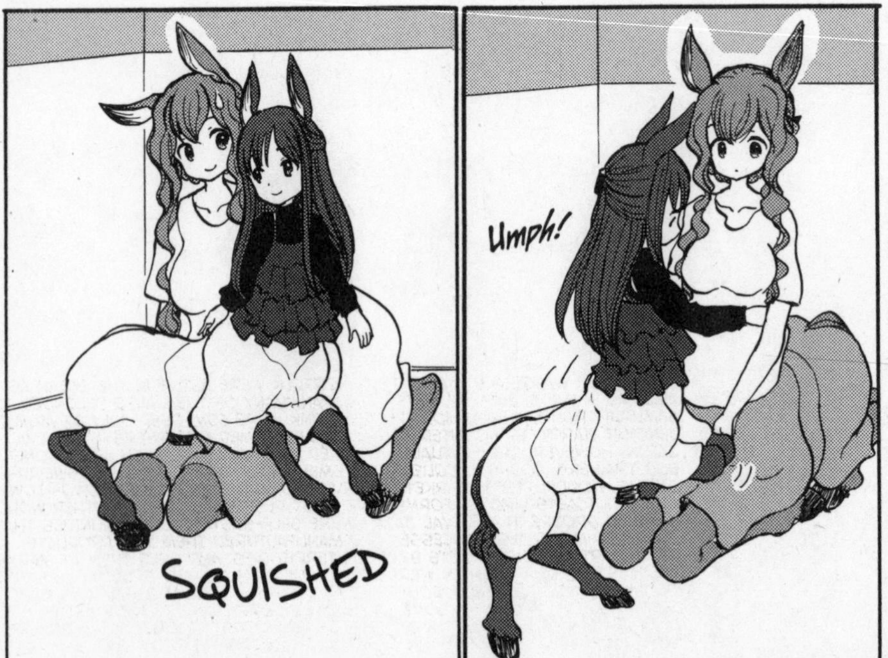
Umph!
SQUISHED

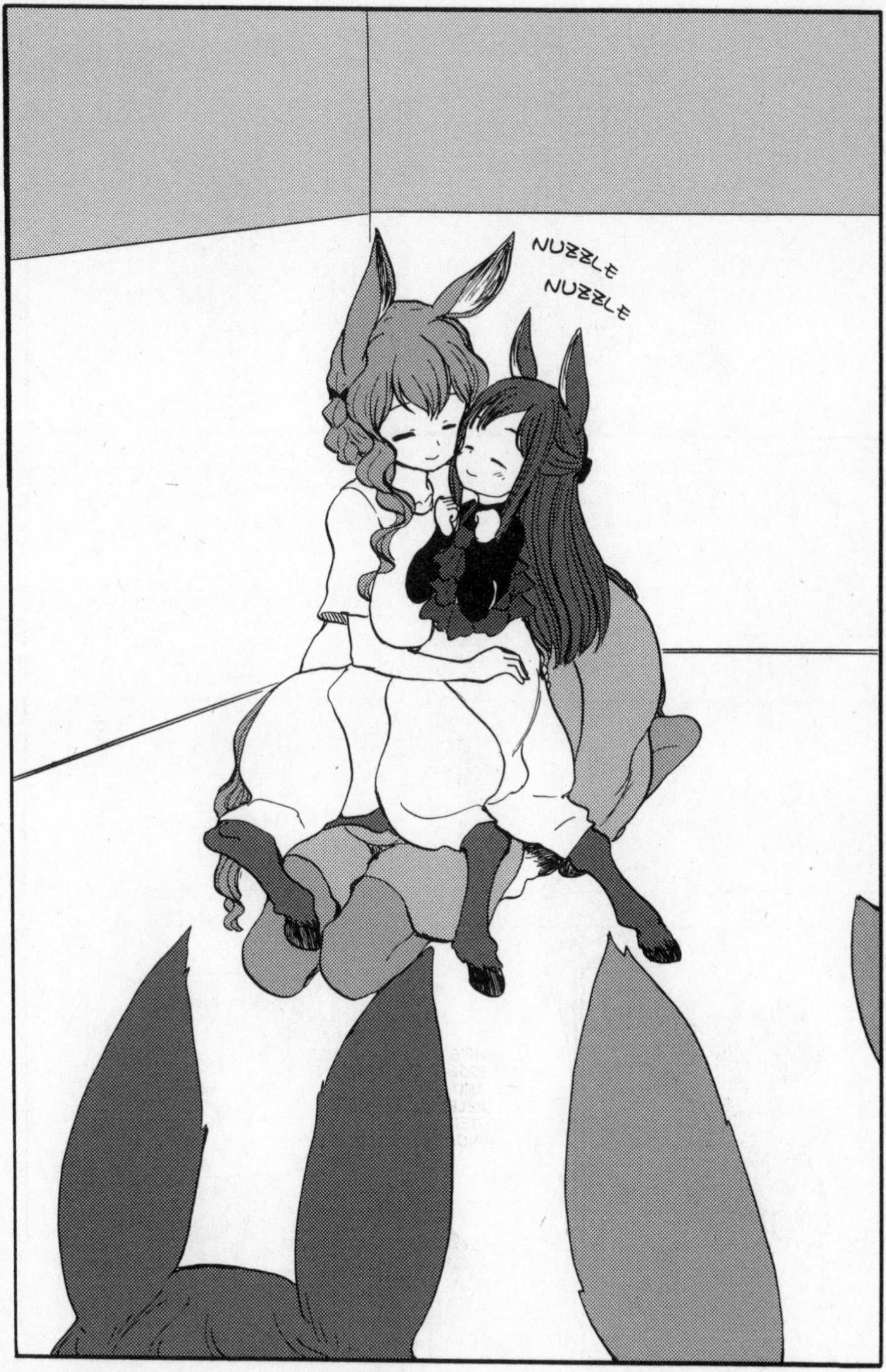
NUZZLE
NUZZLE

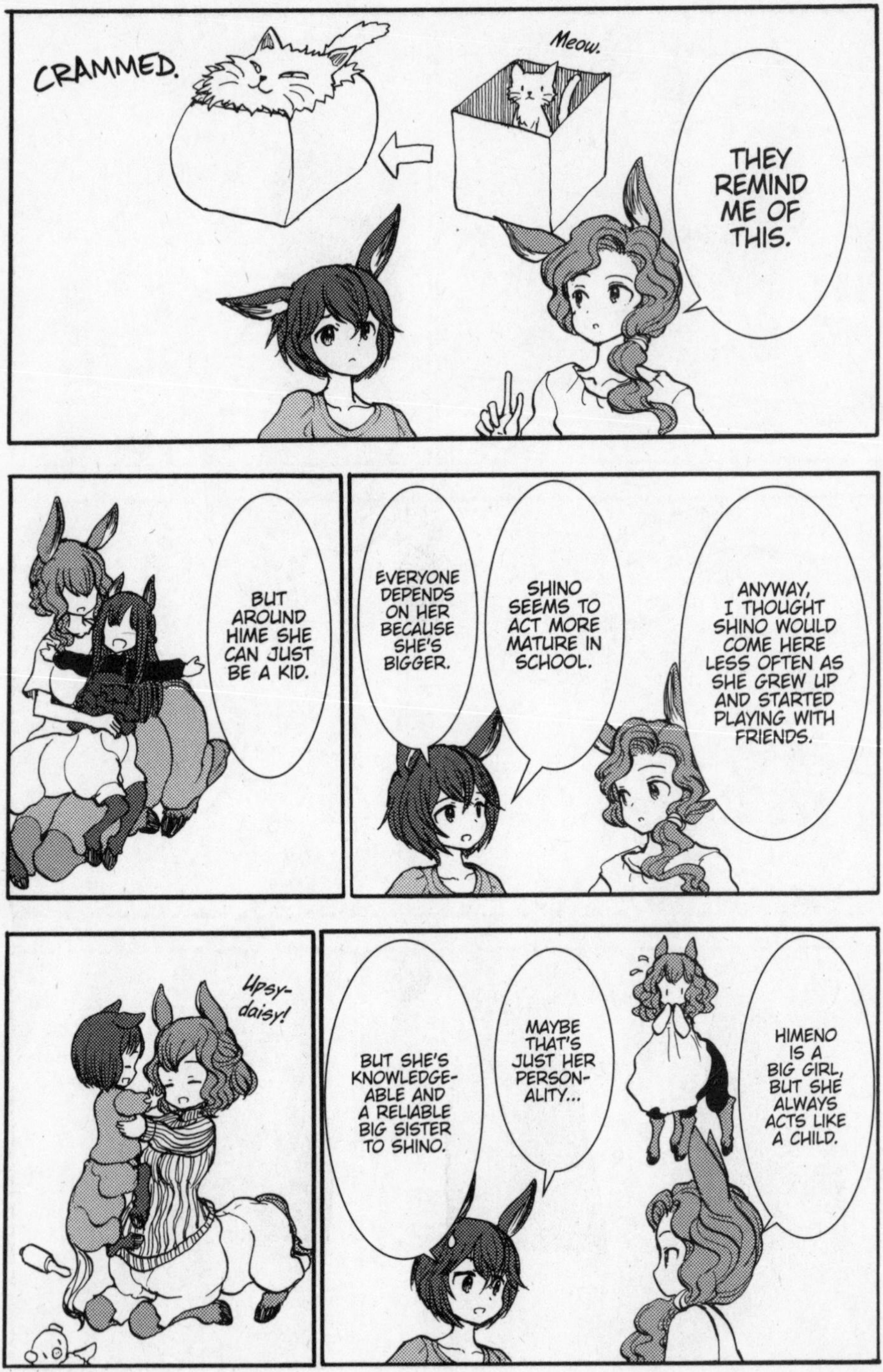
THEY REMIND ME OF THIS.
Meow.
CRAMMED.
ANYWAY, I THOUGHT SHINO WOULD COME HERE LESS OFTEN AS SHE GREW UP AND STARTED PLAYING WITH FRIENDS.
SHINO SEEMS TO ACT MORE MATURE IN SCHOOL.
EVERYONE DEPENDS ON HER BECAUSE SHE'S BIGGER.
BUT AROUND HIME SHE CAN JUST BE A KID.
HIMENO IS A BIG GIRL, BUT SHE ALWAYS ACTS LIKE A CHILD.
MAYBE THAT'S JUST HER PERSONALITY...
BUT SHE'S KNOWLEDGEABLE AND A RELIABLE BIG SISTER TO SHINO.
Upsy-daisy!

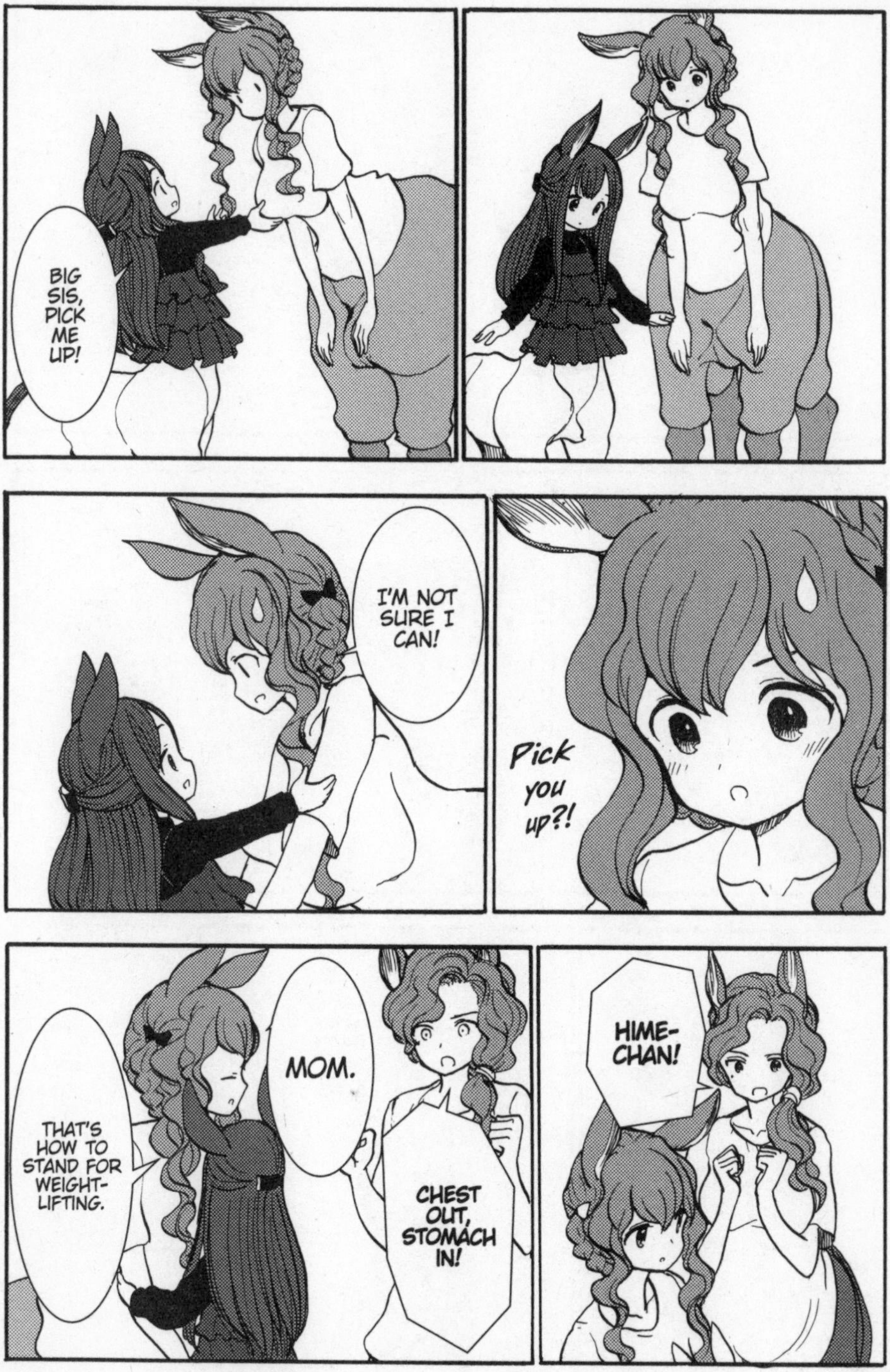
BIG SIS, PICK ME UP!
Pick you up?!
I'M NOT SURE I CAN!
HIME-CHAN!
CHEST OUT, STOMACH IN!
MOM.
THAT'S HOW TO STAND FOR WEIGHT-LIFTING.

A Centaur's Life

SPOTLIGHT ON MERFOLK:
< 6 > THE NAVY

AT THE BEGINNING OF THE WARRING STATES PERIOD,
THE FEUDAL LORDS DROPPED THE CONCEPT OF POSSESSING
MULTIPLE LANDS AND INSTEAD ESTABLISHED A TYPE OF EMPIRE
WITH CENTRALIZED TERRITORIAL CONTROL AND OVERARCHING
LAWS. IN ADDITION, SAMURAI GROUPS SHED THEIR NON-SAMURAI
MEMBERS, WITH SOME EXCEPTIONS. THE MERFOLK ALSO LEFT, BUT
AS A RESULT, MERFOLK COMMUNITIES THAT HAD EXISTED SINCE
ANCIENT TIMES LOST THEIR PROTECTION AND DISAPPEARED FROM
RIVERS AND LAKES. HOWEVER, MERFOLK TRANSPORTATION UNIONS
THAT PARTNERED WITH WITNESSES AND LOCAL INFLUENCERS
WERE ESTABLISHED AT PORTS IN EVERY REGION. IN THE COASTAL
AREAS, A MERFOLK GROUP KNOWN AS THE NAVY WAS BORN.

THE NAVY ESTABLISHED ITS HEADQUARTERS ON A SMALL ISLAND IN ORDER
TO AVOID THREATS FROM LAND. IT OFFERED WATER TRANSPORTATION OR
COLLECTED TOLLS FROM OTHER WATER TRANSPORTATION VENDORS THROUGH
ITS MILITARY PROWESS. IT ALSO TOOK AN ACTIVE ROLE IN CONFLICTS BETWEEN
FEUDAL LORDS OVER NAVAL POWER. ONE LEGENDARY MERFOLK NAVAL TACTIC
WAS TO SINK ENEMY VESSELS BY POURING WATER INTO THEM FROM A LARGE
STEEL BUCKET, BUT THESE STORIES ARE INACCURATE. WHILE THE USE OF STEEL
BUCKETS WAS IN FACT TRUE, WHAT WAS ACTUALLY DUMPED INTO ENEMY VESSELS
WAS A FLAMMABLE CONCOCTION MADE OF SULFUR AND PINE RESIN. SHIPS AT THE
TIME WERE CONSTRUCTED OF WOOD, WHICH MADE THEM EXTREMELY VULNERABLE
TO INCENDIARY ATTACKS. METAL CONTAINERS SIMILAR TO *GANDOU* SEARCHLIGHTS,
WHICH COULD KEEP A CANDLE BURNING UNDERWATER, HAVE ALSO BEEN FOUND.

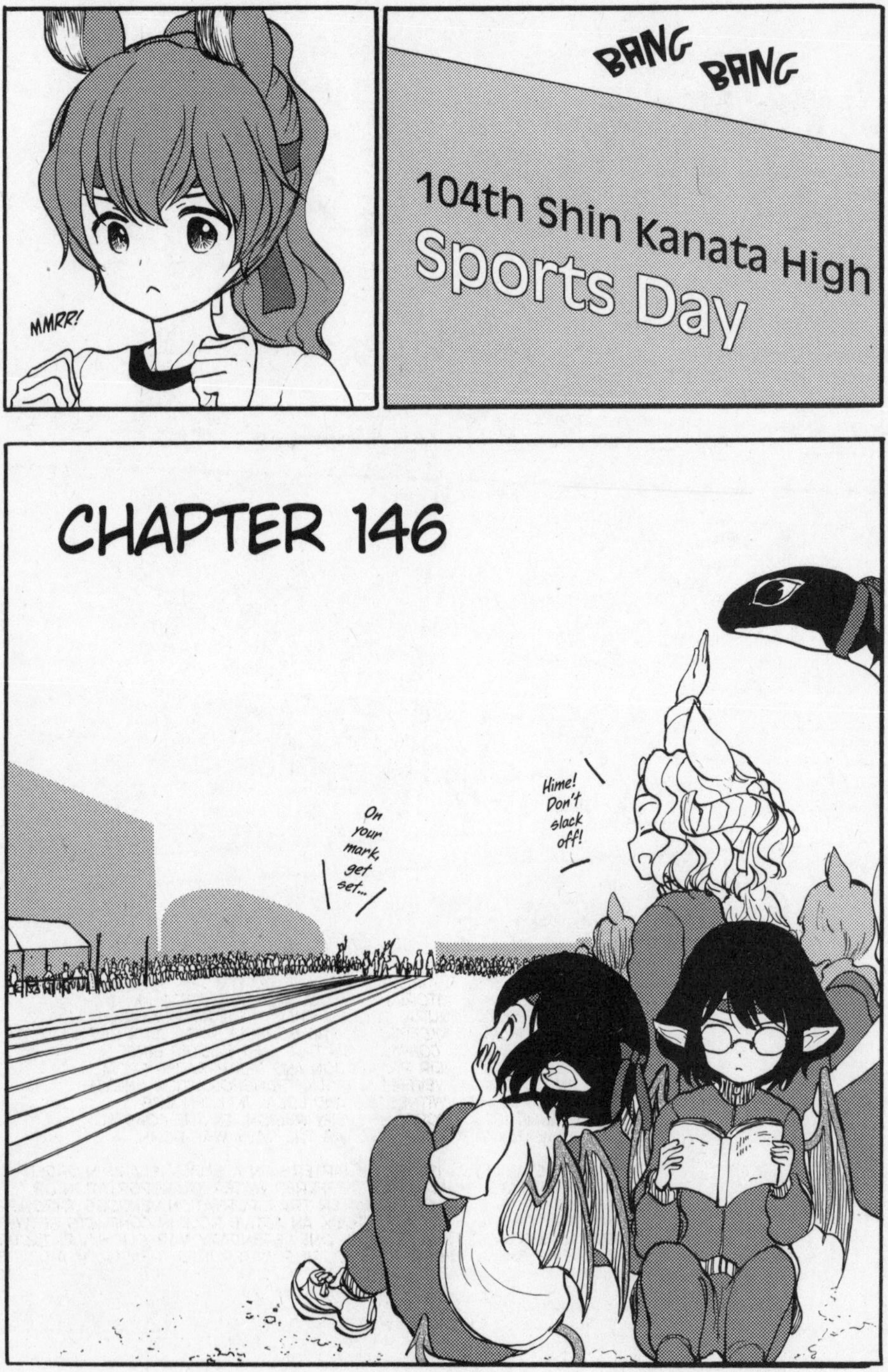
BANG BANG
104th Shin Kanata High
Sports Day
MMRR!
CHAPTER 146
Hime! Don't slack off!
On your mark, get set...

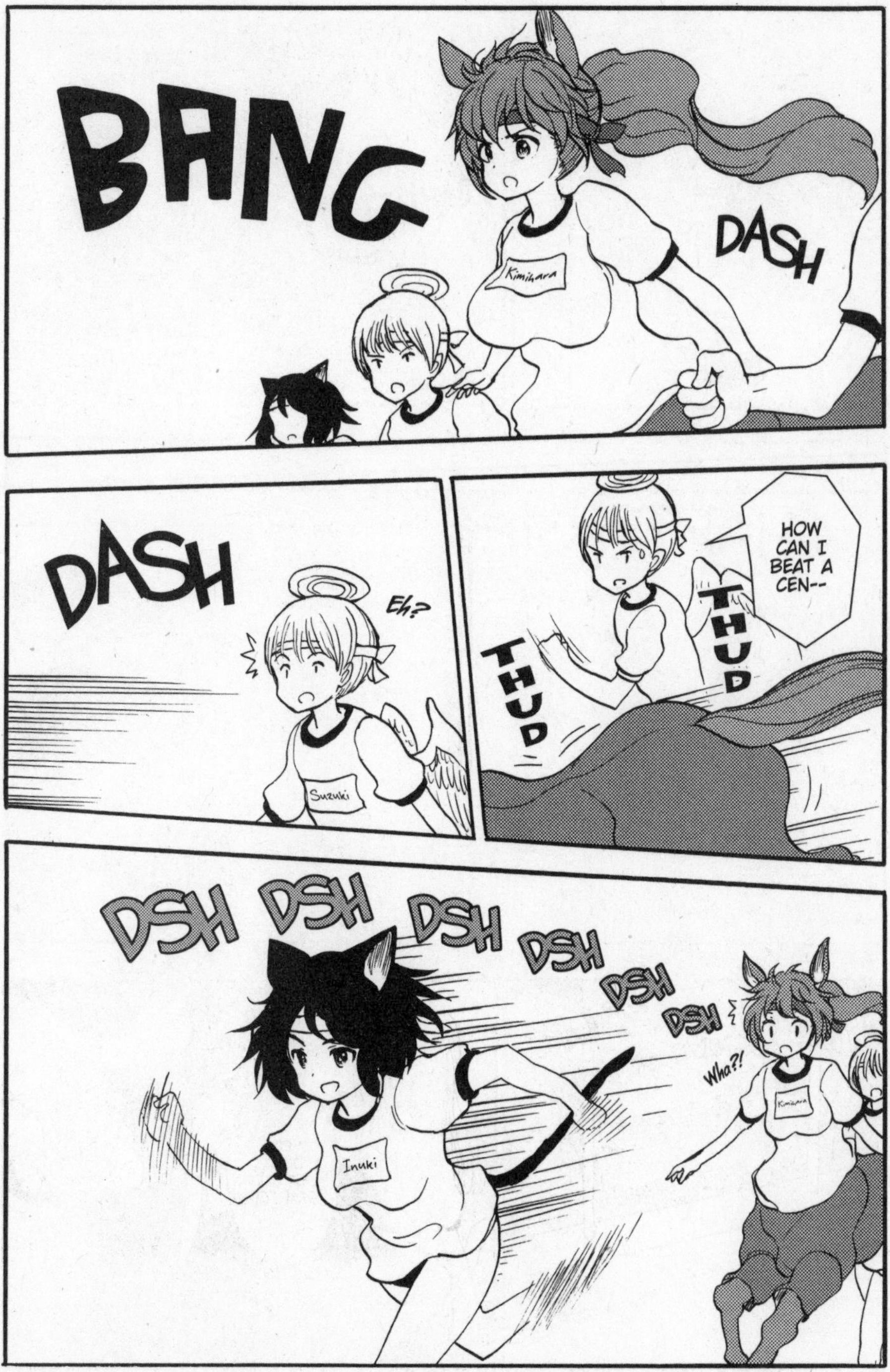
BANG
DASH
Kimihara
HOW CAN I BEAT A CEN--
THUD
THUD
DASH
Eh?
Suzuki
DSH DSH DSH DSH DSH DSH
Wha?!
Kimihara
Inuki

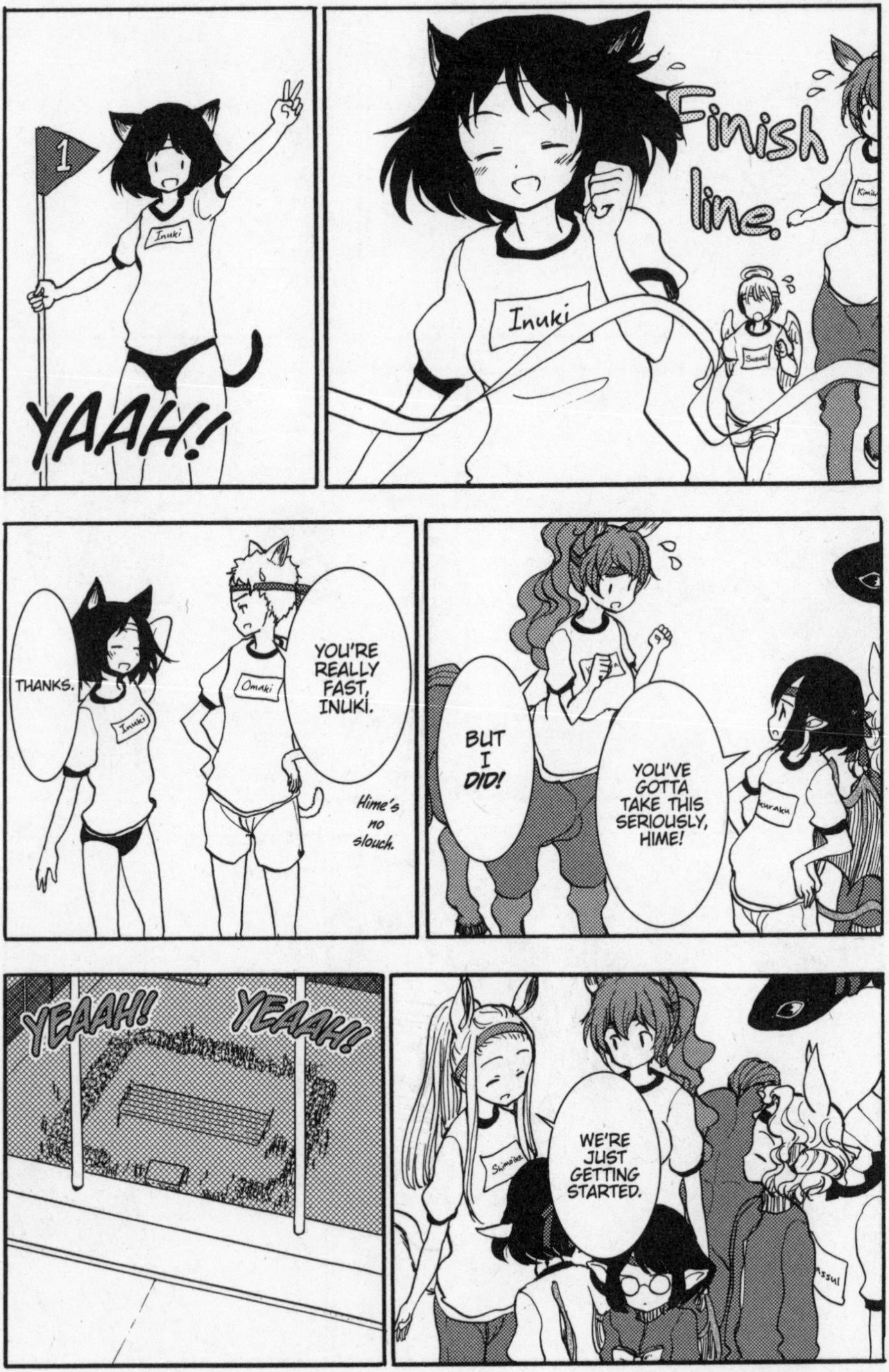
Finish line.
YAAH!
YOU'VE GOTTA TAKE THIS SERIOUSLY, HIME!
BUT I DID!
YOU'RE REALLY FAST, INUKI.
Hime's no slouch.
THANKS.
WE'RE JUST GETTING STARTED.
YEAAH! YEAAH!

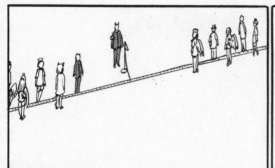

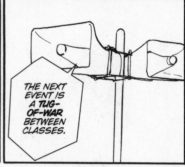

THE NEXT EVENT IS A TUG-OF-WAR BETWEEN CLASSES.
CENTAURS CAN'T CROUCH DOWN.
THAT GIVES US AN EDGE.
Ready, set...
HEAVE!

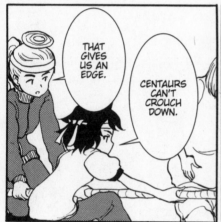

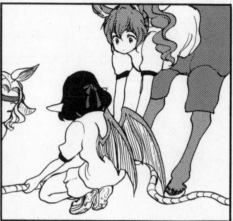

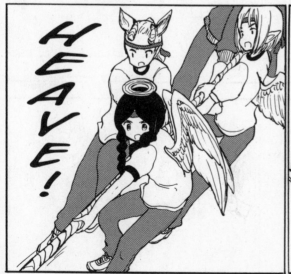

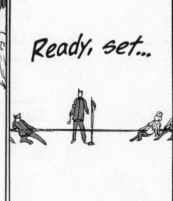

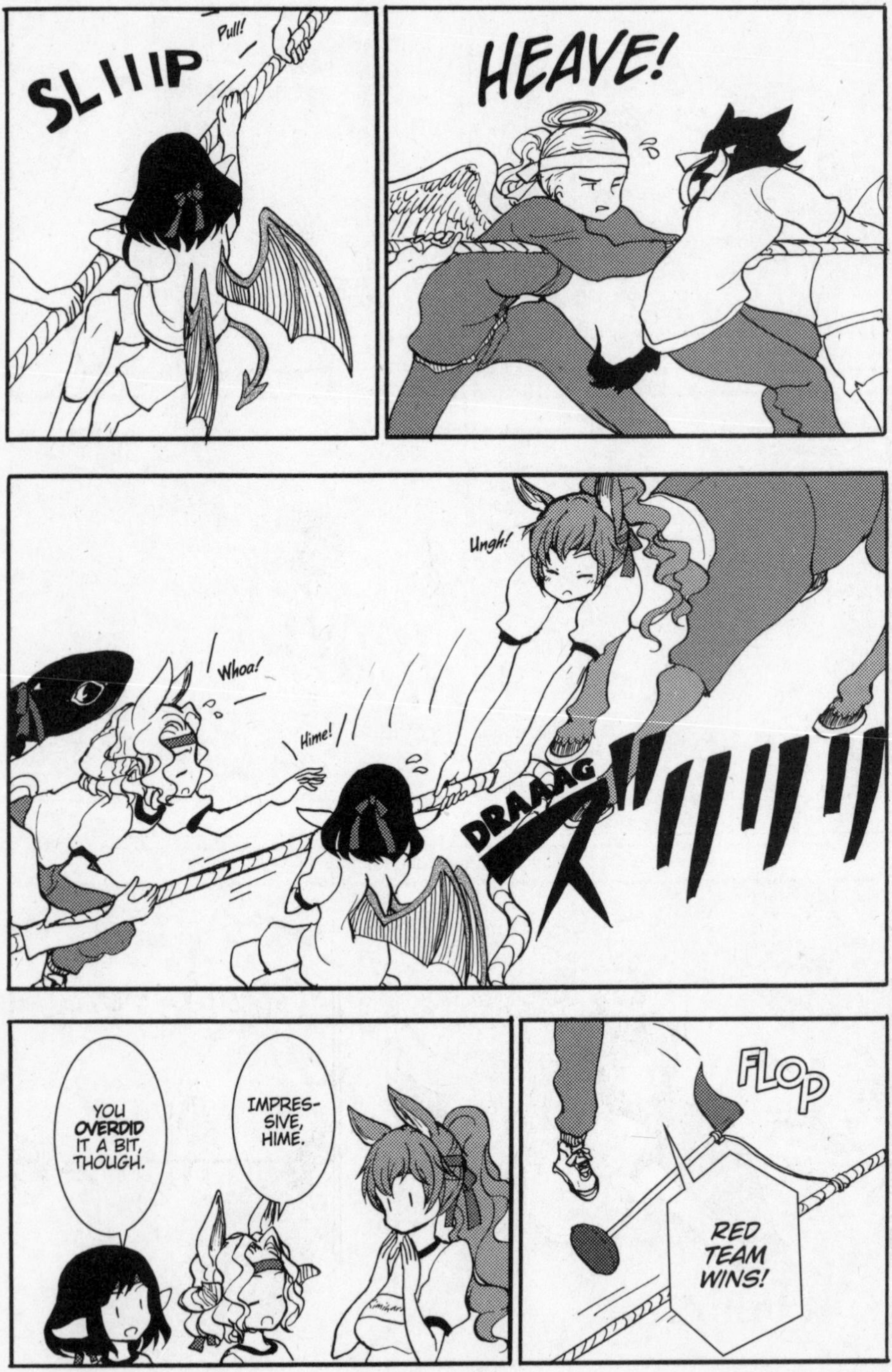
HEAVE!
SLIIIP
Pull!
Ungh!
Whoa!
Hime!
DRAAAG
FLOP
RED TEAM WINS!
IMPRESSIVE, HIME.
YOU OVERDID IT A BIT, THOUGH.

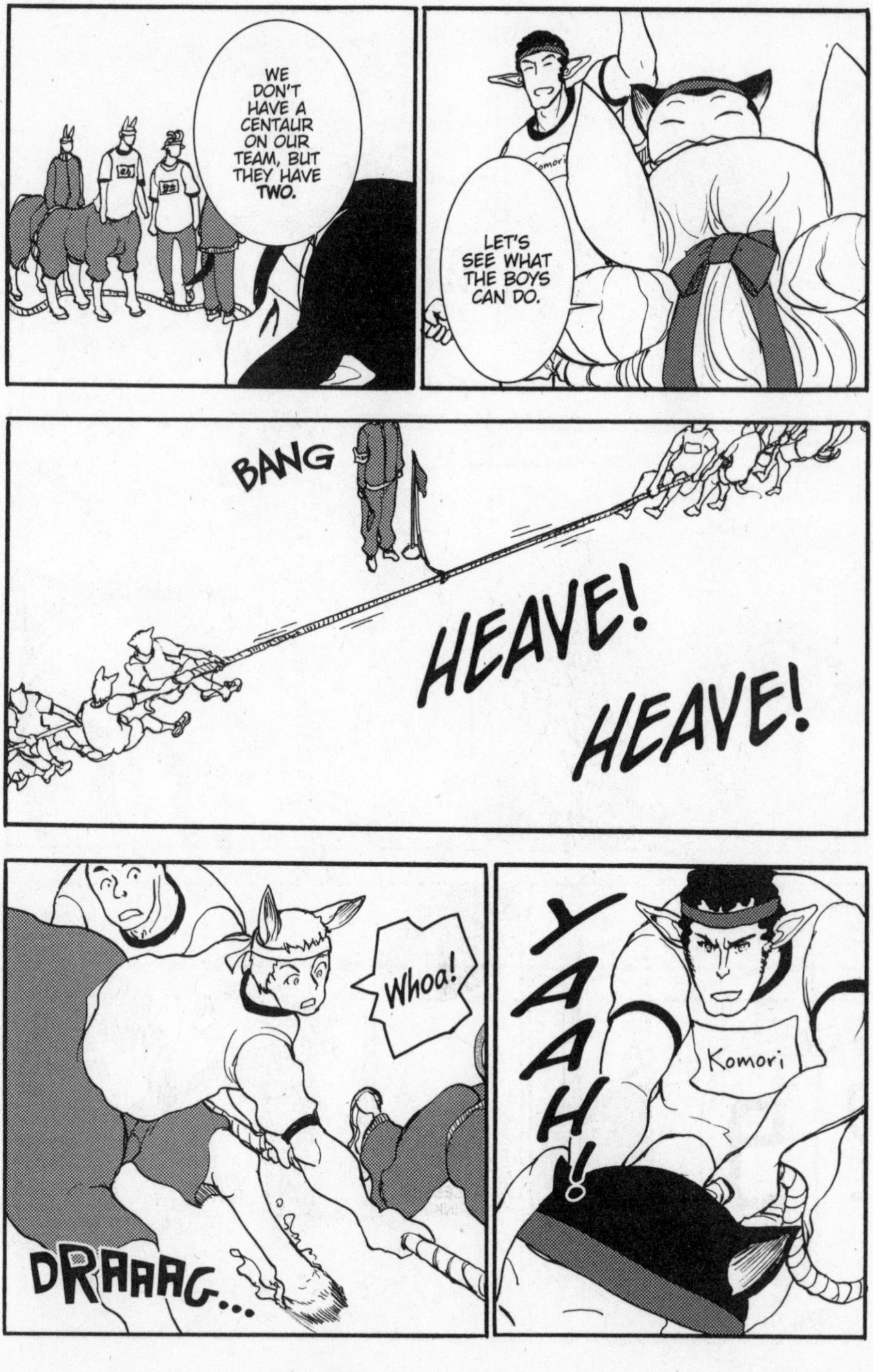

LET'S SEE WHAT THE BOYS CAN DO.
WE DON'T HAVE A CENTAUR ON OUR TEAM, BUT THEY HAVE TWO.
BANG
HEAVE!
HEAVE!
YAAAH!
Komori
Whoa!
DRAAAG...

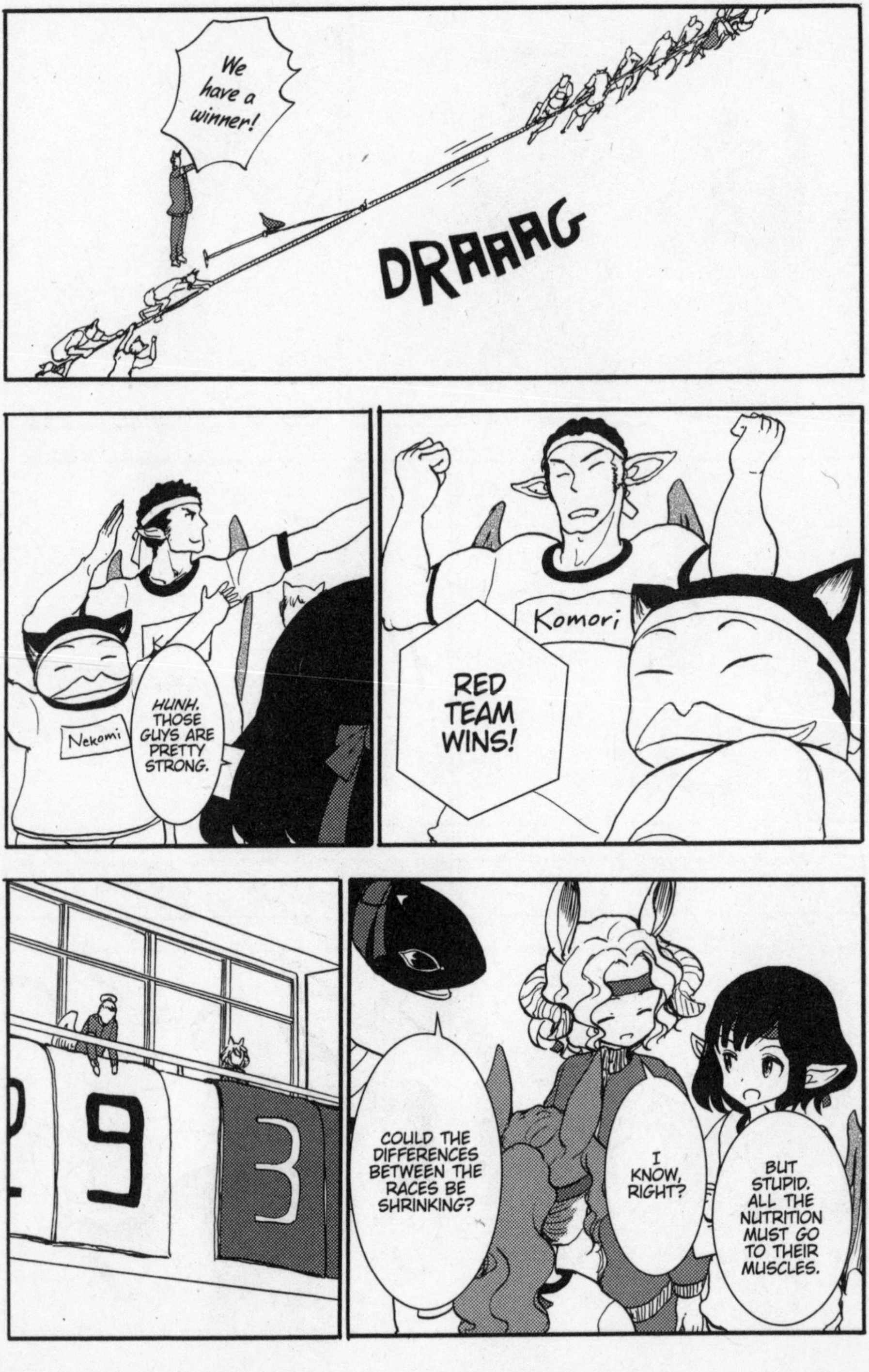
We have a winner!
DRAAAG
Komori
RED TEAM WINS!
Nekomi
HUNH. THOSE GUYS ARE PRETTY STRONG.
BUT STUPID. ALL THE NUTRITION MUST GO TO THEIR MUSCLES.
I KNOW, RIGHT?
COULD THE DIFFERENCES BETWEEN THE RACES BE SHRINKING?
9
3

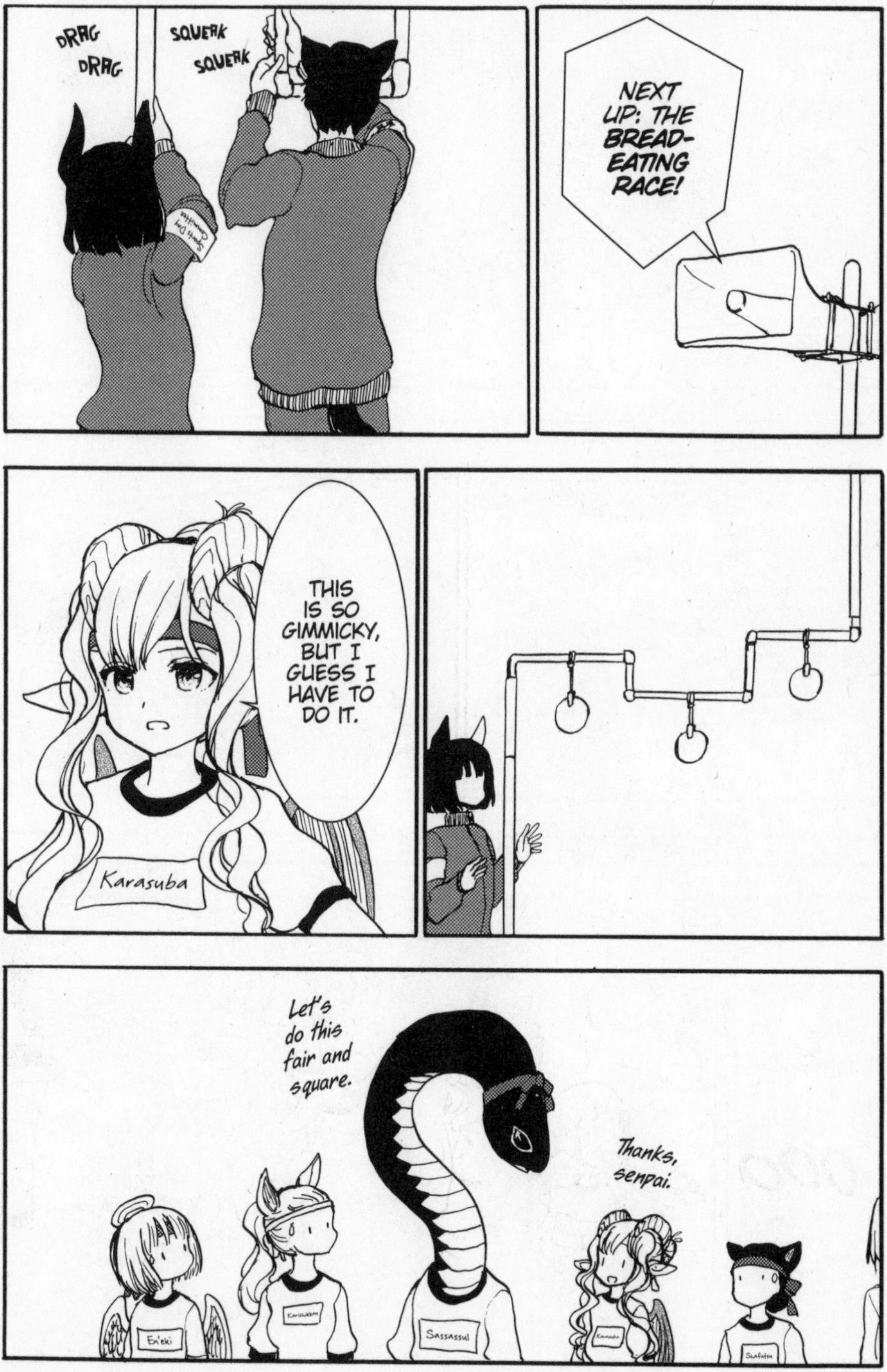
NEXT UP: THE BREAD-EATING RACE!
DRAG DRAG
SQUEAK SQUEAK
THIS IS SO GIMMICKY, BUT I GUESS I HAVE TO DO IT.
Karasuba
Thanks, senpai.
Let's do this fair and square.
Sassassul
En'eki

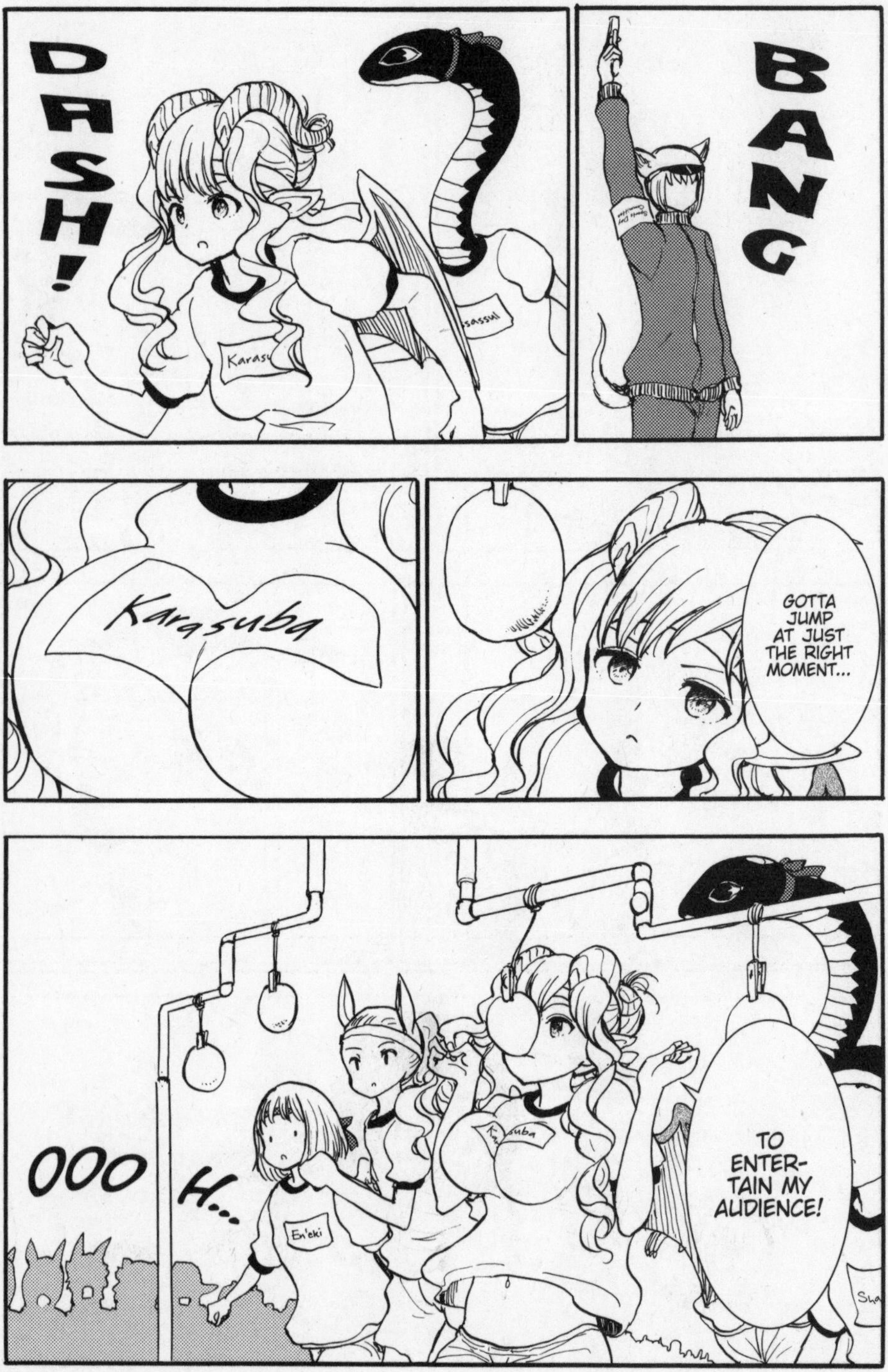
BANG
DASH!
Karasu
GOTTA JUMP AT JUST THE RIGHT MOMENT...
Karasuba
TO ENTER-TAIN MY AUDIENCE!
OOO H...
En'eki

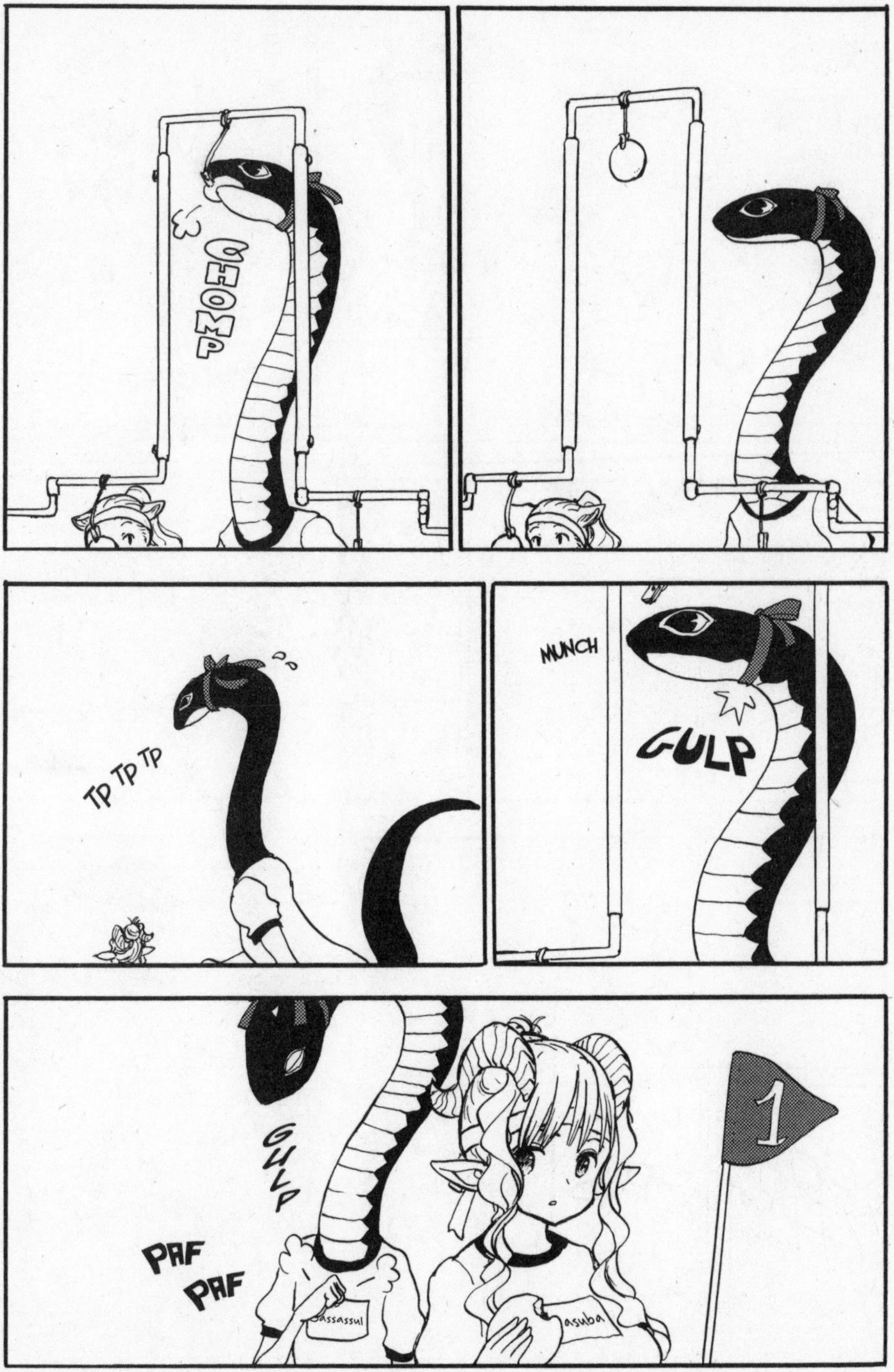
CHOMP
MUNCH
GULP
Tp Tp Tp
GULP
PAF
PAF
1

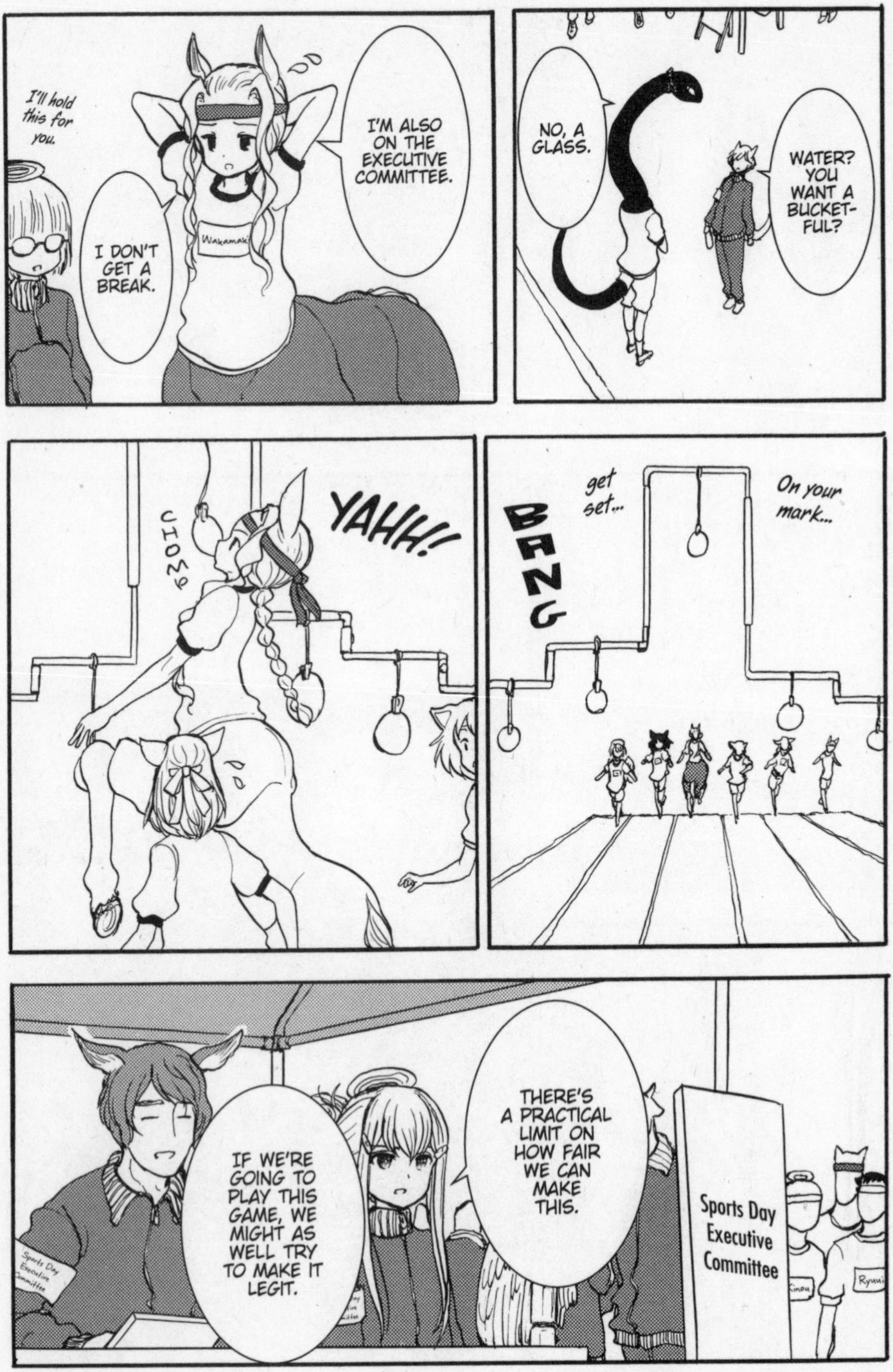
WATER? YOU WANT A BUCKET-FUL?
NO, A GLASS.
I'M ALSO ON THE EXECUTIVE COMMITTEE.
I'll hold this for you.
Wakamaki
I DON'T GET A BREAK.
On your mark...
get set...
BANG
YAHH!!
CHOMP
THERE'S A PRACTICAL LIMIT ON HOW FAIR WE CAN MAKE THIS.
Sports Day Executive Committee
IF WE'RE GOING TO PLAY THIS GAME, WE MIGHT AS WELL TRY TO MAKE IT LEGIT.
Sports Day Executive Committee

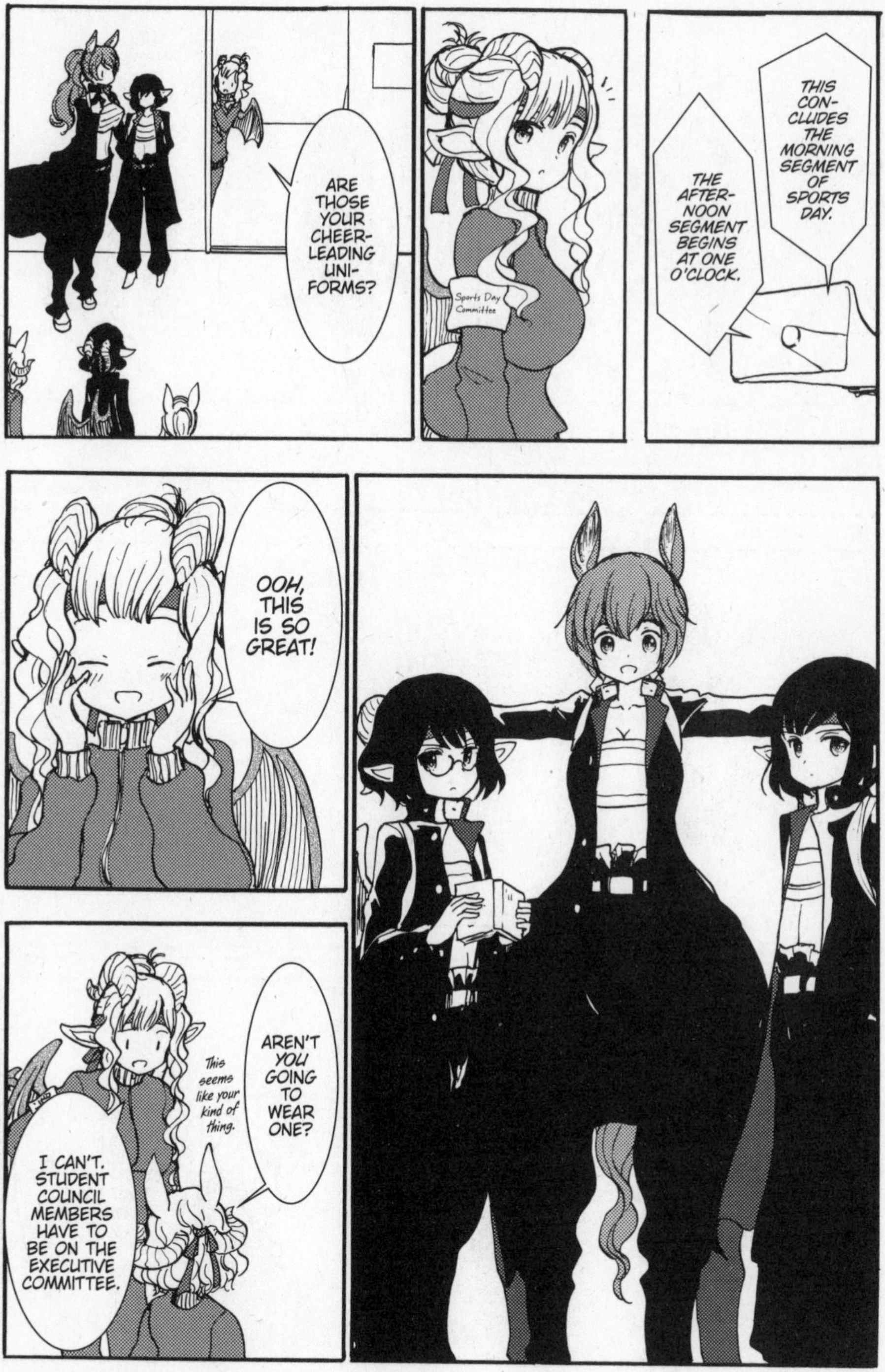
THIS CONCLUDES THE MORNING SEGMENT OF SPORTS DAY.
THE AFTERNOON SEGMENT BEGINS AT ONE O'CLOCK.
Sports Day Committee
ARE THOSE YOUR CHEERLEADING UNIFORMS?
OOH, THIS IS SO GREAT!
AREN'T YOU GOING TO WEAR ONE?
This seems like your kind of thing.
I CAN'T. STUDENT COUNCIL MEMBERS HAVE TO BE ON THE EXECUTIVE COMMITTEE.

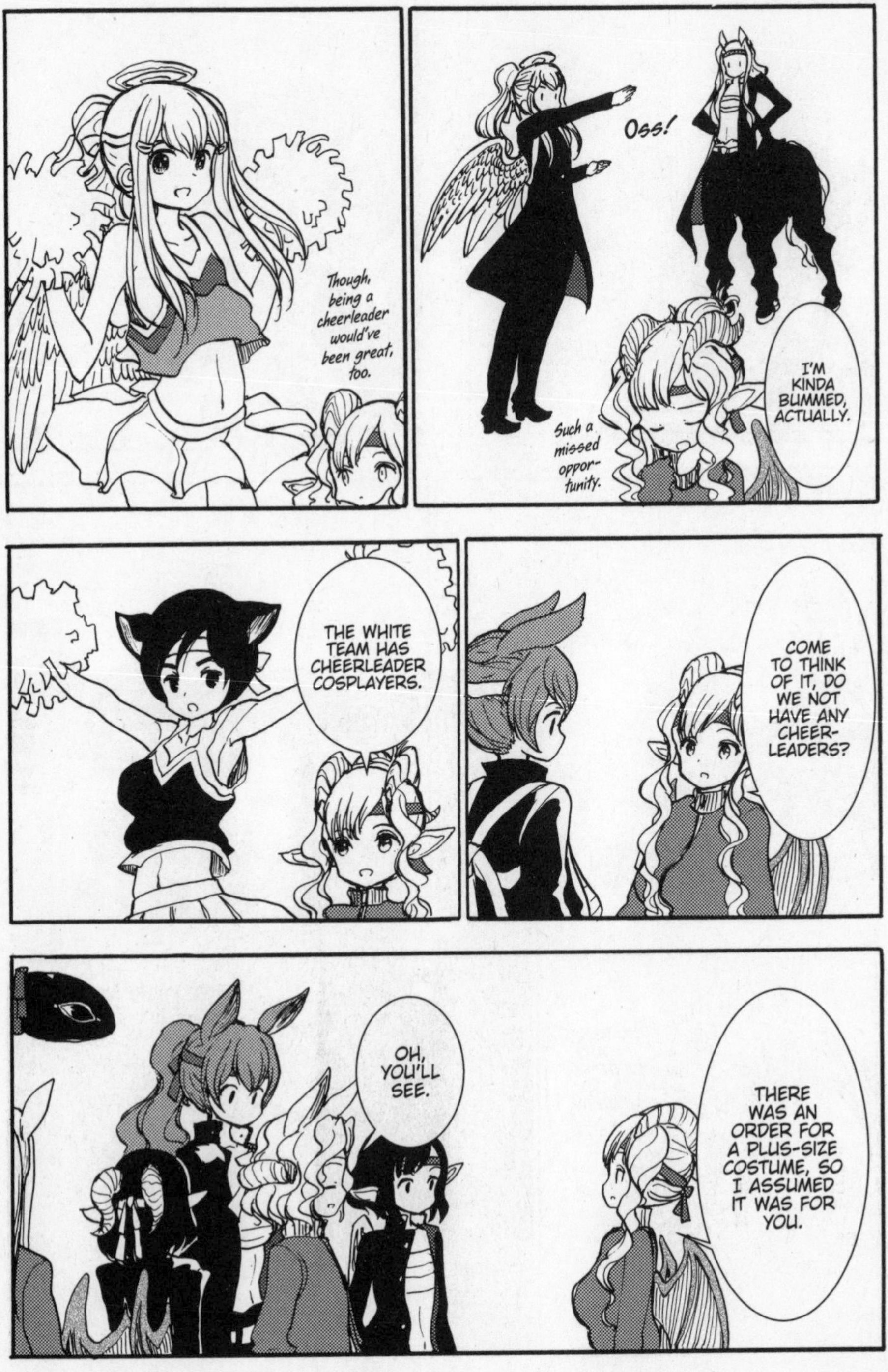
Oss!
I'M KINDA BUMMED, ACTUALLY.
Such a missed opportunity.
Though, being a cheerleader would've been great, too.
COME TO THINK OF IT, DO WE NOT HAVE ANY CHEERLEADERS?
THE WHITE TEAM HAS CHEERLEADER COSPLAYERS.
THERE WAS AN ORDER FOR A PLUS-SIZE COSTUME, SO I ASSUMED IT WAS FOR YOU.
OH, YOU'LL SEE.

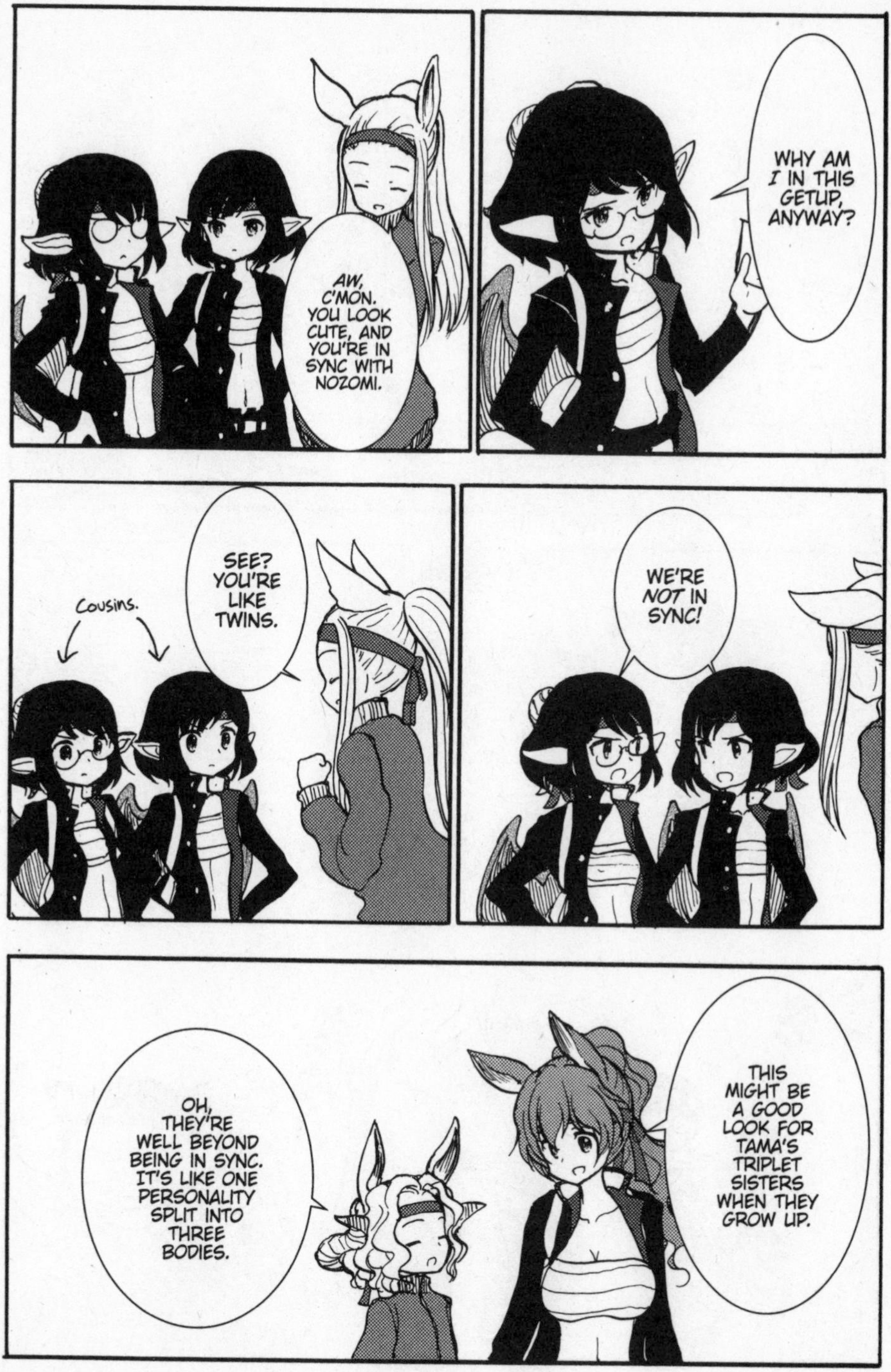
WHY AM *I* IN THIS GETUP, ANYWAY?
AW, C'MON. YOU LOOK CUTE, AND YOU'RE IN SYNC WITH NOZOMI.
WE'RE *NOT* IN SYNC!
SEE? YOU'RE LIKE TWINS.
Cousins.
THIS MIGHT BE A GOOD LOOK FOR TAMA'S TRIPLET SISTERS WHEN THEY GROW UP.
OH, THEY'RE WELL BEYOND BEING IN SYNC. IT'S LIKE ONE PERSONALITY SPLIT INTO THREE BODIES.

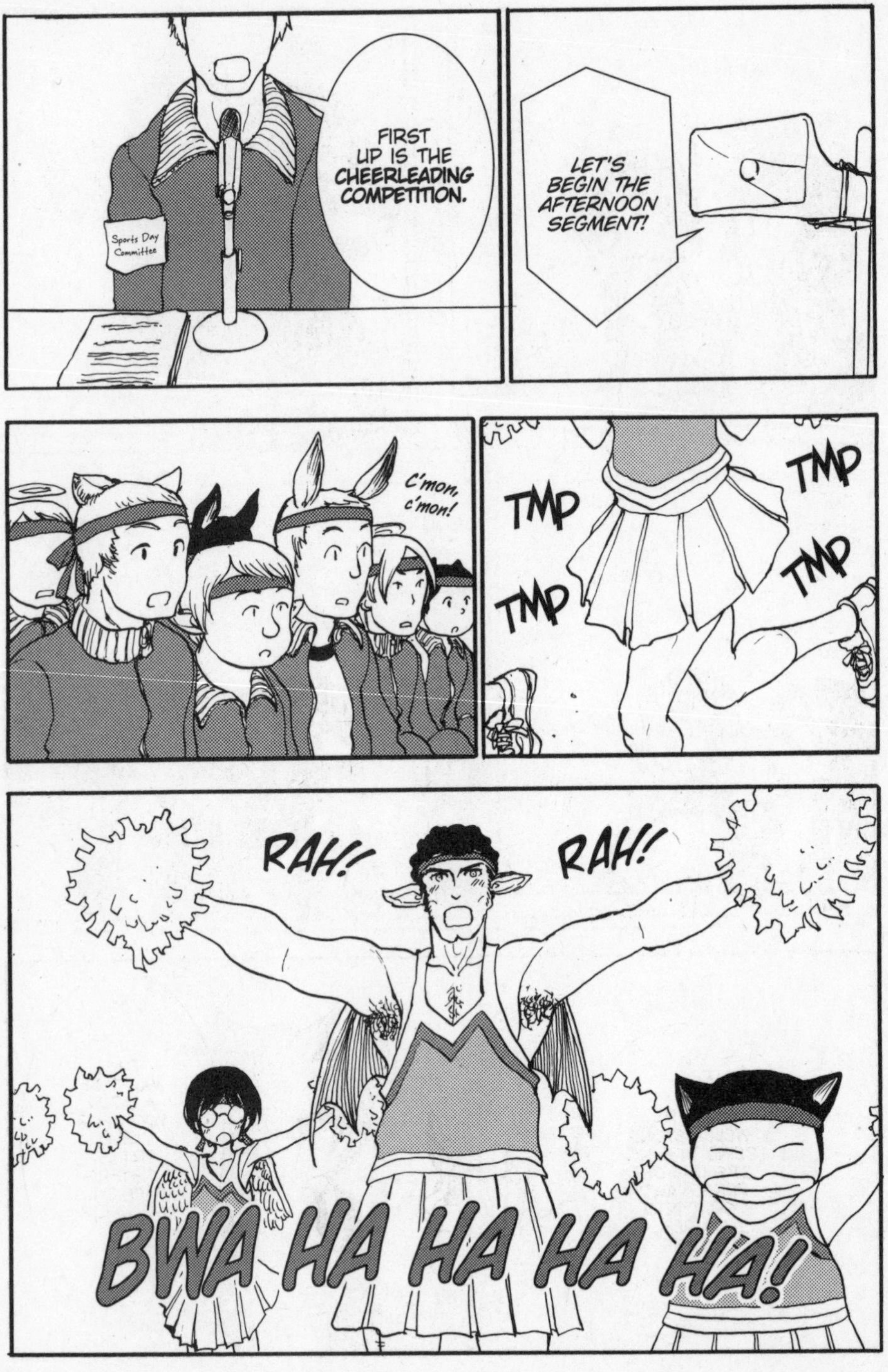

LET'S BEGIN THE AFTERNOON SEGMENT!
Sports Day Committee
FIRST UP IS THE CHEERLEADING COMPETITION.
TMP
TMP
TMP
TMP
C'mon, c'mon!
RAH!
RAH!
BWA HA HA HA HA HA!

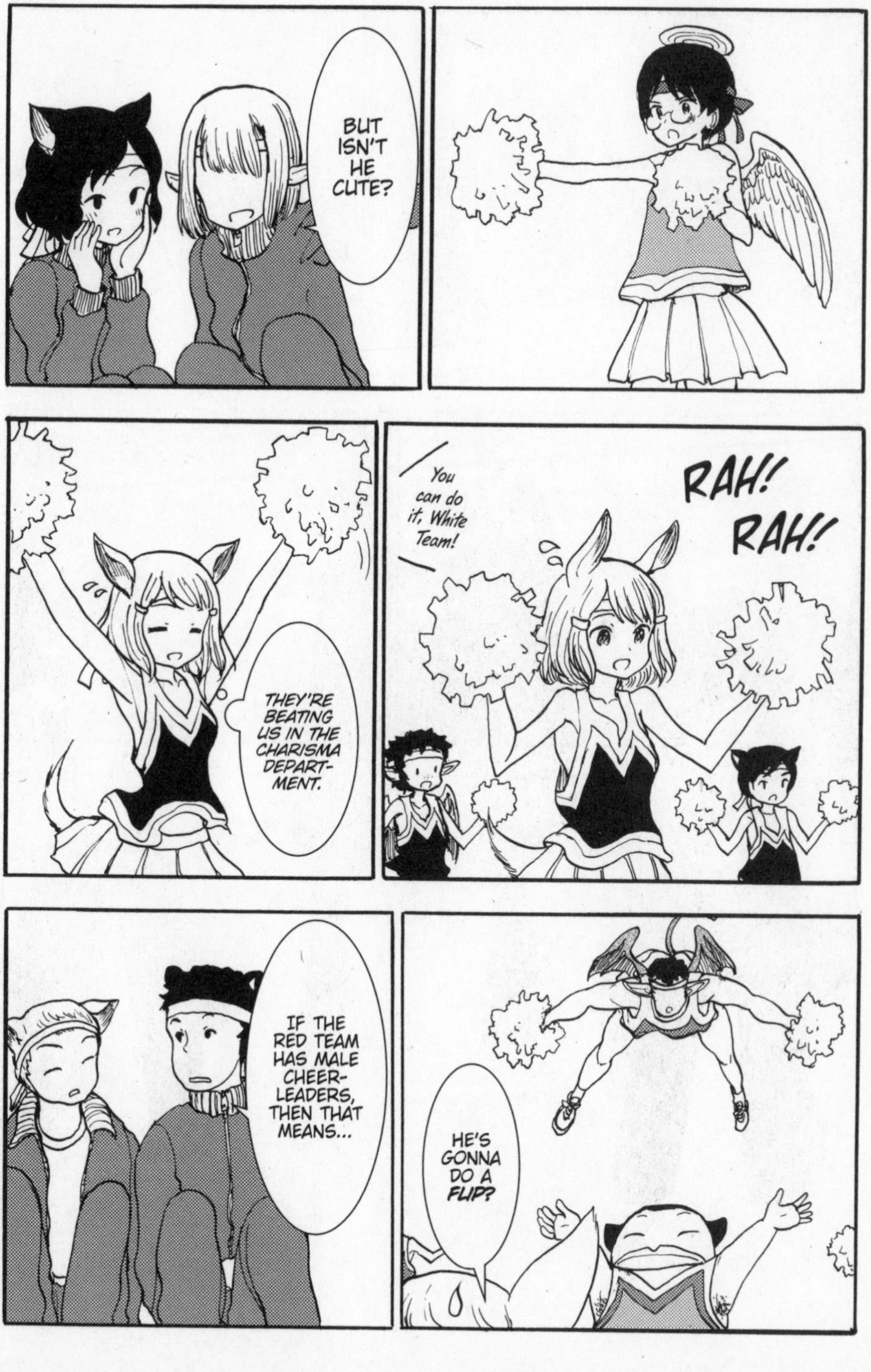
BUT ISN'T HE CUTE?
RAH! RAH!
You can do it, White Team!
THEY'RE BEATING US IN THE CHARISMA DEPARTMENT.
HE'S GONNA DO A *FLIP?*
IF THE RED TEAM HAS MALE CHEERLEADERS, THEN THAT MEANS...

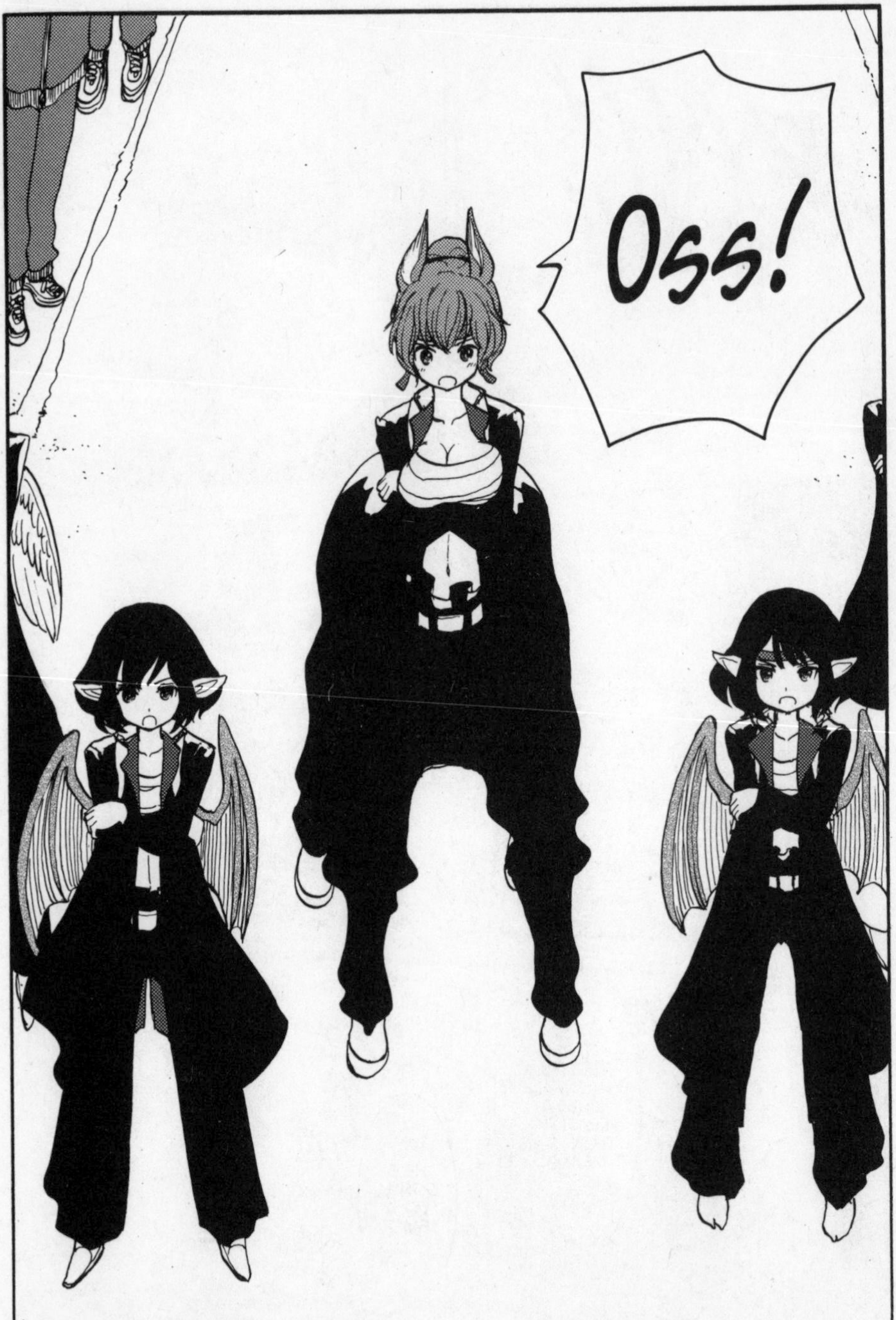
Oss!

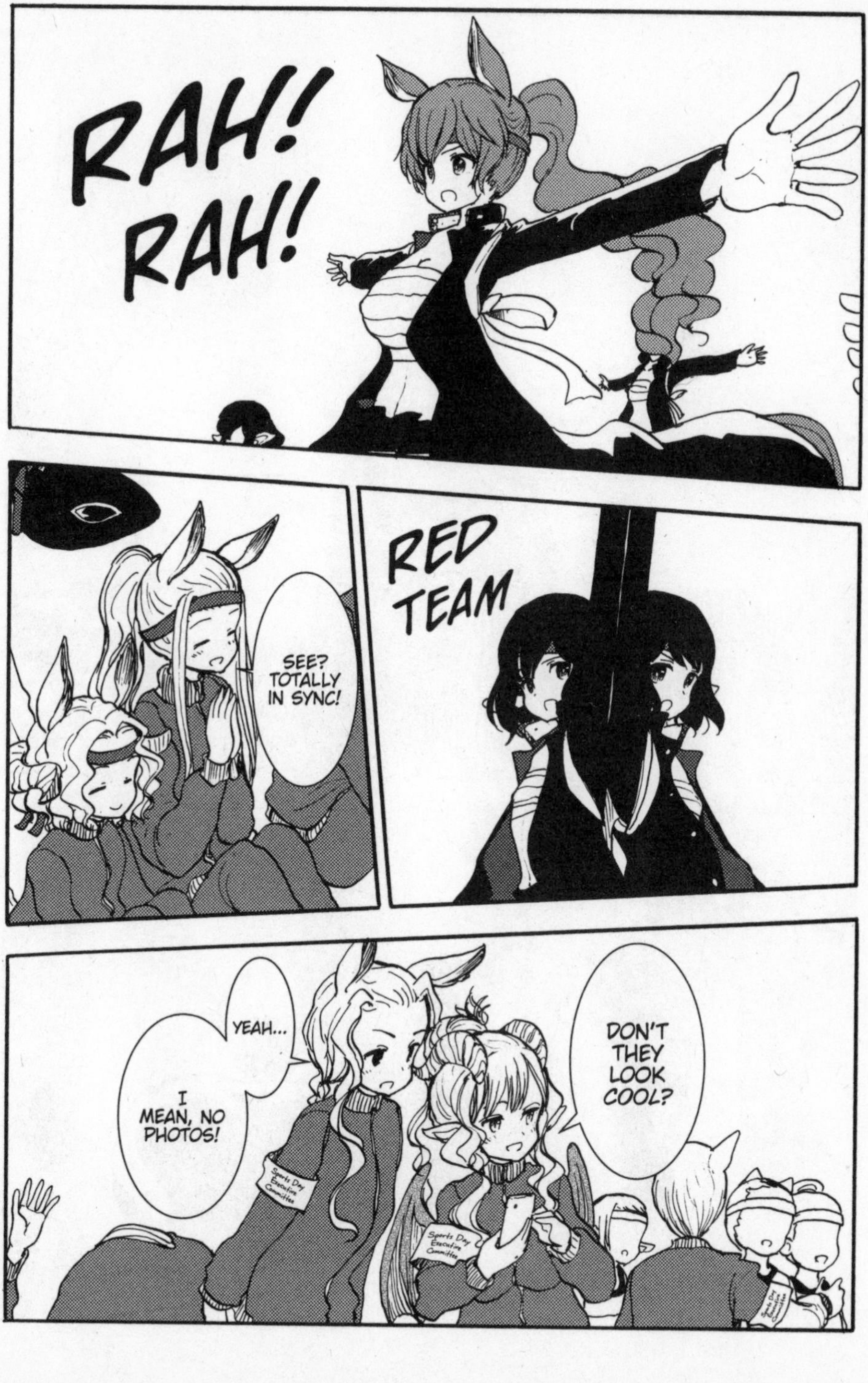
RAH! RAH!
RED TEAM
SEE? TOTALLY IN SYNC!
DON'T THEY LOOK COOL?
YEAH...
I MEAN, NO PHOTOS!
Sports Day Executive Committee
Sports Day Executive Committee

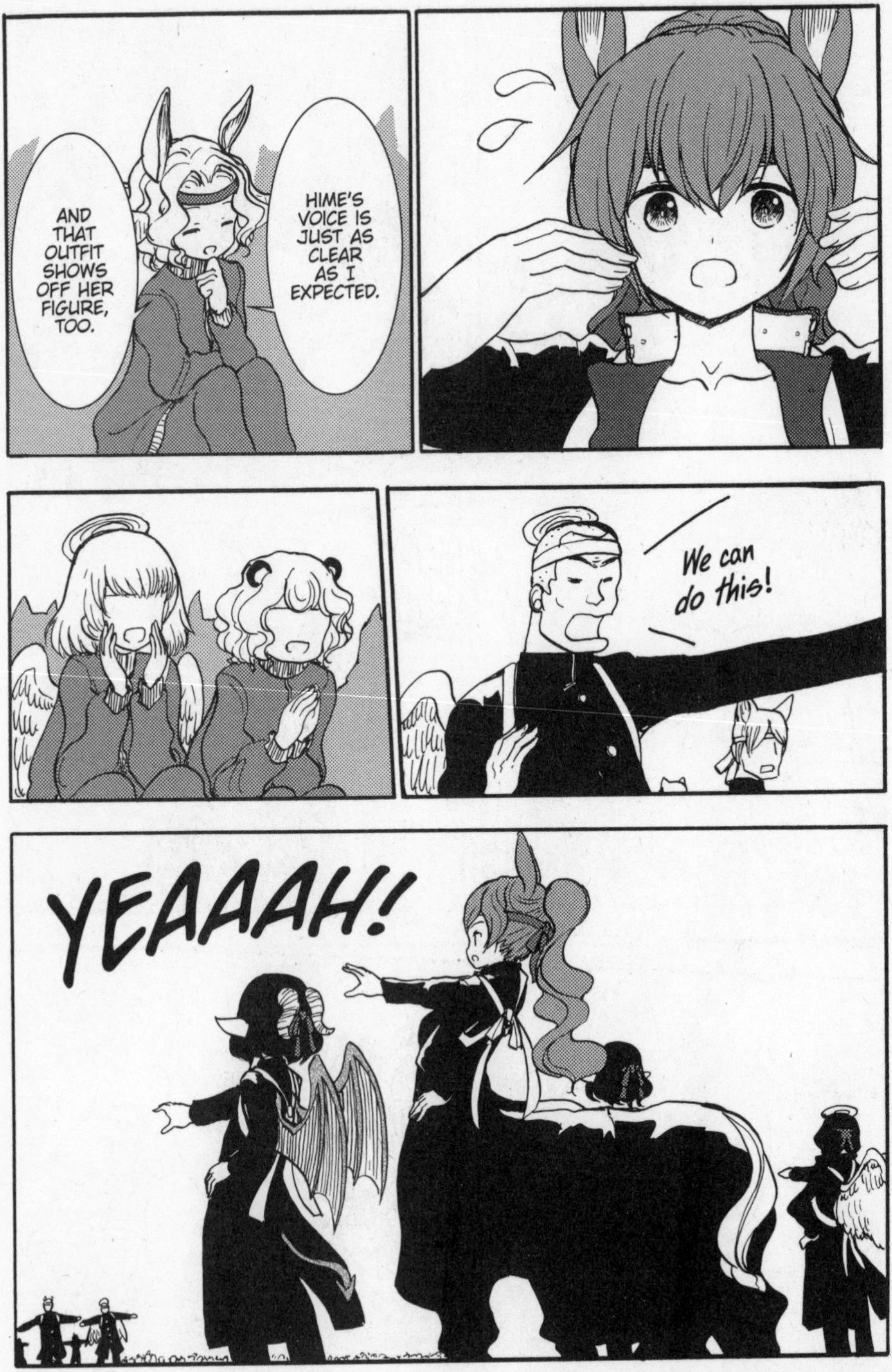
HIME'S VOICE IS JUST AS CLEAR AS I EXPECTED.
AND THAT OUTFIT SHOWS OFF HER FIGURE, TOO.
We can do this!
YEAAAH!

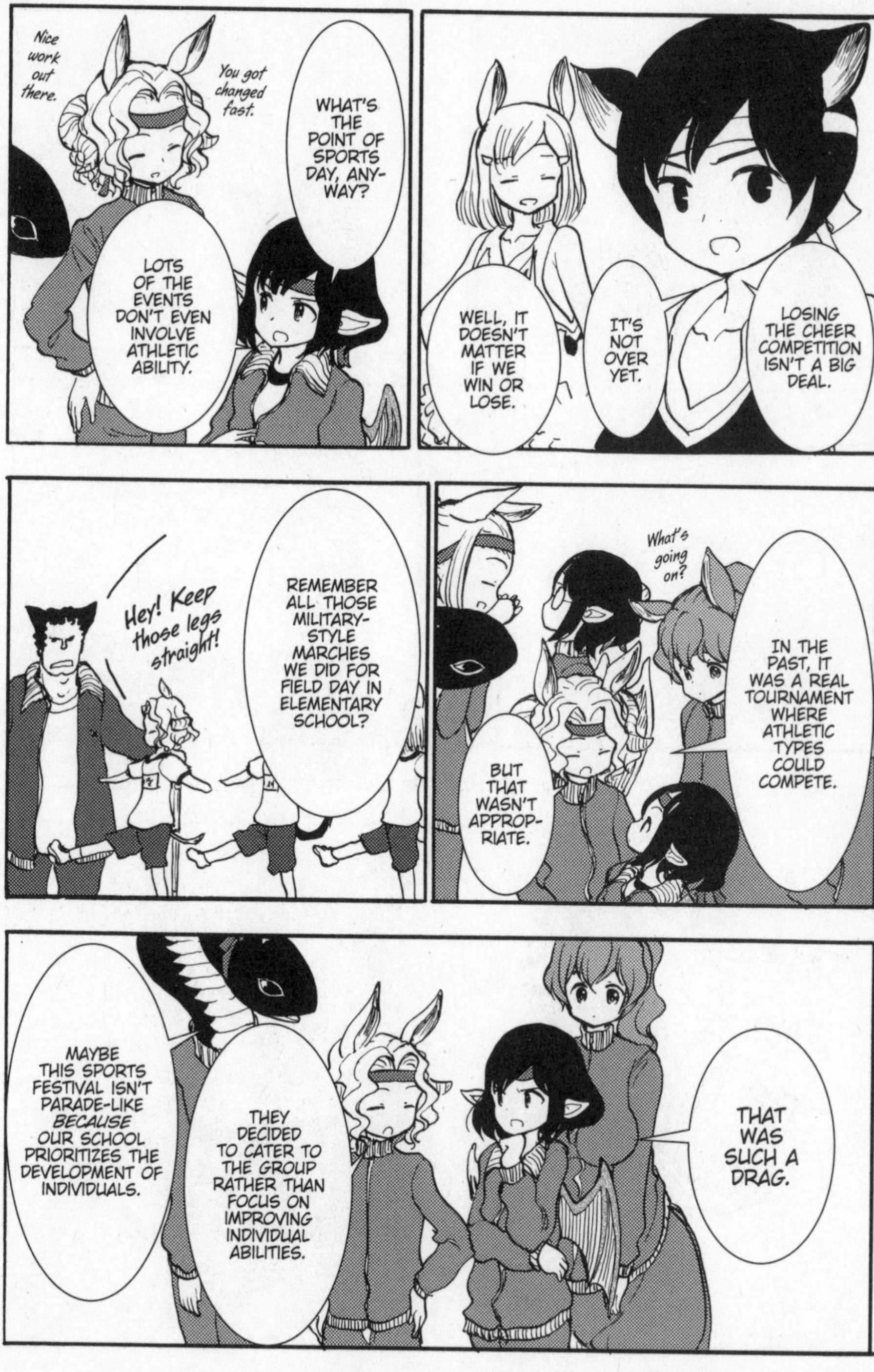
LOSING THE CHEER COMPETITION ISN'T A BIG DEAL.
IT'S NOT OVER YET.
WELL, IT DOESN'T MATTER IF WE WIN OR LOSE.
WHAT'S THE POINT OF SPORTS DAY, ANYWAY?
You got changed fast.
Nice work out there.
LOTS OF THE EVENTS DON'T EVEN INVOLVE ATHLETIC ABILITY.
What's going on?
IN THE PAST, IT WAS A REAL TOURNAMENT WHERE ATHLETIC TYPES COULD COMPETE.
BUT THAT WASN'T APPROPRIATE.
REMEMBER ALL THOSE MILITARY-STYLE MARCHES WE DID FOR FIELD DAY IN ELEMENTARY SCHOOL?
Hey! Keep those legs straight!
THAT WAS SUCH A DRAG.
THEY DECIDED TO CATER TO THE GROUP RATHER THAN FOCUS ON IMPROVING INDIVIDUAL ABILITIES.
MAYBE THIS SPORTS FESTIVAL ISN'T PARADE-LIKE *BECAUSE* OUR SCHOOL PRIORITIZES THE DEVELOPMENT OF INDIVIDUALS.

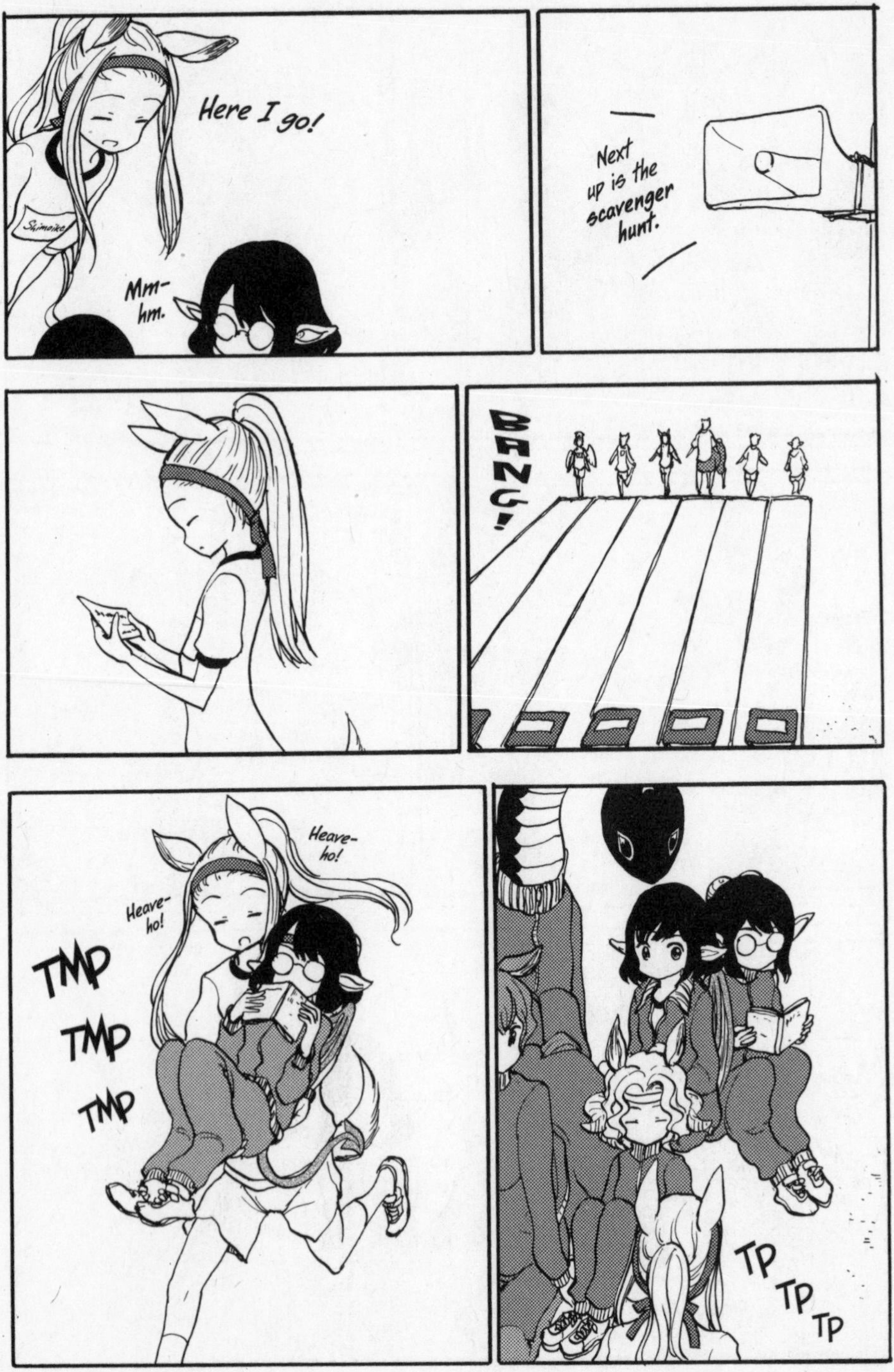
Next up is the scavenger hunt.
Here I go!
Shimoike
Mm-hm.
BANG!
TP TP TP
Heave-ho!
Heave-ho!
TMP TMP TMP

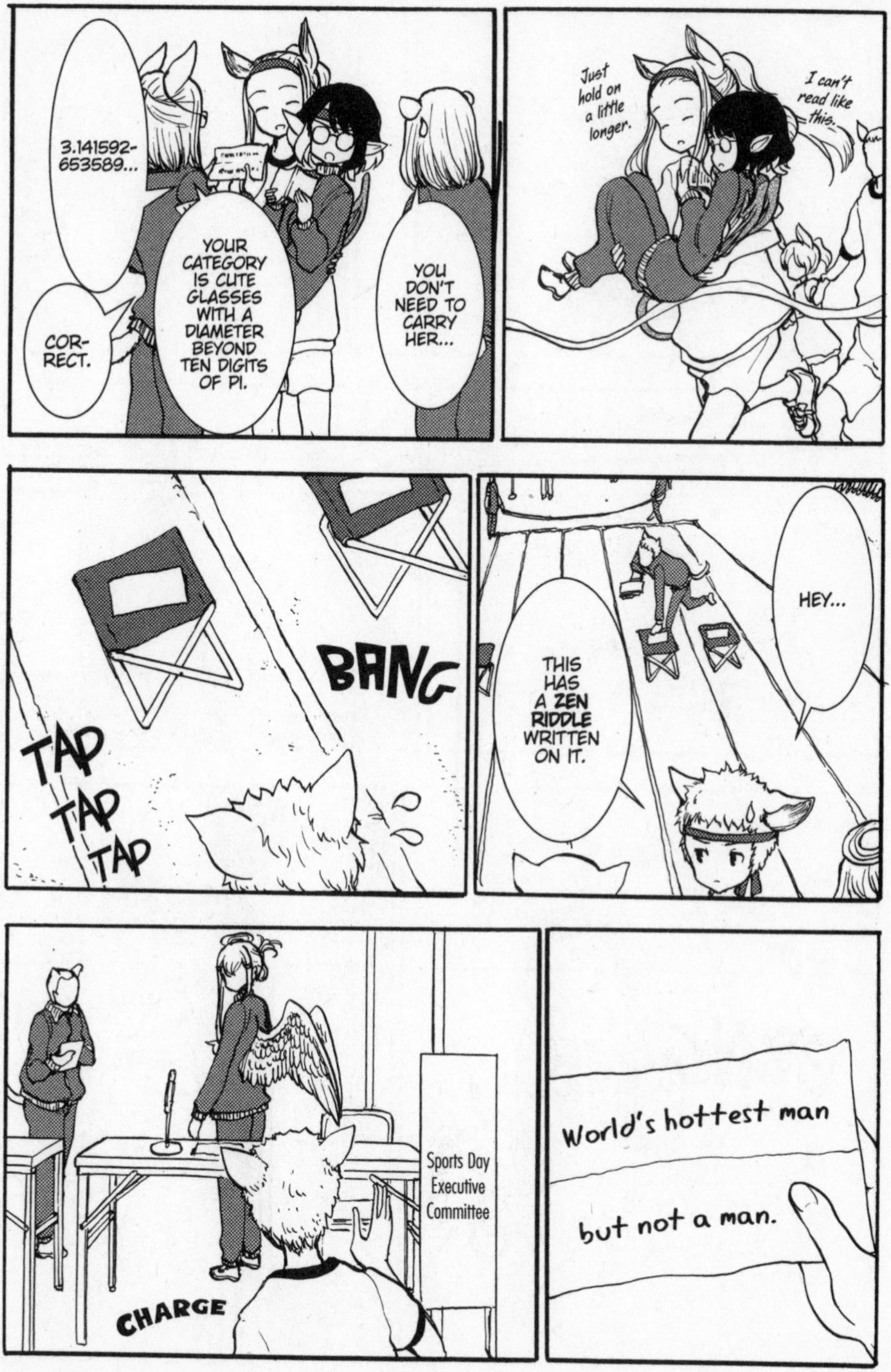
I can't read like this.
Just hold on a little longer.
3.141592-653589...
COR-RECT.
YOUR CATEGORY IS CUTE GLASSES WITH A DIAMETER BEYOND TEN DIGITS OF PI.
YOU DON'T NEED TO CARRY HER...
HEY...
THIS HAS A ZEN RIDDLE WRITTEN ON IT.
BANG
TAP TAP TAP
World's hottest man
but not a man.
Sports Day Executive Committee
CHARGE

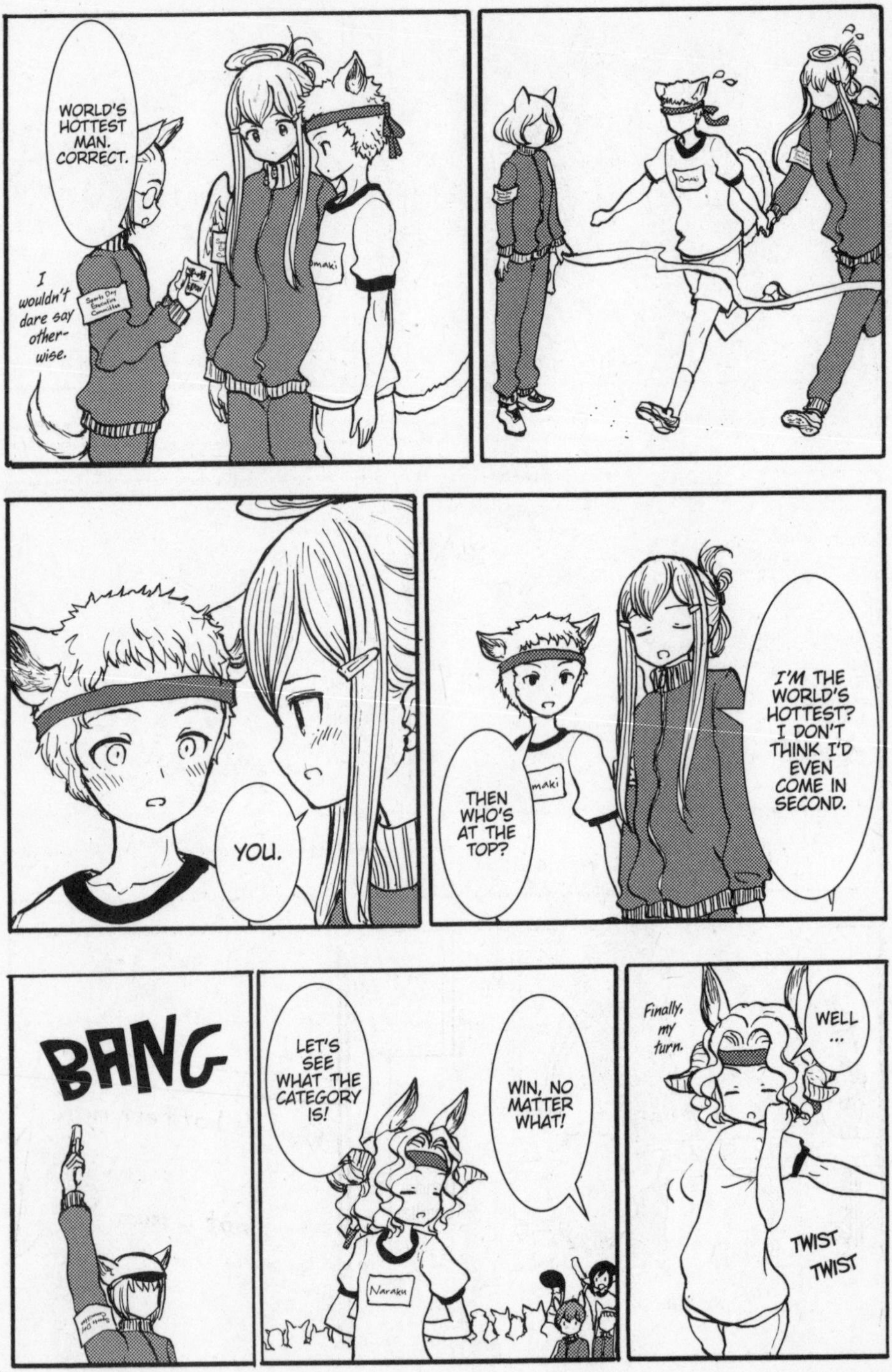
WORLD'S HOTTEST MAN. CORRECT.
I wouldn't dare say other-wise.
I'M THE WORLD'S HOTTEST? I DON'T THINK I'D EVEN COME IN SECOND.
THEN WHO'S AT THE TOP?
YOU.
WELL ...
Finally, my turn.
TWIST TWIST
WIN, NO MATTER WHAT!
LET'S SEE WHAT THE CATEGORY IS!
BANG

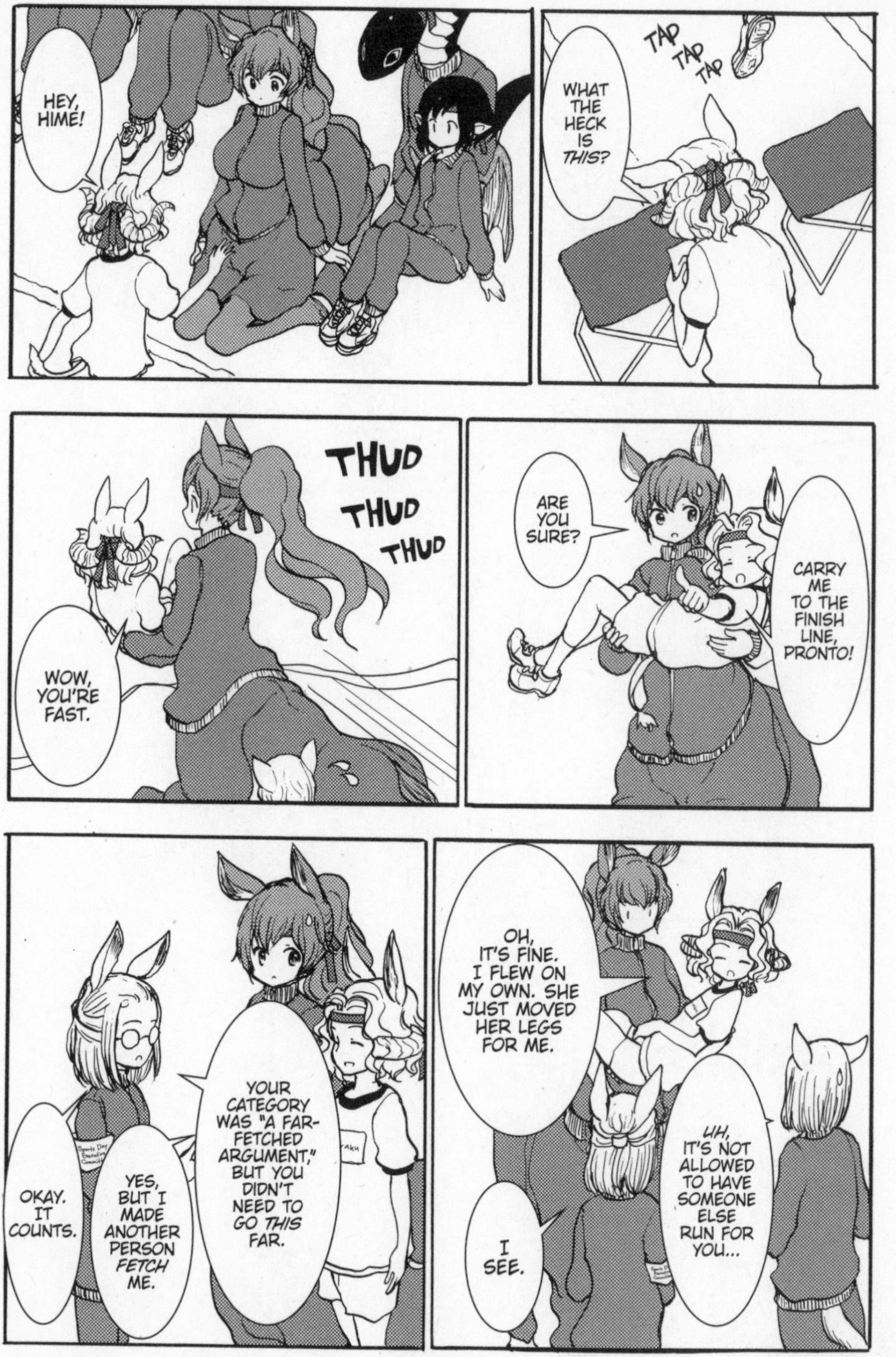
TAP TAP TAP
WHAT THE HECK IS *THIS*?
HEY, HIME!
CARRY ME TO THE FINISH LINE, PRONTO!
ARE YOU SURE?
THUD THUD THUD
WOW, YOU'RE FAST.
UH, IT'S NOT ALLOWED TO HAVE SOMEONE ELSE RUN FOR YOU...
OH, IT'S FINE. I FLEW ON MY OWN. SHE JUST MOVED HER LEGS FOR ME.
I SEE.
YOUR CATEGORY WAS "A FAR-FETCHED ARGUMENT," BUT YOU DIDN'T NEED TO GO *THIS* FAR.
YES, BUT I MADE ANOTHER PERSON *FETCH* ME.
OKAY. IT COUNTS.

A CentaUr's Life

SPOTLIGHT ON MERFOLK:
< 7 > MERFOLK IN THE
SHOGUNATE SYSTEM

AS THE WARRING STATES PERIOD CAME TO AN END AND THE PERIOD
OF NATIONAL ISOLATION BEGAN, OPPORTUNITIES FOR MERFOLK SHRANK.
THIS WAS BECAUSE THE EDO SHOGUNATE WAS SUSPICIOUS OF THE MERFOLK,
WHOSE ACTIVITIES WERE OFTEN HIDDEN FROM SIGHT, AND CONSIDERED THEM
DANGEROUS. NOT A SINGLE MERFOLK BECAME A FEUDAL LORD; INDEED, EVEN THE
FORMER CHIEF OF THE MERFOLK NAVY WAS APPOINTED AS A MERE RETAINER.
IN ADDITION, INTERMARRIAGE WITH OTHER RACES OF MAMMALIAN HUMANS LED
TO THE DISAPPEARANCE OF THE MERFOLK FORM IN THAT FAMILY LINE AFTER
SEVERAL GENERATIONS. A NON-MERFOLK MAGISTRATE WAS DISPATCHED TO RULE
OVER AN ISLAND WITH PREDOMINANTLY MERFOLK RESIDENTS. MERFOLK RITUALS
WERE HELD IN LARGE LAKES, AND MANY OF THE COMMUNITIES THAT HAD CEASED
TO EXIST DURING THE WARRING STATES PERIOD WERE RESTORED DURING THIS
TIME. HOWEVER, THESE COMMUNITIES WERE SMALL, AND OFTEN GRADUALLY
DISAPPEARED OR SURVIVED ONLY BY BRINGING IN PRIESTS TO PERFORM
CEREMONIES. DESPITE THEIR POPULATION DECLINE, MERFOLK COULD STILL BE
FOUND WORKING AS BARGE-HAULERS IN CANALS AND LARGE RIVERS. THEIR
LONG-DISTANCE SWIMMING SKILLS WERE ALSO INVALUABLE IN SMUGGLING.
FUNDING FOR THE LATER ANTI-SHOGUNATE MOVEMENT WOULD NOT
HAVE BEEN POSSIBLE WITHOUT THE MERFOLK'S ACTIVE ROLE.

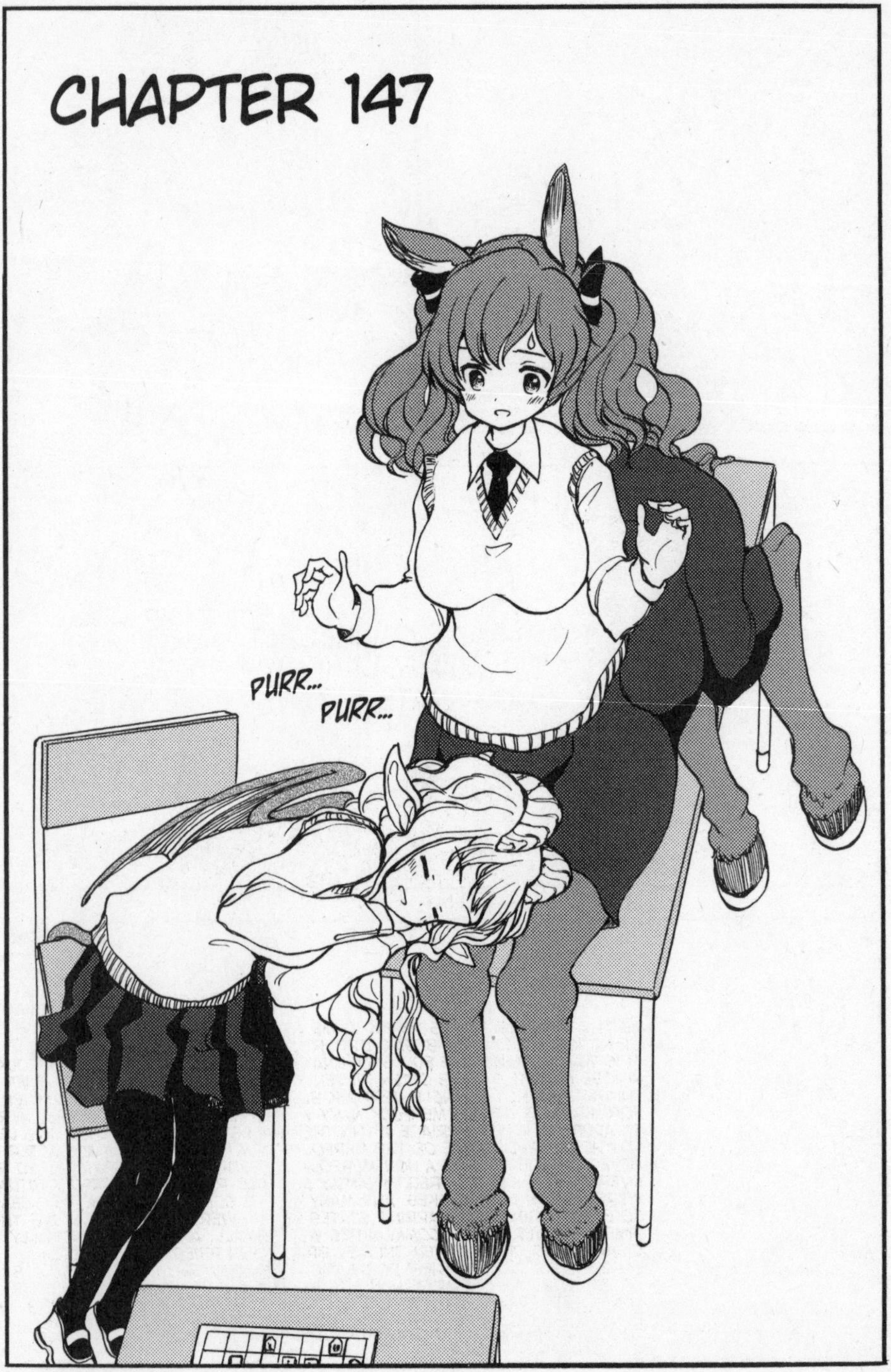
CHAPTER 147
PURR...
PURR...

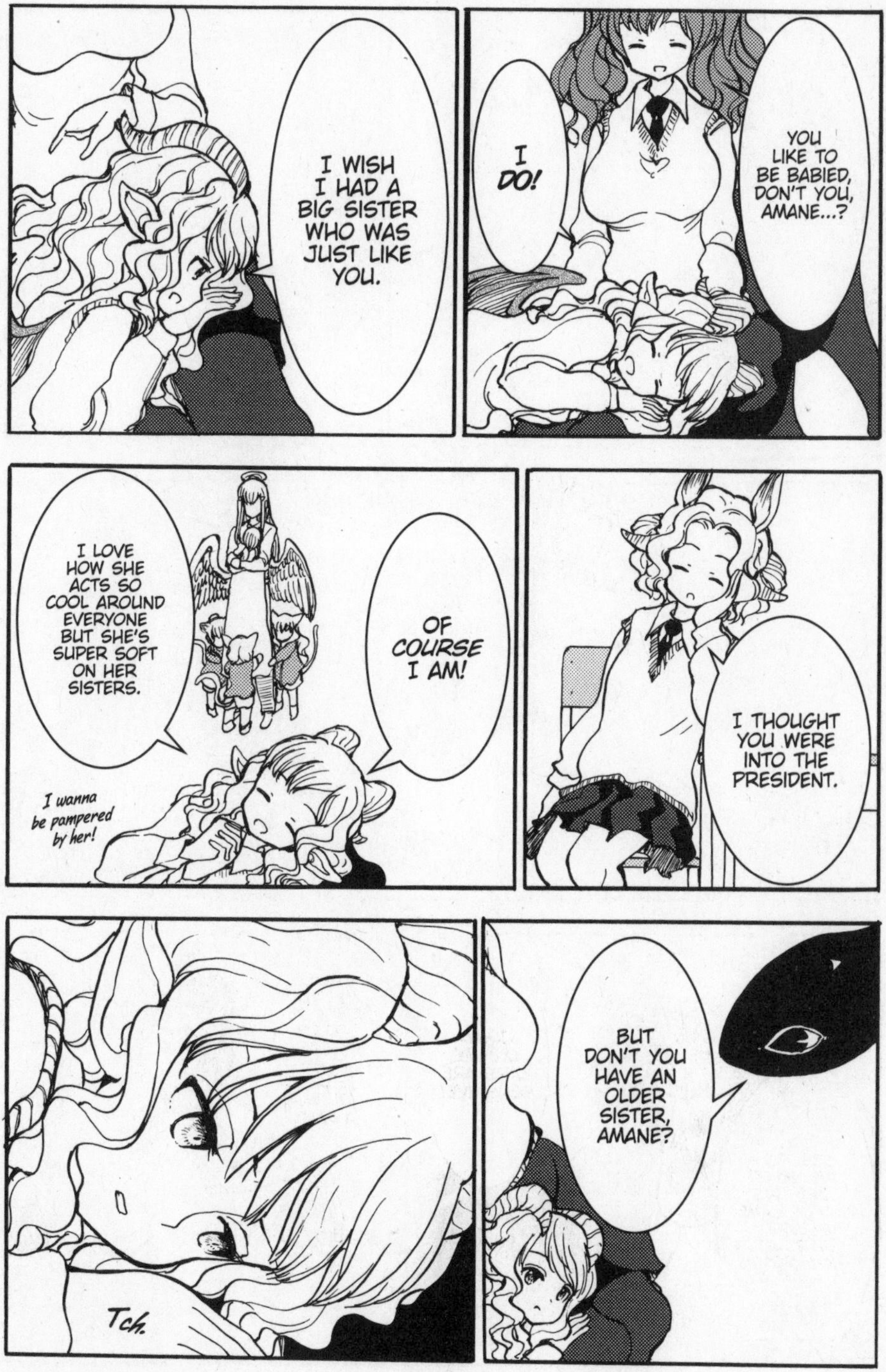
YOU LIKE TO BE BABIED, DON'T YOU, AMANE...?
I DO!
I WISH I HAD A BIG SISTER WHO WAS JUST LIKE YOU.
I THOUGHT YOU WERE INTO THE PRESIDENT.
OF COURSE I AM!
I LOVE HOW SHE ACTS SO COOL AROUND EVERYONE BUT SHE'S SUPER SOFT ON HER SISTERS.
I wanna be pampered by her!
BUT DON'T YOU HAVE AN OLDER SISTER, AMANE?
Tch.

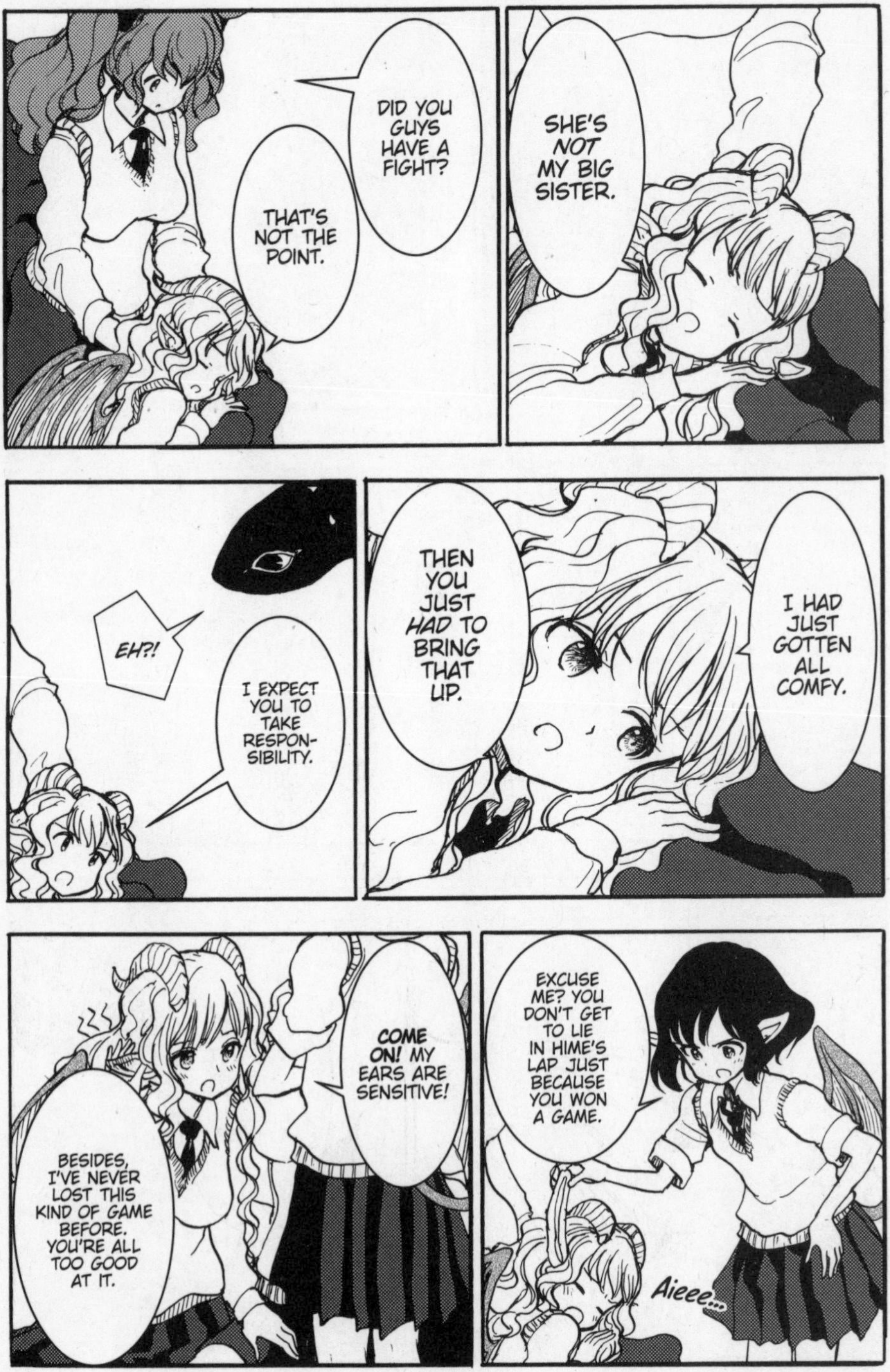
SHE'S *NOT* MY BIG SISTER.
DID YOU GUYS HAVE A FIGHT?
THAT'S NOT THE POINT.
I HAD JUST GOTTEN ALL COMFY.
THEN YOU JUST *HAD* TO BRING THAT UP.
I EXPECT YOU TO TAKE RESPON-SIBILITY.
EH?!
EXCUSE ME? YOU DON'T GET TO LIE IN HIME'S LAP JUST BECAUSE YOU WON A GAME.
Aieee...
COME ON! MY EARS ARE SENSITIVE!
BESIDES, I'VE NEVER LOST THIS KIND OF GAME BEFORE. YOU'RE ALL TOO GOOD AT IT.

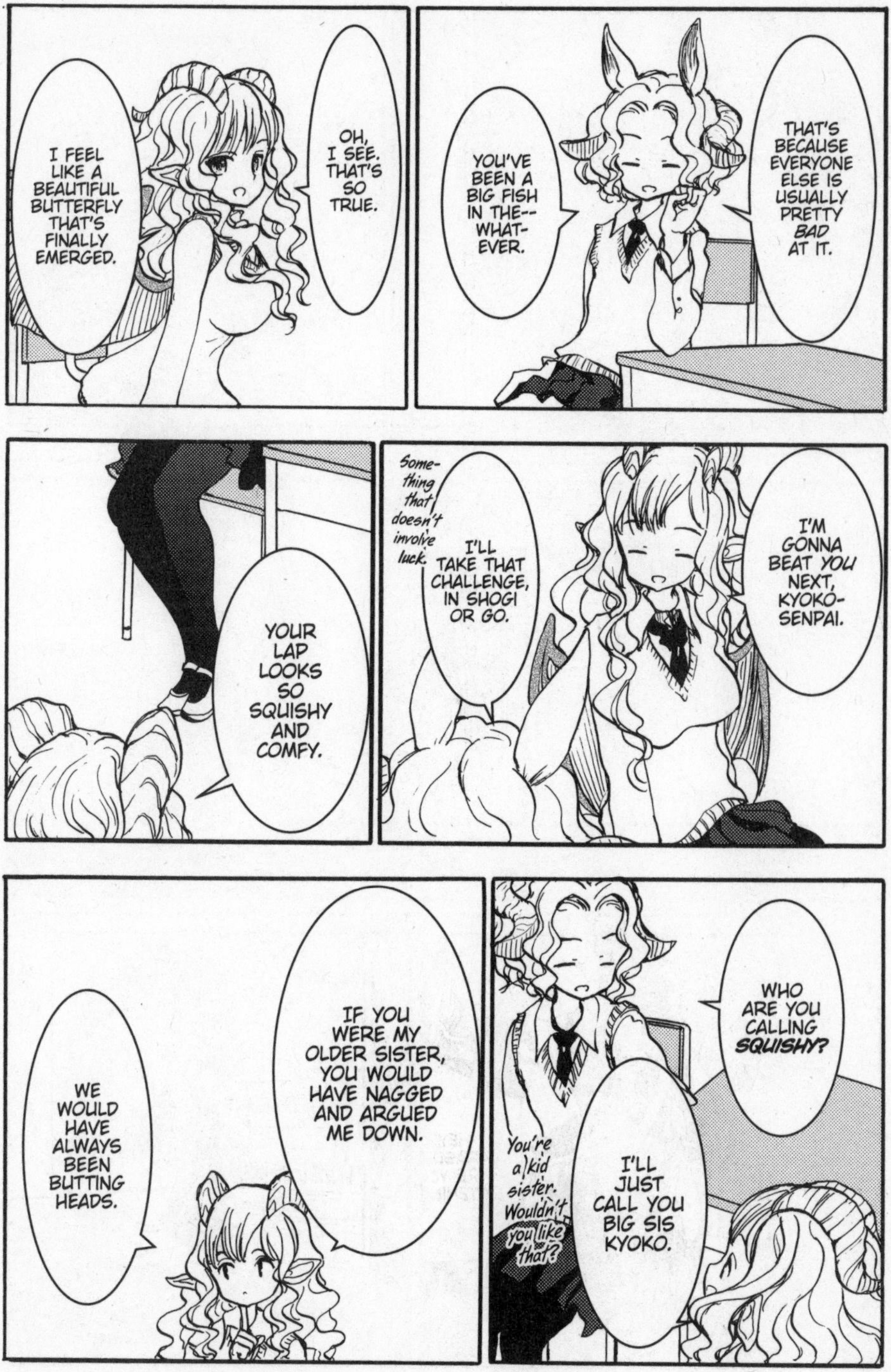
THAT'S BECAUSE EVERYONE ELSE IS USUALLY PRETTY *BAD* AT IT.
YOU'VE BEEN A BIG FISH IN THE-- WHAT-EVER.
OH, I SEE. THAT'S SO TRUE.
I FEEL LIKE A BEAUTIFUL BUTTERFLY THAT'S FINALLY EMERGED.
I'M GONNA BEAT *YOU* NEXT, KYOKO-SENPAI.
I'LL TAKE THAT CHALLENGE, IN SHOGI OR GO.
Some-thing that doesn't involve luck.
YOUR LAP LOOKS SO SQUISHY AND COMFY.
WHO ARE YOU CALLING ***SQUISHY?***
I'LL JUST CALL YOU BIG SIS KYOKO.
You're a kid sister. Wouldn't you like that?
IF YOU WERE MY OLDER SISTER, YOU WOULD HAVE NAGGED AND ARGUED ME DOWN.
WE WOULD HAVE ALWAYS BEEN BUTTING HEADS.

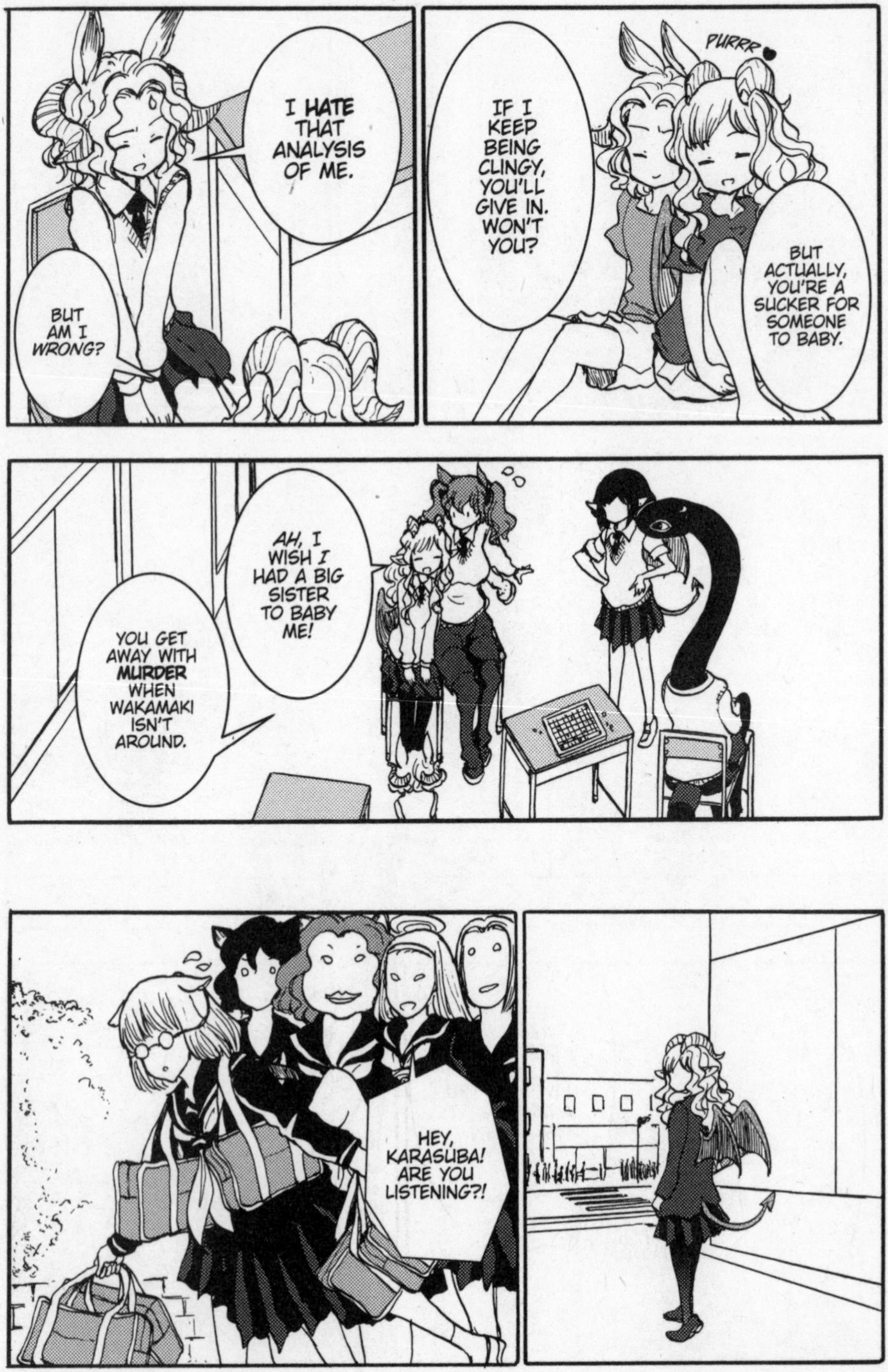
PURRR
BUT ACTUALLY, YOU'RE A SUCKER FOR SOMEONE TO BABY.
IF I KEEP BEING CLINGY, YOU'LL GIVE IN. WON'T YOU?
I HATE THAT ANALYSIS OF ME.
BUT AM I WRONG?
AH, I WISH I HAD A BIG SISTER TO BABY ME!
YOU GET AWAY WITH MURDER WHEN WAKAMAKI ISN'T AROUND.
HEY, KARASUBA! ARE YOU LISTENING?!

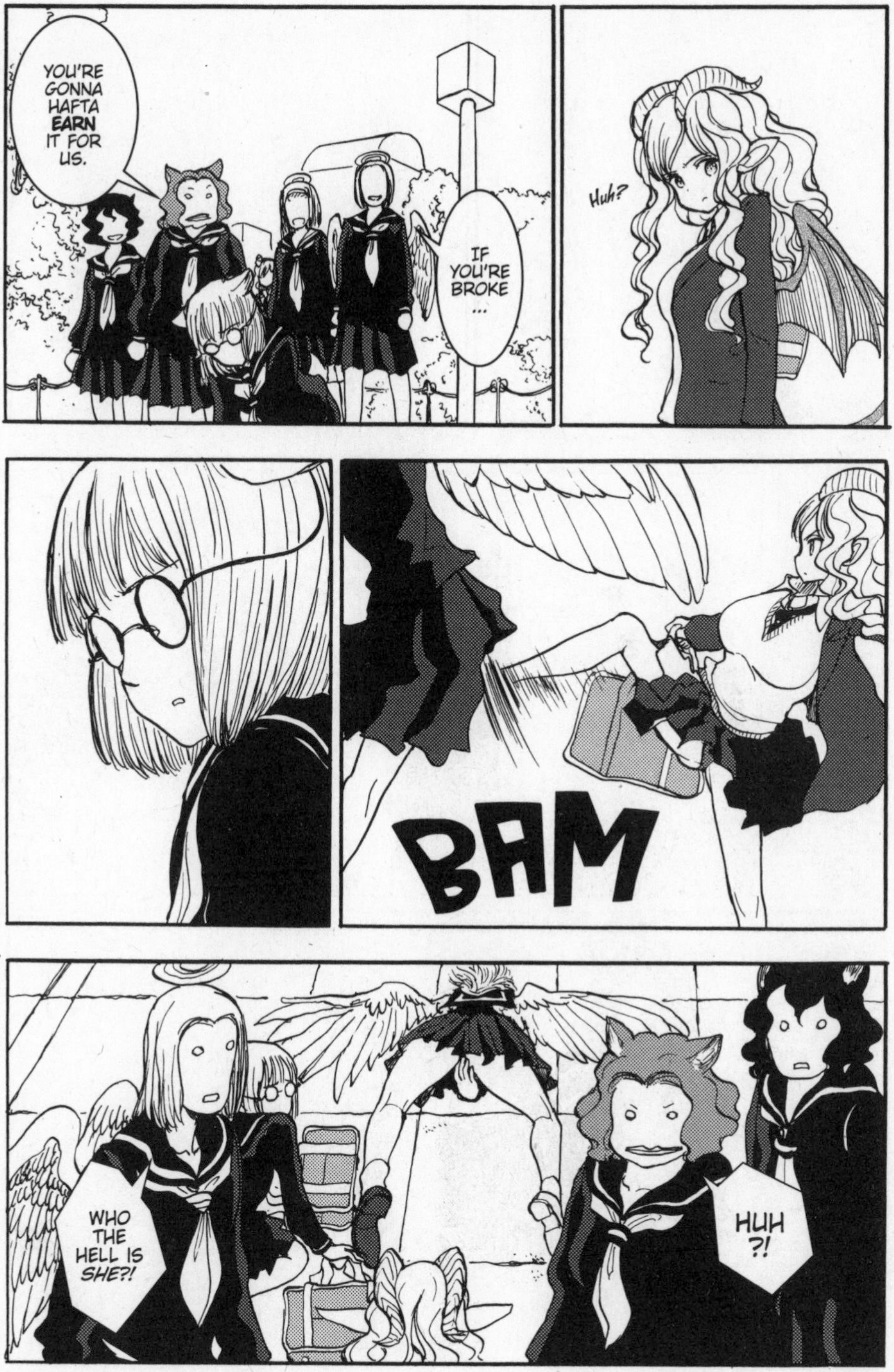
Huh?
IF YOU'RE BROKE ...
YOU'RE GONNA HAFTA EARN IT FOR US.
BAM
HUH ?!
WHO THE HELL IS SHE?!

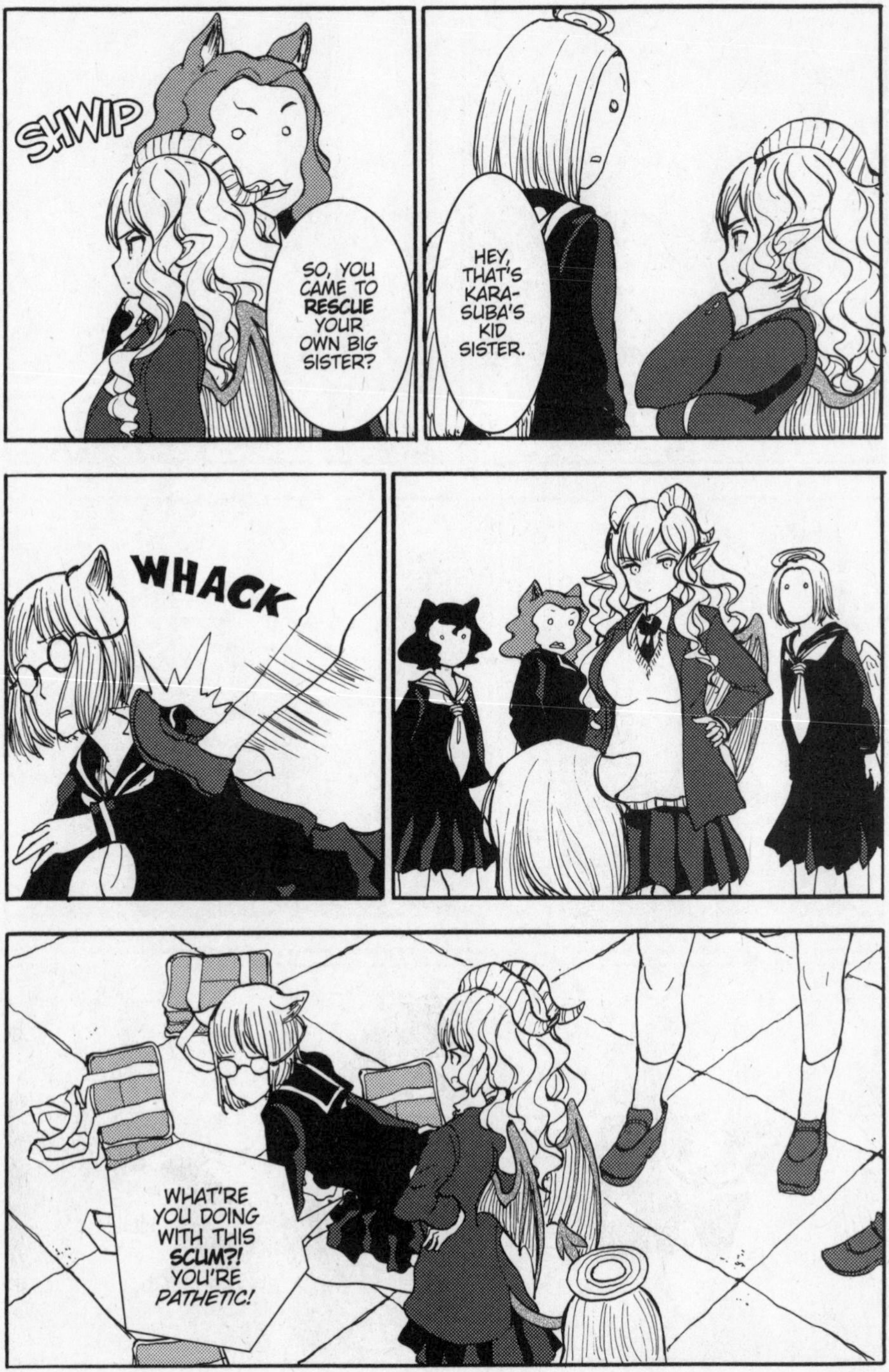
HEY, THAT'S KARA-SUBA'S KID SISTER.
SHWIP
SO, YOU CAME TO RESCUE YOUR OWN BIG SISTER?
WHACK
WHAT'RE YOU DOING WITH THIS SCUM?! YOU'RE PATHETIC!

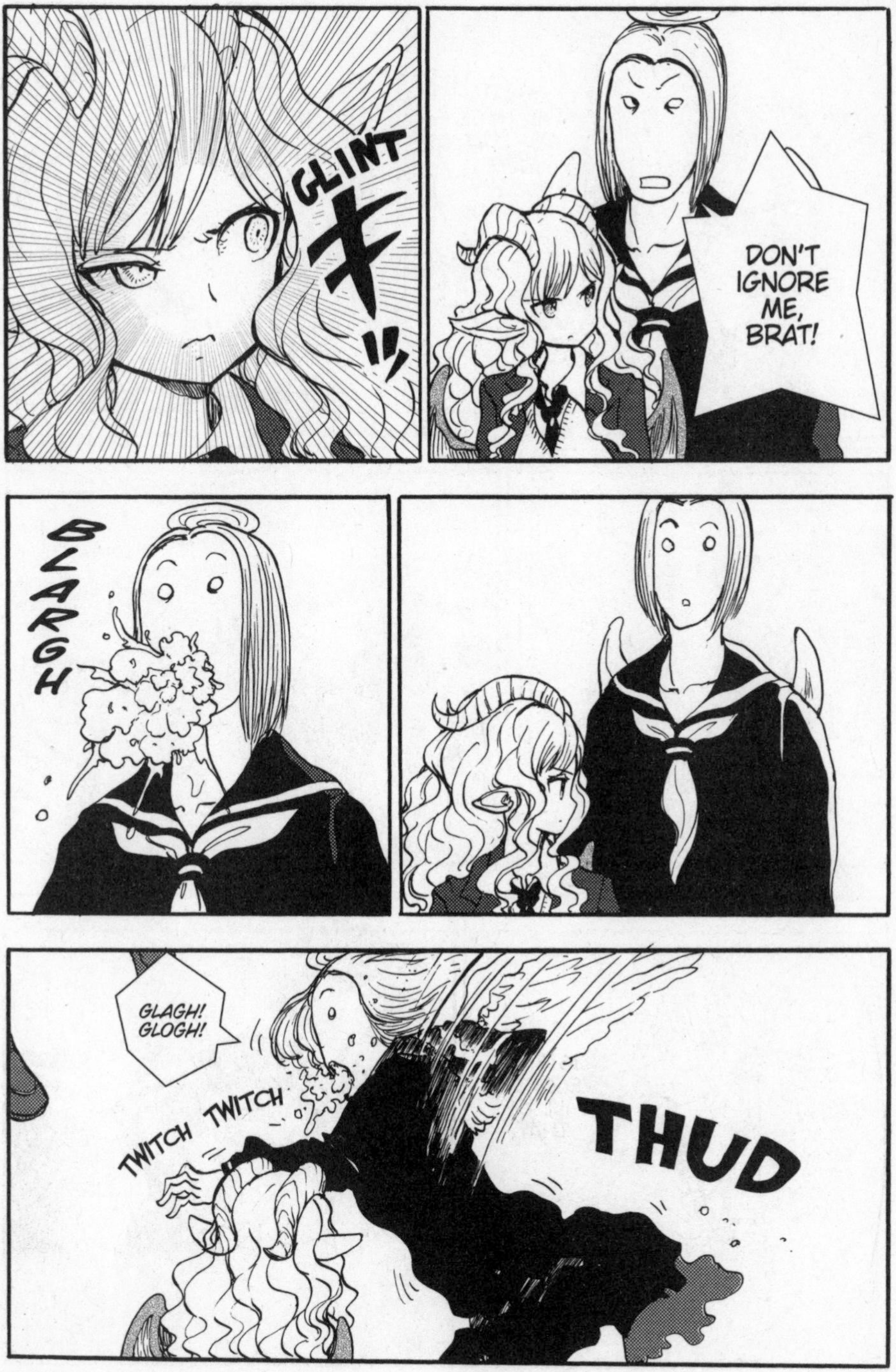
DON'T IGNORE ME, BRAT!
GLINT
キッ
BLARGH
GLAGH! GLOGH!
THUD
TWITCH TWITCH

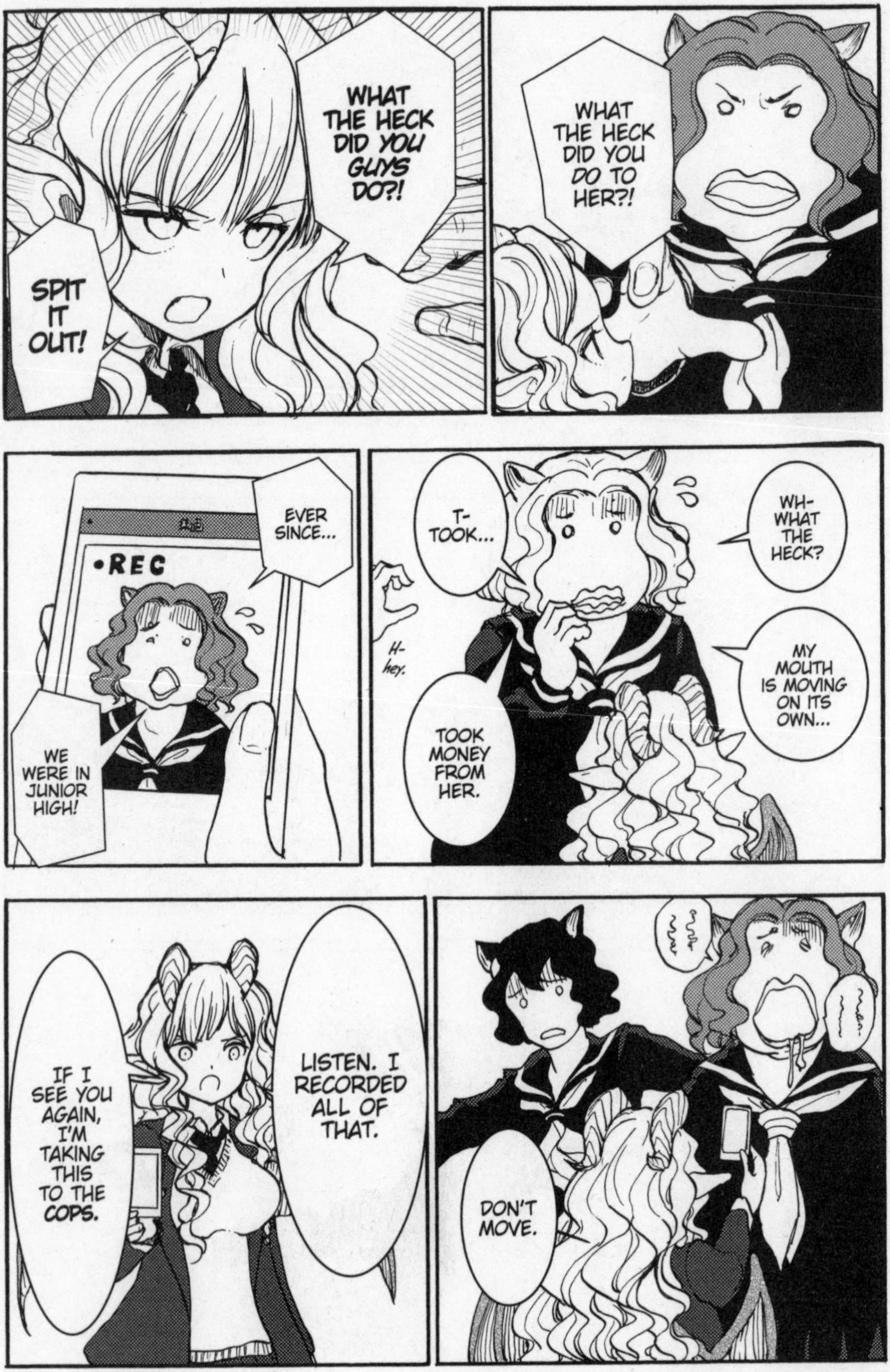
WHAT THE HECK DID YOU DO TO HER?!
WHAT THE HECK DID YOU GUYS DO?!
SPIT IT OUT!
WH- WHAT THE HECK?
MY MOUTH IS MOVING ON ITS OWN...
T- TOOK...
TOOK MONEY FROM HER.
H- hey.
EVER SINCE...
•REC
WE WERE IN JUNIOR HIGH!
DON'T MOVE.
LISTEN. I RECORDED ALL OF THAT.
IF I SEE YOU AGAIN, I'M TAKING THIS TO THE COPS.

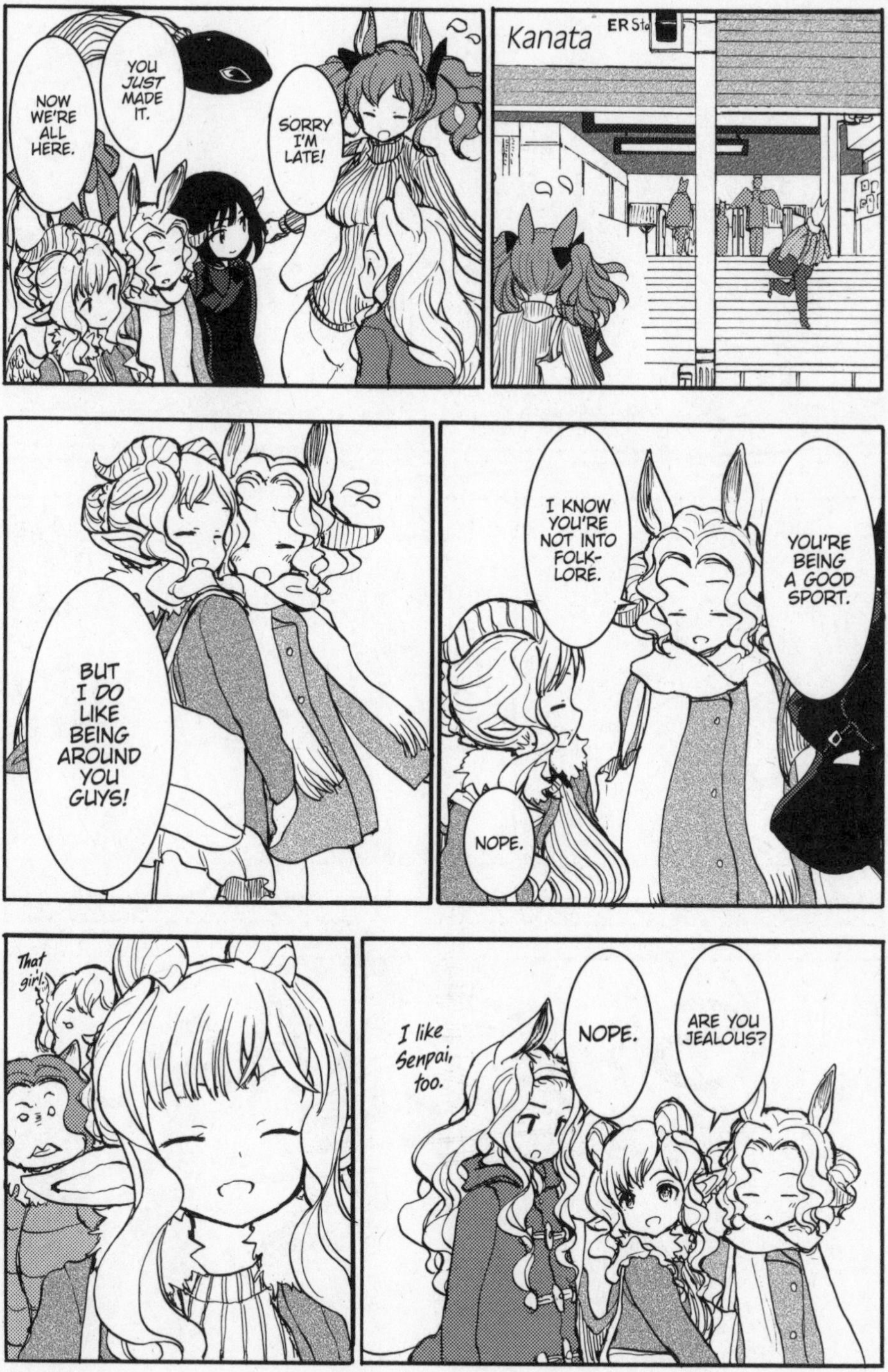
Kanata
ER Sta
SORRY I'M LATE!
YOU JUST MADE IT.
NOW WE'RE ALL HERE.
YOU'RE BEING A GOOD SPORT.
I KNOW YOU'RE NOT INTO FOLK-LORE.
NOPE.
BUT I DO LIKE BEING AROUND YOU GUYS!
ARE YOU JEALOUS?
NOPE.
I like Senpai, too.
That girl...

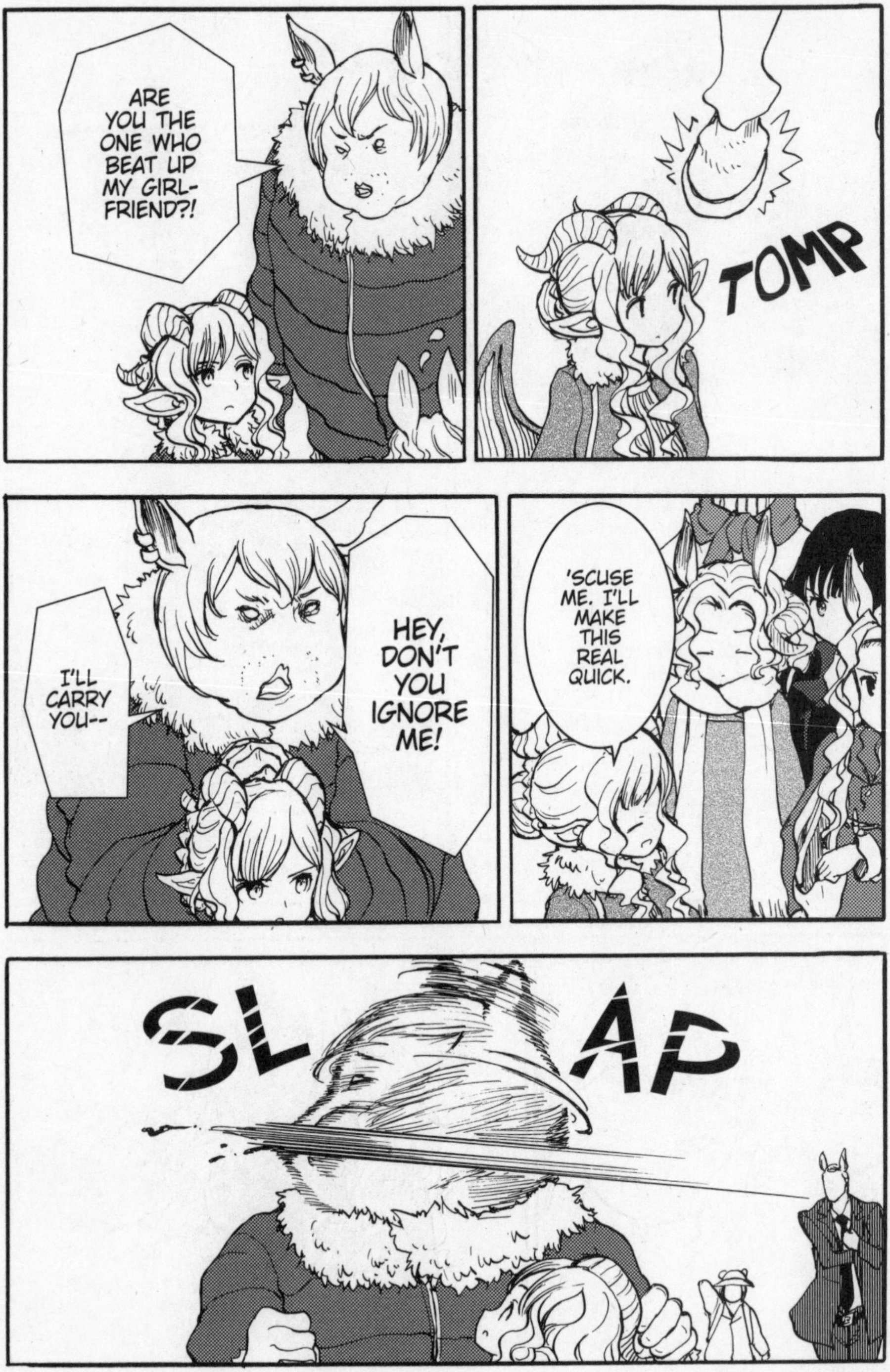
TOMP
ARE YOU THE ONE WHO BEAT UP MY GIRL-FRIEND?!
'SCUSE ME. I'LL MAKE THIS REAL QUICK.
HEY, DON'T YOU IGNORE ME!
I'LL CARRY YOU--
SLAP

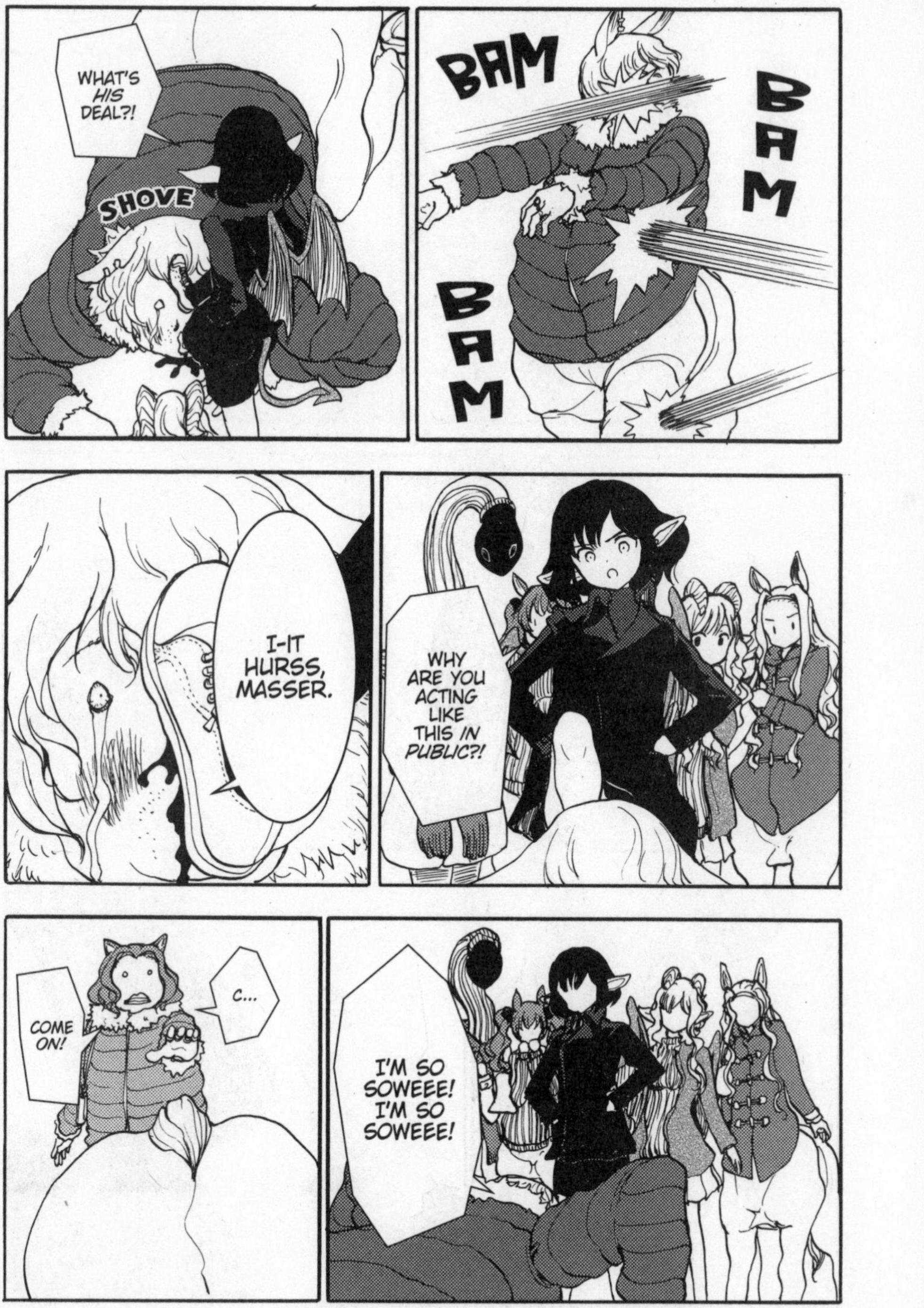
BAM
BAM
BAM
WHAT'S *HIS* DEAL?!
SHOVE
WHY ARE YOU ACTING LIKE THIS *IN PUBLIC*?!
I-IT HURSS, MASSER.
I'M SO SOWEEE! I'M SO SOWEEE!
C...
COME ON!

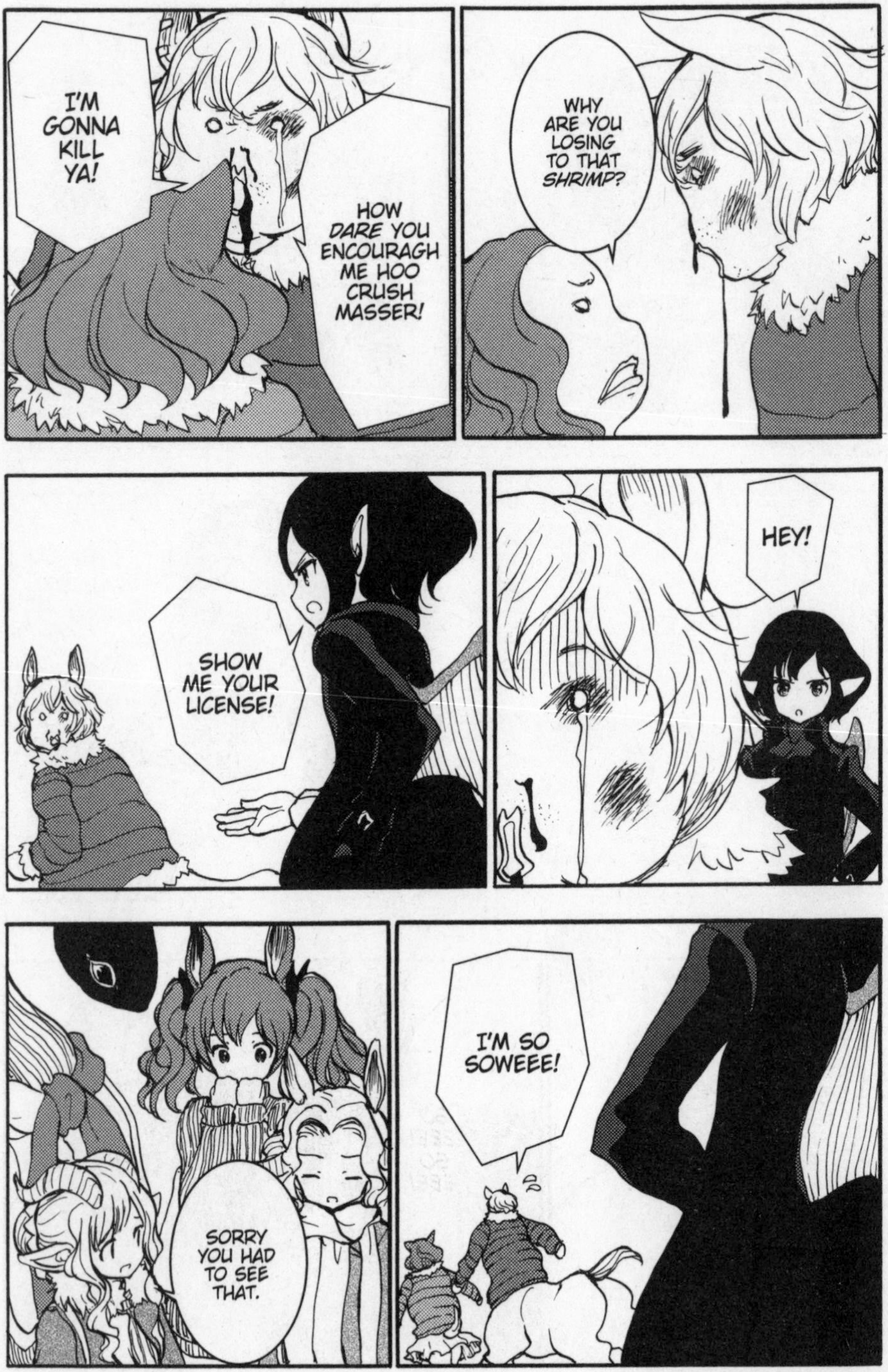
WHY ARE YOU LOSING TO THAT *SHRIMP?*
HOW *DARE* YOU ENCOURAGH ME HOO CRUSH MASSER!
I'M GONNA KILL YA!
HEY!
SHOW ME YOUR LICENSE!
I'M SO SOWEEE!
SORRY YOU HAD TO SEE THAT.

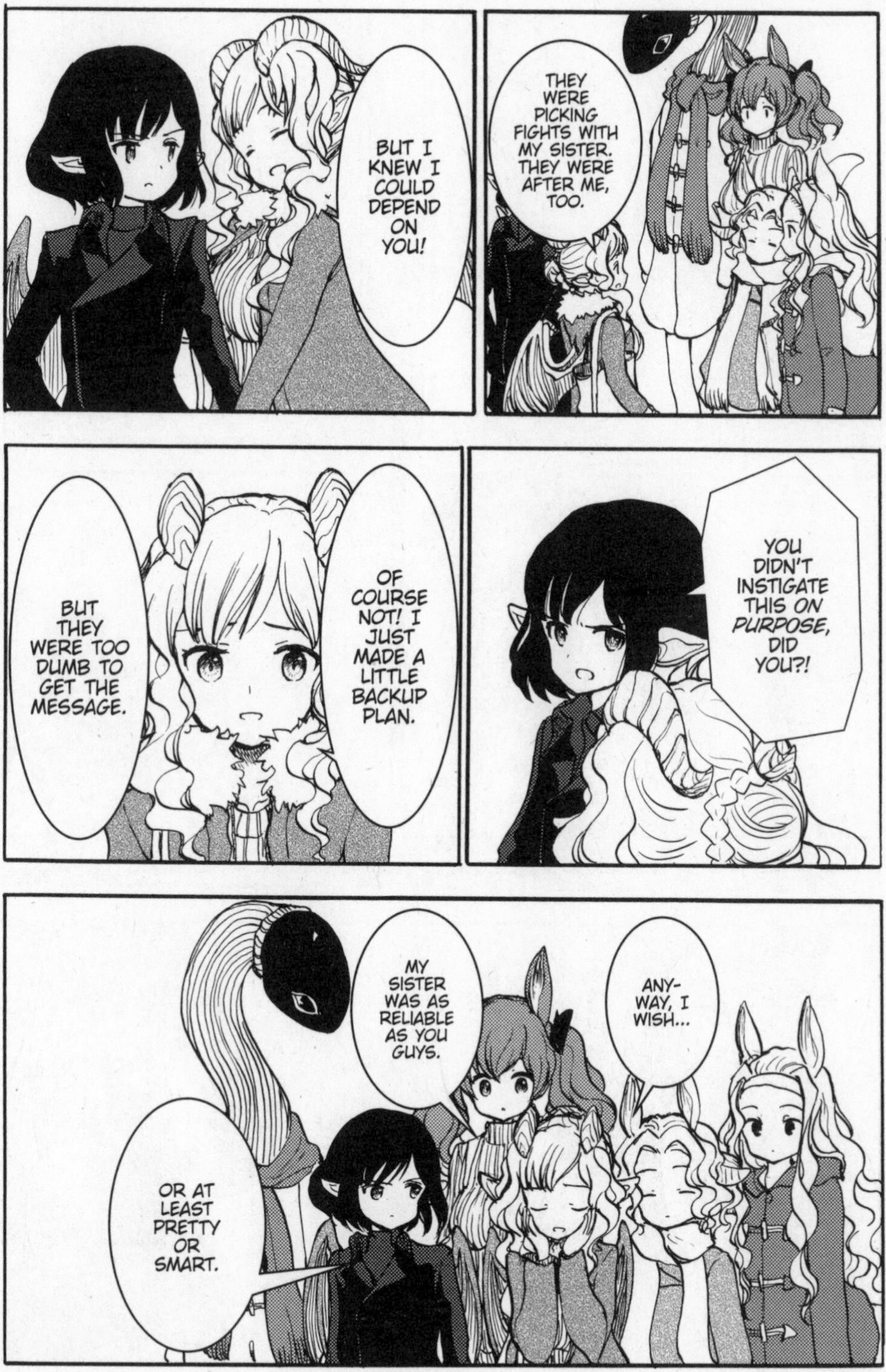
THEY WERE PICKING FIGHTS WITH MY SISTER. THEY WERE AFTER ME, TOO.
BUT I KNEW I COULD DEPEND ON YOU!
YOU DIDN'T INSTIGATE THIS *ON PURPOSE*, DID YOU?!
OF COURSE NOT! I JUST MADE A LITTLE BACKUP PLAN.
BUT THEY WERE TOO DUMB TO GET THE MESSAGE.
ANY-WAY, I WISH...
MY SISTER WAS AS RELIABLE AS YOU GUYS.
OR AT LEAST PRETTY OR SMART.

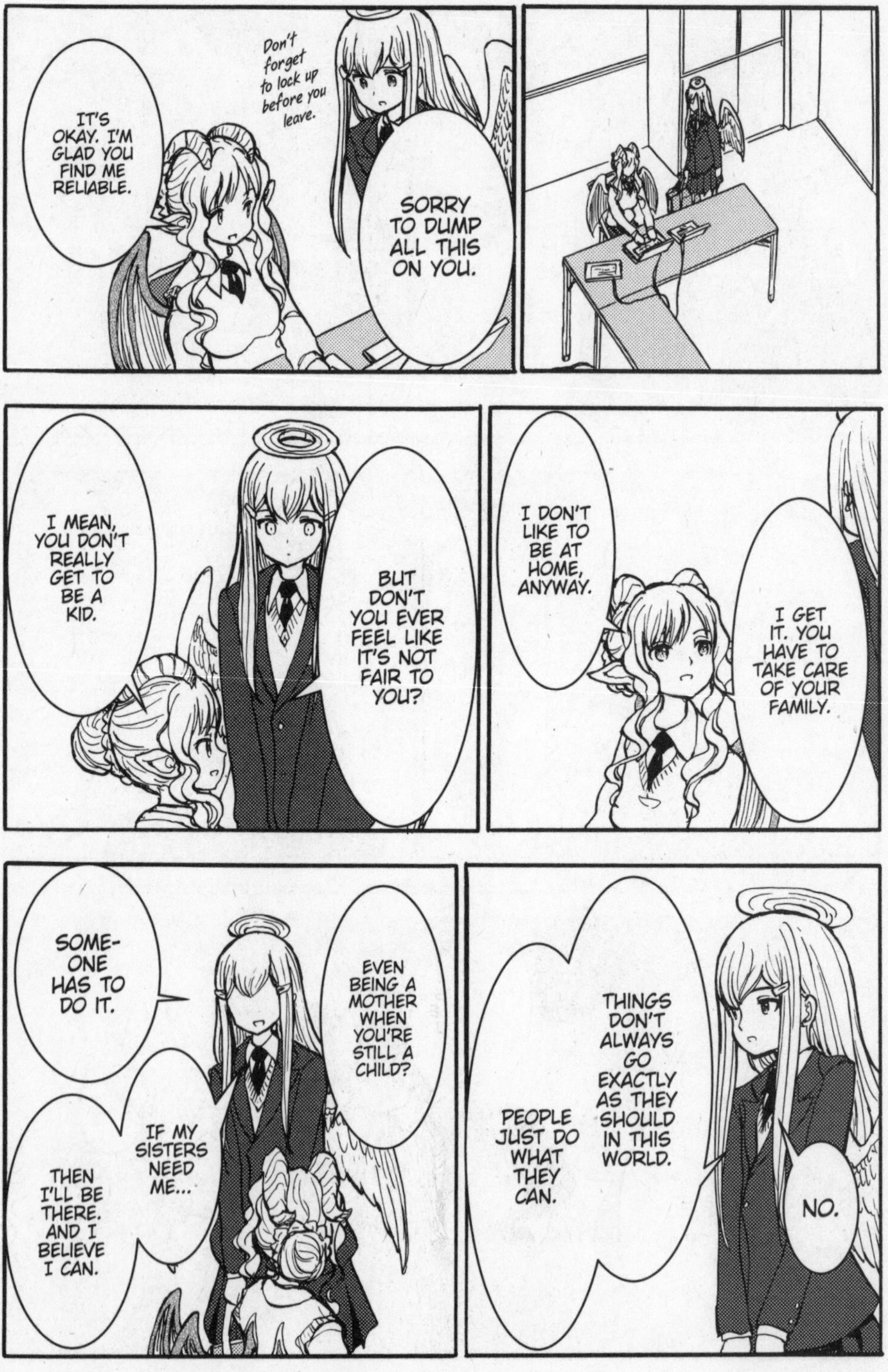
Don't forget to lock up before you leave.
SORRY TO DUMP ALL THIS ON YOU.
IT'S OKAY. I'M GLAD YOU FIND ME RELIABLE.
I GET IT. YOU HAVE TO TAKE CARE OF YOUR FAMILY.
I DON'T LIKE TO BE AT HOME, ANYWAY.
BUT DON'T YOU EVER FEEL LIKE IT'S NOT FAIR TO YOU?
I MEAN, YOU DON'T REALLY GET TO BE A KID.
NO.
THINGS DON'T ALWAYS GO EXACTLY AS THEY SHOULD IN THIS WORLD.
PEOPLE JUST DO WHAT THEY CAN.
EVEN BEING A MOTHER WHEN YOU'RE STILL A CHILD?
SOME-ONE HAS TO DO IT.
IF MY SISTERS NEED ME...
THEN I'LL BE THERE. AND I BELIEVE I CAN.

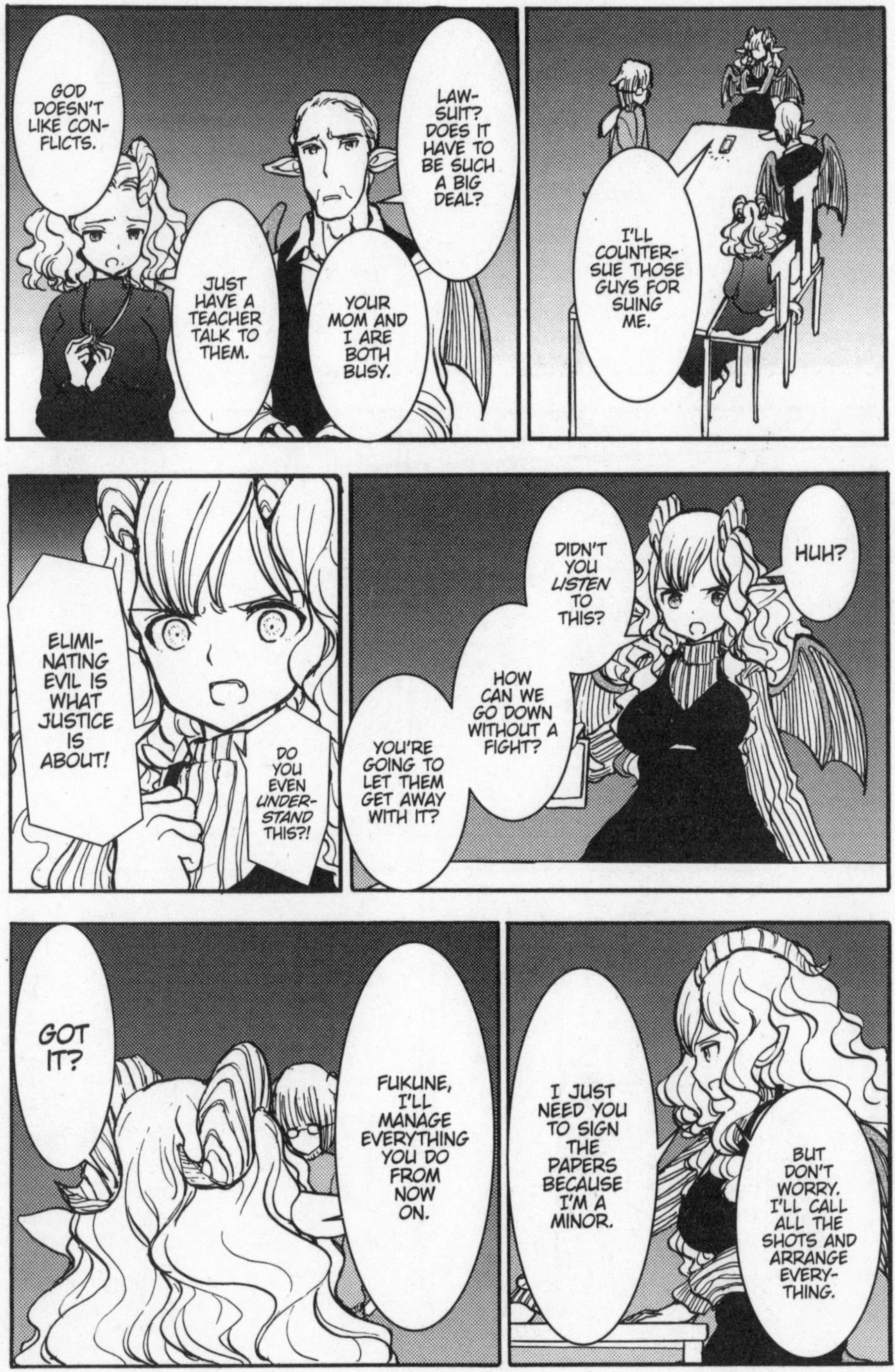
I'LL COUNTER-SUE THOSE GUYS FOR SUING ME.
LAW-SUIT? DOES IT HAVE TO BE SUCH A BIG DEAL?
GOD DOESN'T LIKE CON-FLICTS.
YOUR MOM AND I ARE BOTH BUSY.
JUST HAVE A TEACHER TALK TO THEM.
HUH?
DIDN'T YOU *LISTEN* TO THIS?
HOW CAN WE GO DOWN WITHOUT A FIGHT?
YOU'RE GOING TO LET THEM GET AWAY WITH IT?
DO YOU EVEN *UNDER-STAND* THIS?!
ELIMI-NATING EVIL IS WHAT JUSTICE IS ABOUT!
BUT DON'T WORRY. I'LL CALL ALL THE SHOTS AND ARRANGE EVERY-THING.
I JUST NEED YOU TO SIGN THE PAPERS BECAUSE I'M A MINOR.
FUKUNE, I'LL MANAGE EVERYTHING YOU DO FROM NOW ON.
GOT IT?

A Centaur's Life

SPOTLIGHT ON MERFOLK:
< 8 > MERFOLK'S LIFE BEFORE WAR

IN THE PERIOD AFTER THE MEIJI RESTORATION, THE MERFOLK WERE NO LONGER UNDER SCRUTINY AND HAD GAINED COMPLETE FREEDOM. HOWEVER, THE SHIPPING SERVICES THEY HAD BEEN PROVIDING WERE REPLACED BY STEAMSHIPS. JUST AS THE FASTEST HORSE WAS UNABLE TO COMPETE WITH A TRAIN OR AN AUTOMOBILE, MERFOLK SIMPLY COULD NOT COMPETE WITH STEAM ENGINES. THEIR MONOPOLY OVER RITUAL LAKE SERVICES ERODED, AND THEY WERE SOON REPLACED BY OTHER MAMMALIAN HUMAN RACES. THOUGH MERFOLK WEREN'T EXCLUDED FROM RITUAL SERVICES AT LAKE KYOU AND LAKE KOUJOU, WHICH WERE CONSIDERED STATE RELIGION, THE LACK OF PROTECTION FROM THE STATE WOULD LEAD TO IMMEDIATE ELIMINATION OF THE ALREADY-SPARSE POPULATION OF MERFOLK.

WITH THE EXCEPTION OF LAKE KYOU AND LAKE KOUJOU, MERFOLK COMMUNITIES LARGELY DISAPPEARED FROM AREAS OTHER THAN THE PACIFIC COAST. THOUGH THEIR AMA DIVERS BECAME FAMOUS FOR FISHING THROUGH FREEDIVING, MERFOLK GENERALLY LOST THEIR ROLE IN LARGE-SCALE FISHING TO MACHINE-POWERED SHIPS AND TRAWLS.

HUMAN IMPACT ON THE ENVIRONMENT WAS STILL MINIMAL IN THIS PERIOD. HAVING NEVER EXPERIENCED OVERPOPULATION, MERFOLK WERE MOSTLY ABLE TO AVOID FOOD SHORTAGES. THEY ALSO MANAGED TO SURVIVE THE GREAT FAMINE OF TOHOKU IN THE SHOWA PERIOD. THE SURVIVAL OF THEIR RELIGION AND THEIR LACK OF OBVIOUS WEALTH INDICATED THAT ACTION AGAINST MERFOLK, SUCH AS ATTACKS OR LOOTING, WAS RARE.

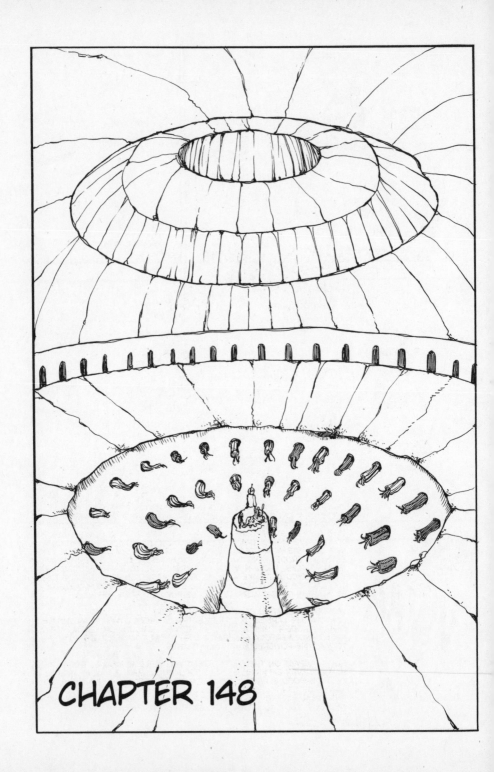

CHAPTER 148

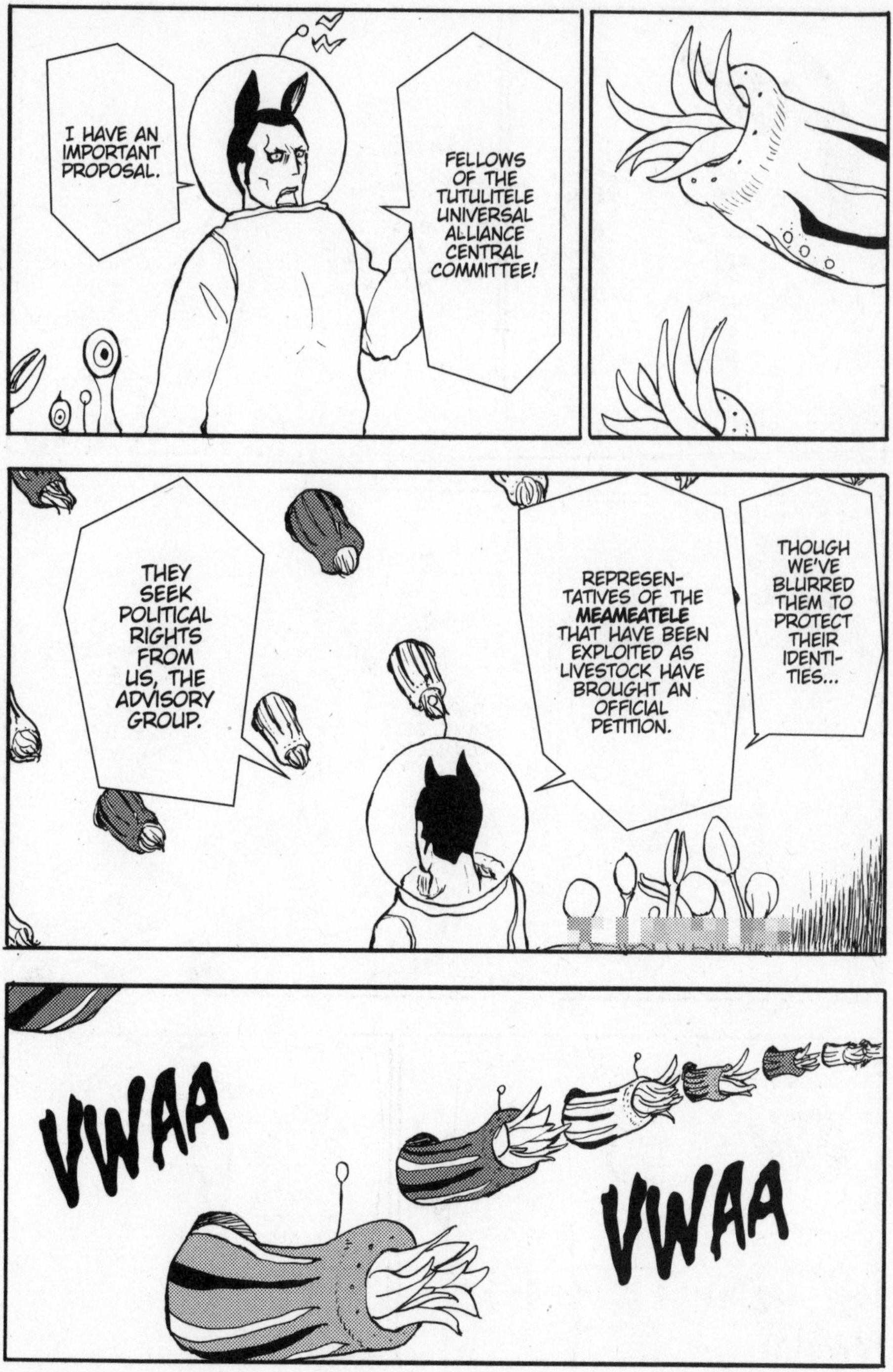
FELLOWS OF THE TUTULITELE UNIVERSAL ALLIANCE CENTRAL COMMITTEE!
I HAVE AN IMPORTANT PROPOSAL.
THOUGH WE'VE BLURRED THEM TO PROTECT THEIR IDENTI-TIES...
REPRESEN-TATIVES OF THE **MEAMEATELE** THAT HAVE BEEN EXPLOITED AS LIVESTOCK HAVE BROUGHT AN OFFICIAL PETITION.
THEY SEEK POLITICAL RIGHTS FROM US, THE ADVISORY GROUP.
VWAA
VWAA

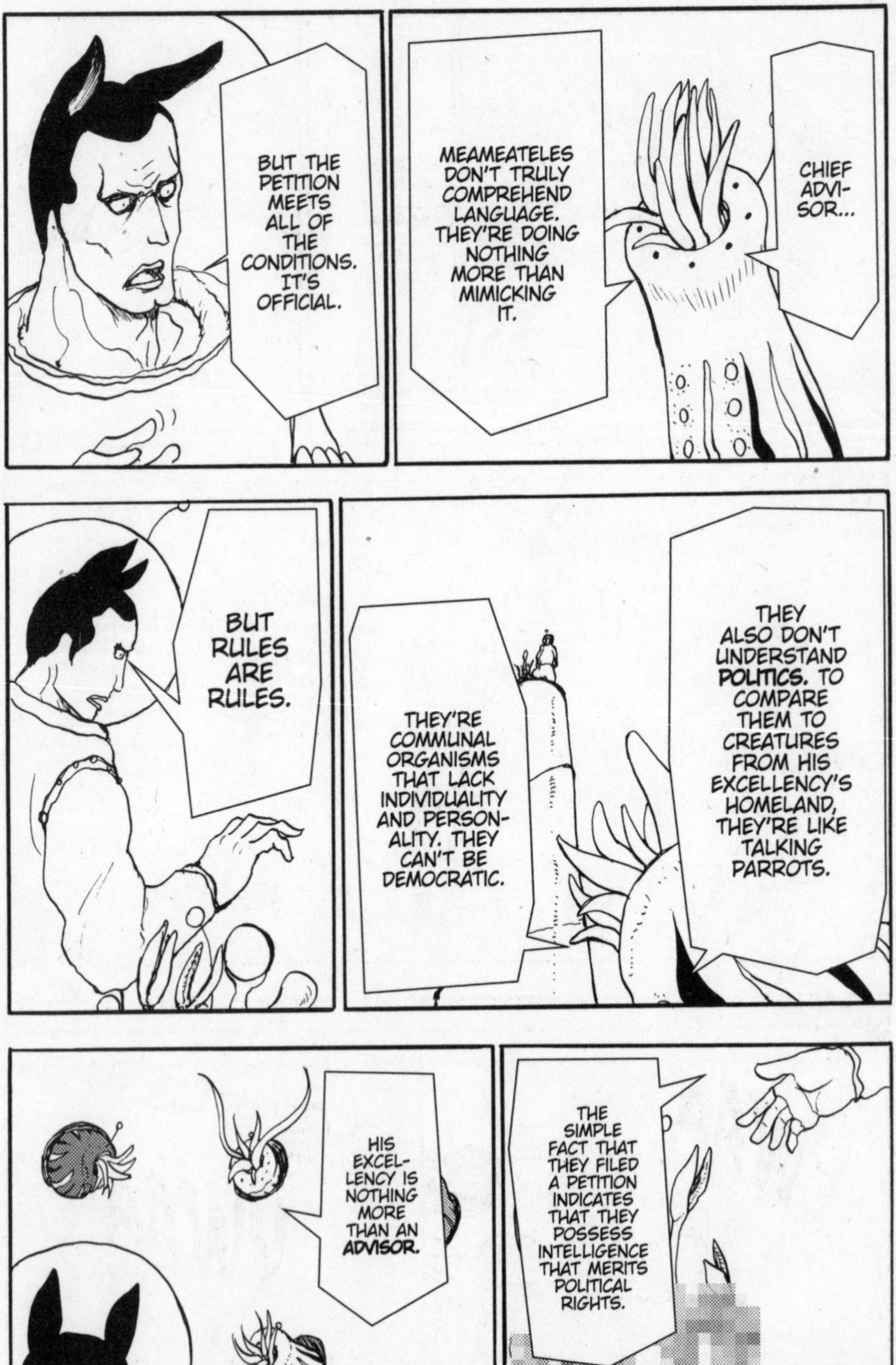
CHIEF ADVISOR...
MEAMEATELES DON'T TRULY COMPREHEND LANGUAGE. THEY'RE DOING NOTHING MORE THAN MIMICKING IT.
BUT THE PETITION MEETS ALL OF THE CONDITIONS. IT'S OFFICIAL.
THEY ALSO DON'T UNDERSTAND **POLITICS.** TO COMPARE THEM TO CREATURES FROM HIS EXCELLENCY'S HOMELAND, THEY'RE LIKE TALKING PARROTS.
THEY'RE COMMUNAL ORGANISMS THAT LACK INDIVIDUALITY AND PERSONALITY. THEY CAN'T BE DEMOCRATIC.
BUT RULES ARE RULES.
THE SIMPLE FACT THAT THEY FILED A PETITION INDICATES THAT THEY POSSESS INTELLIGENCE THAT MERITS POLITICAL RIGHTS.
HIS EXCELLENCY IS NOTHING MORE THAN AN **ADVISOR.**

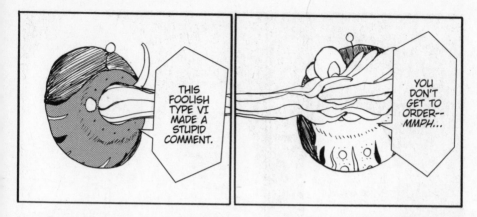

YOU DON'T GET TO ORDER-- MMPH...
THIS FOOLISH TYPE VI MADE A STUPID COMMENT.
THE CENTRAL COMMITTEE AND ALL THE FELLOWS OF TUTULITELE VALUE YOUR ADVICE.
WE SHOULDN'T QUIBBLE OVER WHETHER THIS IS RIGHT OR WRONG.
INSTEAD, LET'S DISCUSS HOW TO MAKE THIS WORK IN OUR FAVOR WITH A POSITIVE ATTITUDE.
THAT MORON BORROWED AUTHORITY FROM OON.
POLITICALLY EXPERIENCED BUT DOESN'T GET THE PRINCIPLES.
THAT CLUELESS TYPE VI...

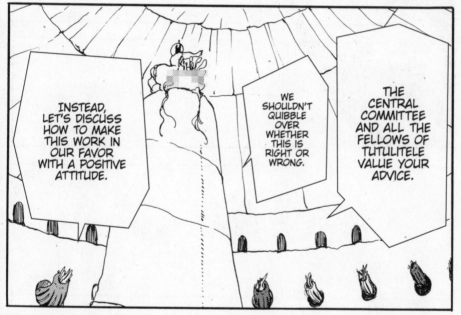

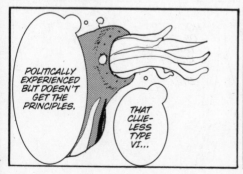

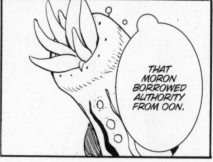

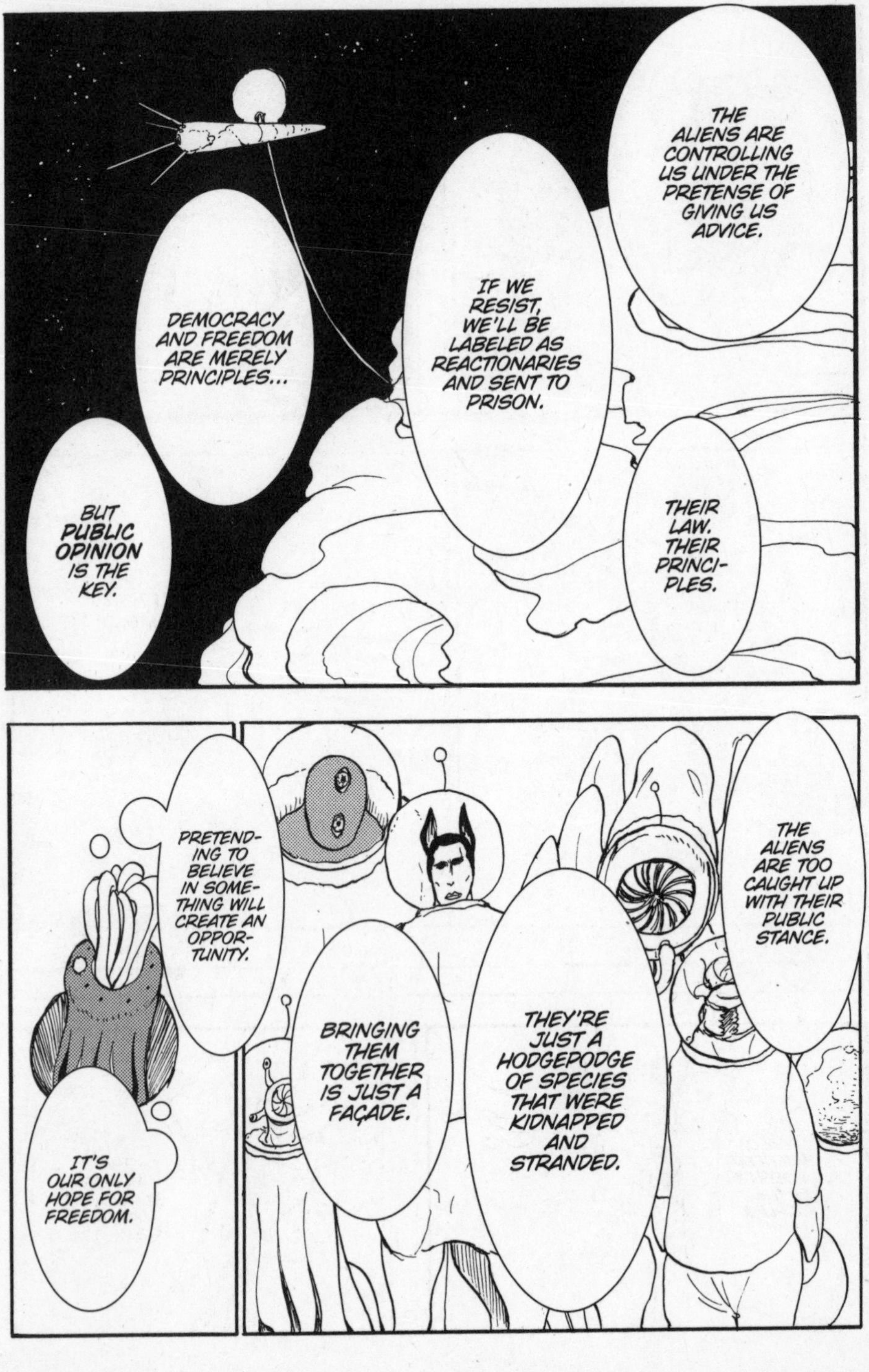
THE ALIENS ARE CONTROLLING US UNDER THE PRETENSE OF GIVING US ADVICE.
IF WE RESIST, WE'LL BE LABELED AS REACTIONARIES AND SENT TO PRISON.
THEIR LAW. THEIR PRINCI-PLES.
DEMOCRACY AND FREEDOM ARE MERELY PRINCIPLES...
BUT PUBLIC OPINION IS THE KEY.
THE ALIENS ARE TOO CAUGHT UP WITH THEIR PUBLIC STANCE.
THEY'RE JUST A HODGEPODGE OF SPECIES THAT WERE KIDNAPPED AND STRANDED.
BRINGING THEM TOGETHER IS JUST A FAÇADE.
PRETEND-ING TO BELIEVE IN SOME-THING WILL CREATE AN OPPOR-TUNITY.
IT'S OUR ONLY HOPE FOR FREEDOM.

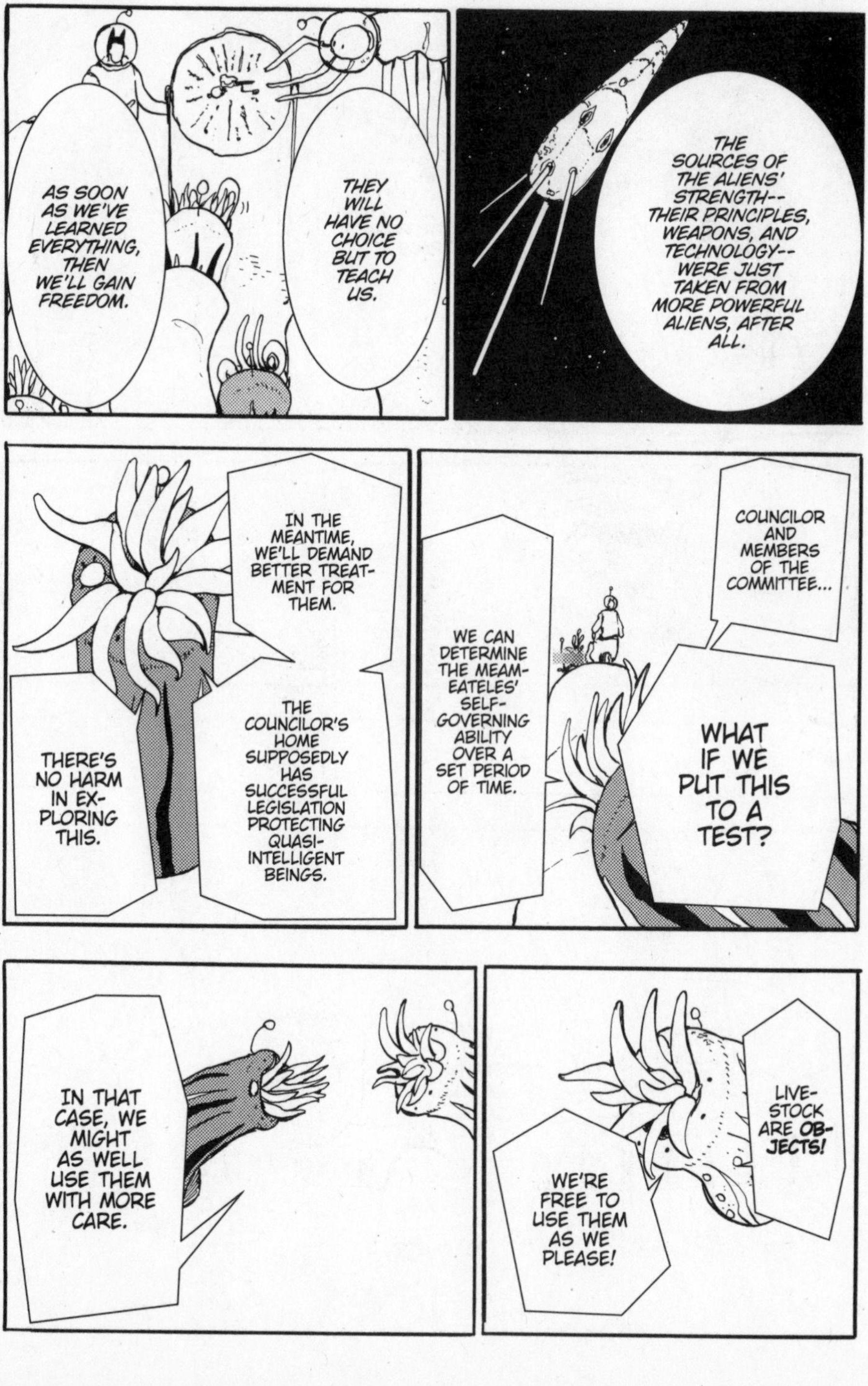
THE SOURCES OF THE ALIENS' STRENGTH--THEIR PRINCIPLES, WEAPONS, AND TECHNOLOGY--WERE JUST TAKEN FROM MORE POWERFUL ALIENS, AFTER ALL.
THEY WILL HAVE NO CHOICE BUT TO TEACH US.
AS SOON AS WE'VE LEARNED EVERYTHING, THEN WE'LL GAIN FREEDOM.
COUNCILOR AND MEMBERS OF THE COMMITTEE...
WHAT IF WE PUT THIS TO A TEST?
WE CAN DETERMINE THE MEAMEATELES' SELF-GOVERNING ABILITY OVER A SET PERIOD OF TIME.
IN THE MEANTIME, WE'LL DEMAND BETTER TREATMENT FOR THEM.
THE COUNCILOR'S HOME SUPPOSEDLY HAS SUCCESSFUL LEGISLATION PROTECTING QUASI-INTELLIGENT BEINGS.
THERE'S NO HARM IN EXPLORING THIS.
LIVESTOCK ARE OBJECTS!
WE'RE FREE TO USE THEM AS WE PLEASE!
IN THAT CASE, WE MIGHT AS WELL USE THEM WITH MORE CARE.

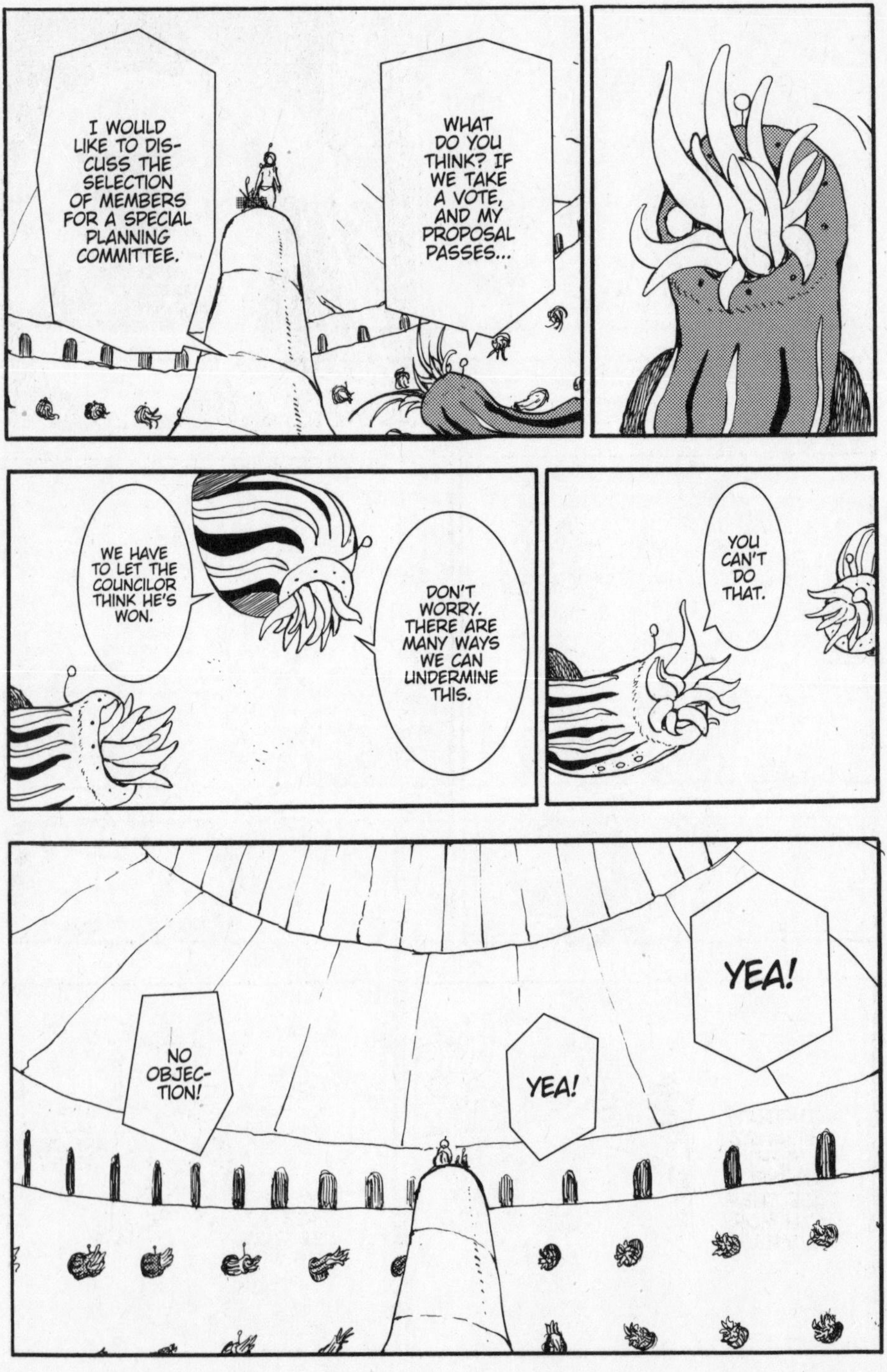
I WOULD LIKE TO DISCUSS THE SELECTION OF MEMBERS FOR A SPECIAL PLANNING COMMITTEE.
WHAT DO YOU THINK? IF WE TAKE A VOTE, AND MY PROPOSAL PASSES...
YOU CAN'T DO THAT.
DON'T WORRY. THERE ARE MANY WAYS WE CAN UNDERMINE THIS.
WE HAVE TO LET THE COUNCILOR THINK HE'S WON.
YEA!
YEA!
NO OBJECTION!

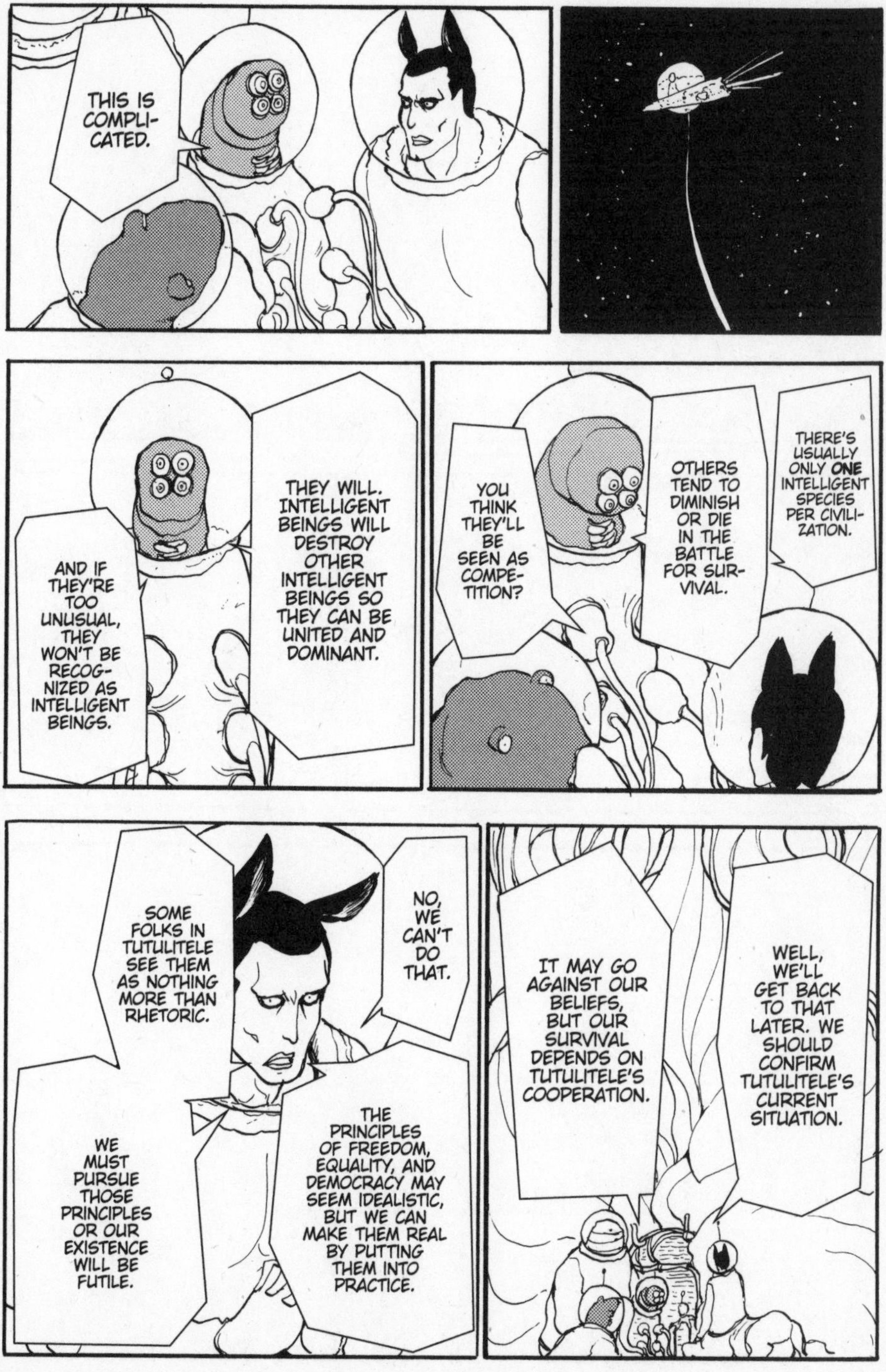
THIS IS COMPLICATED.
THERE'S USUALLY ONLY **ONE** INTELLIGENT SPECIES PER CIVILIZATION.
OTHERS TEND TO DIMINISH OR DIE IN THE BATTLE FOR SURVIVAL.
YOU THINK THEY'LL BE SEEN AS COMPETITION?
THEY WILL. INTELLIGENT BEINGS WILL DESTROY OTHER INTELLIGENT BEINGS SO THEY CAN BE UNITED AND DOMINANT.
AND IF THEY'RE TOO UNUSUAL, THEY WON'T BE RECOGNIZED AS INTELLIGENT BEINGS.
WELL, WE'LL GET BACK TO THAT LATER. WE SHOULD CONFIRM TUTULITELE'S CURRENT SITUATION.
IT MAY GO AGAINST OUR BELIEFS, BUT OUR SURVIVAL DEPENDS ON TUTULITELE'S COOPERATION.
NO, WE CAN'T DO THAT.
SOME FOLKS IN TUTULITELE SEE THEM AS NOTHING MORE THAN RHETORIC.
THE PRINCIPLES OF FREEDOM, EQUALITY, AND DEMOCRACY MAY SEEM IDEALISTIC, BUT WE CAN MAKE THEM REAL BY PUTTING THEM INTO PRACTICE.
WE MUST PURSUE THOSE PRINCIPLES OR OUR EXISTENCE WILL BE FUTILE.

A CentaUr's Life

SPOTLIGHT ON MERFOLK:
< 9 > DURING THE WAR

AFTER THE OUTBREAK OF THE PACIFIC WAR, SOME DESCENDANTS
OF MERFOLK NAVY VETERANS SERVED IN THE NAVY, WHICH EXPANDED
ITS POWER IN THE PACIFIC. SOME PARTICIPATED ACTIVELY AS PILOTS
OF MARITIME PATROL AIRCRAFTS. HOWEVER, THE IDEA THAT MERFOLK
WOULD BE ABLE TO SWIM AWAY IF THEY CRASHED IN FOREIGN WATERS
WAS NOTHING MORE THAN WISHFUL THINKING. INTERRACIAL COOPERA-
TION PROPAGANDA IS BELIEVED TO HAVE BEEN A MAJOR FACTOR IN THE
PERPETUATION OF THAT STORY. IN THE NAVY, WHICH HELD CONTROL OF
THE SEAS EXCEPT FOR THE COASTS IN THE LATER STAGES OF THE WAR,
MERFOLK WERE KNOWN FOR THEIR ROLES IN PATROL AND SURVEILLANCE
ACTIVITIES AND FOR THEIR INFAMOUS SPECIAL TORPEDO ATTACK. THEY
WERE, HOWEVER, POWERLESS AGAINST MODERN WARSHIPS.

MERFOLK SOLDIERS WERE MORE ACTIVE IN THE ARMY. THEY EXCELLED AT
CATCHING ENEMIES IN MAJOR RIVERS AS WELL AS SMALL WATERWAYS.
HOWEVER, ON THE SOUTHERN FRONT, THEY WERE ATTACKED BY
ALLIGATORS AND SUFFERED MANY CASUALTIES.

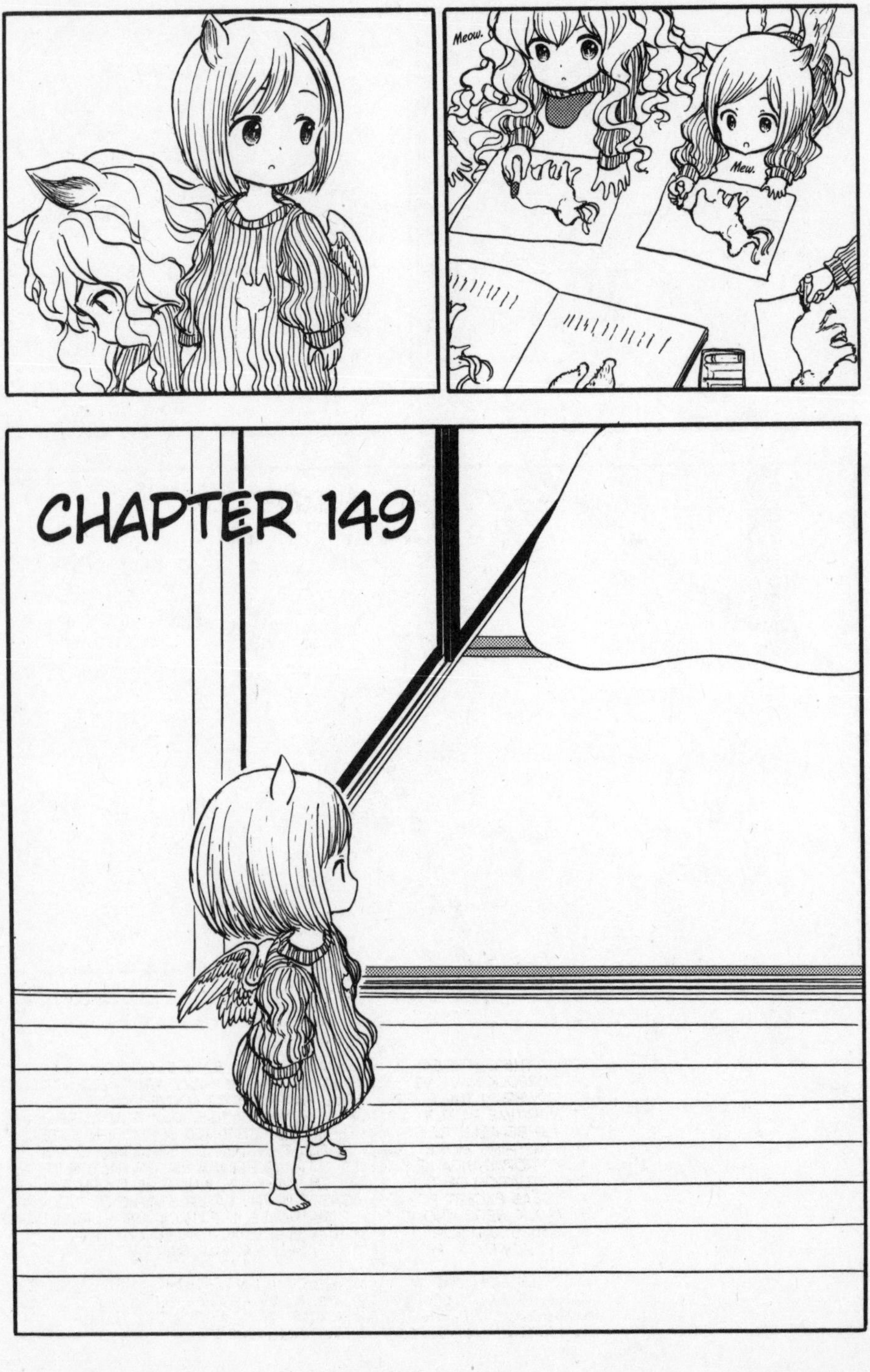
Mew.
Meow.
CHAPTER 149

IT SMELLS LIKE SUN-SHINE!
WARM
WUMF
Loves the bed.
MEOW.

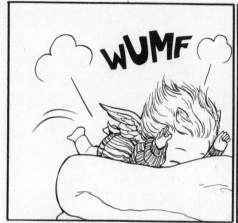

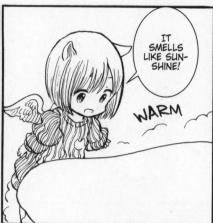

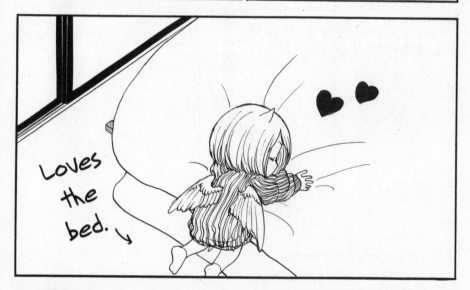

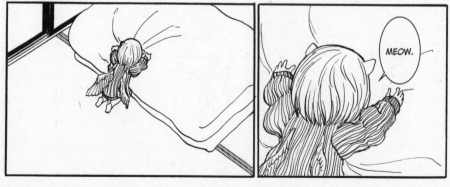

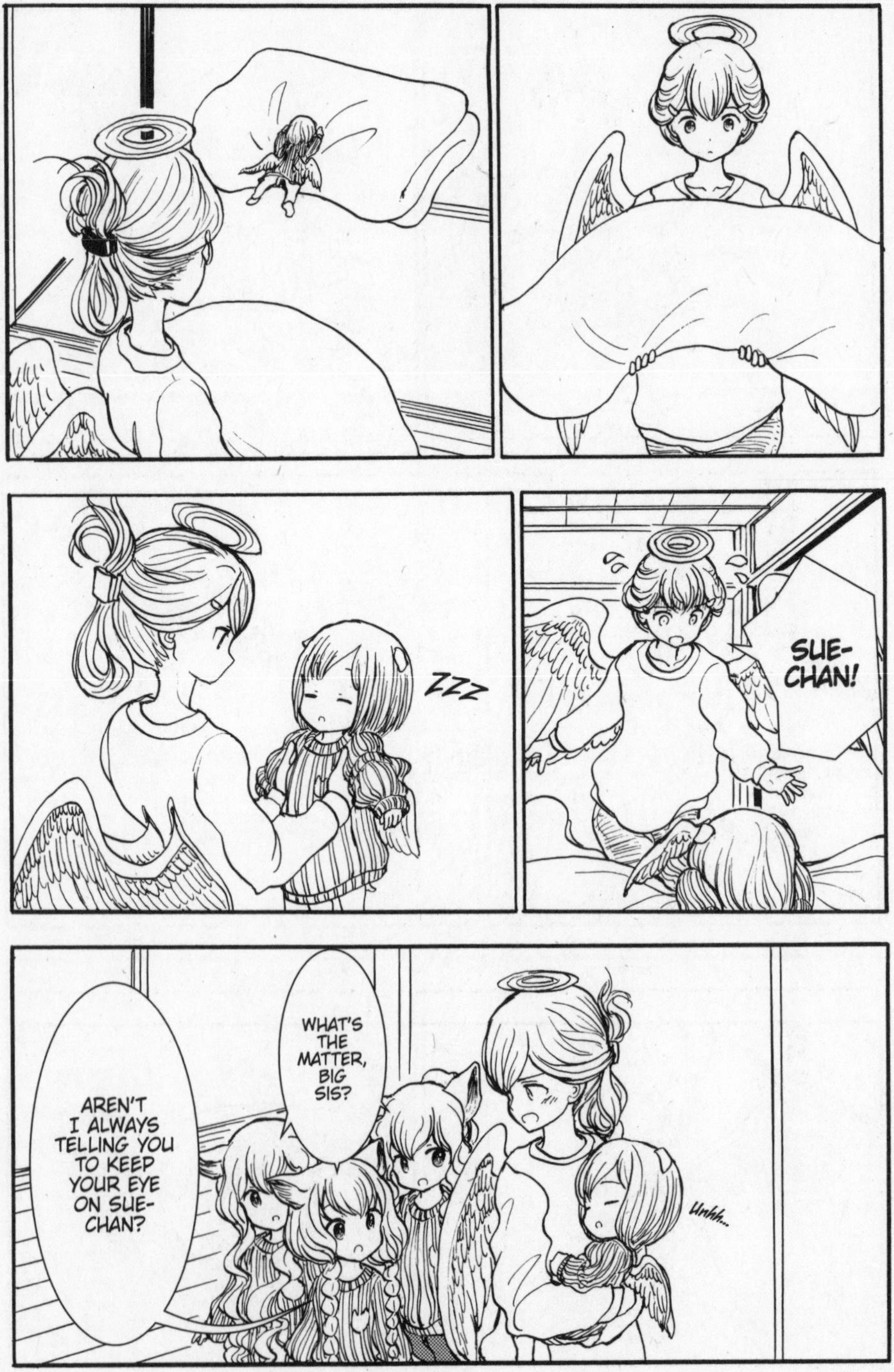
SUE-CHAN!
ZZZ
WHAT'S THE MATTER, BIG SIS?
AREN'T I ALWAYS TELLING YOU TO KEEP YOUR EYE ON SUE-CHAN?
Unhh...

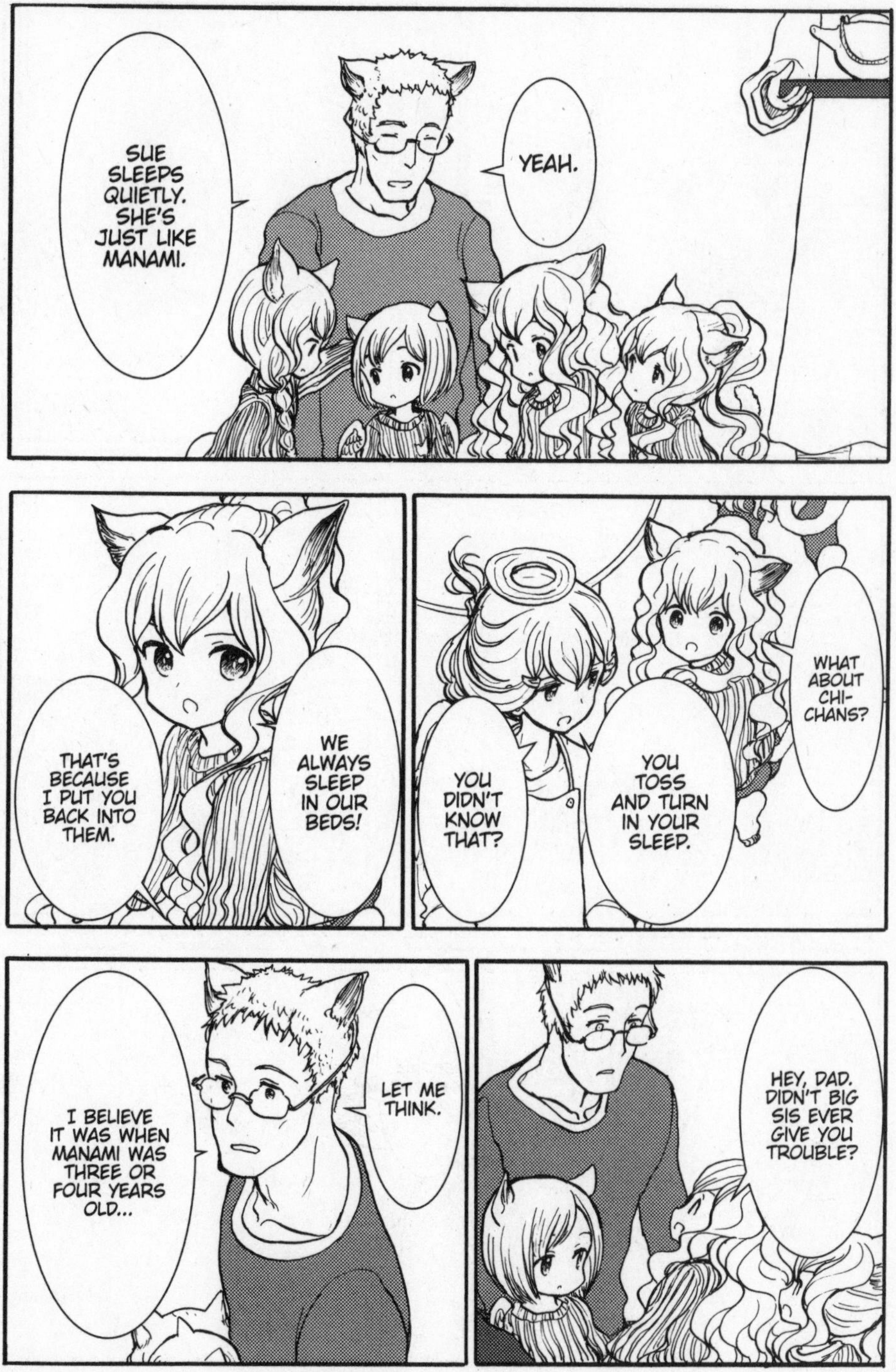
YEAH.
SUE SLEEPS QUIETLY. SHE'S JUST LIKE MANAMI.
WHAT ABOUT CHI-CHANS?
YOU TOSS AND TURN IN YOUR SLEEP.
YOU DIDN'T KNOW THAT?
WE ALWAYS SLEEP IN OUR BEDS!
THAT'S BECAUSE I PUT YOU BACK INTO THEM.
HEY, DAD. DIDN'T BIG SIS EVER GIVE YOU TROUBLE?
LET ME THINK.
I BELIEVE IT WAS WHEN MANAMI WAS THREE OR FOUR YEARS OLD...

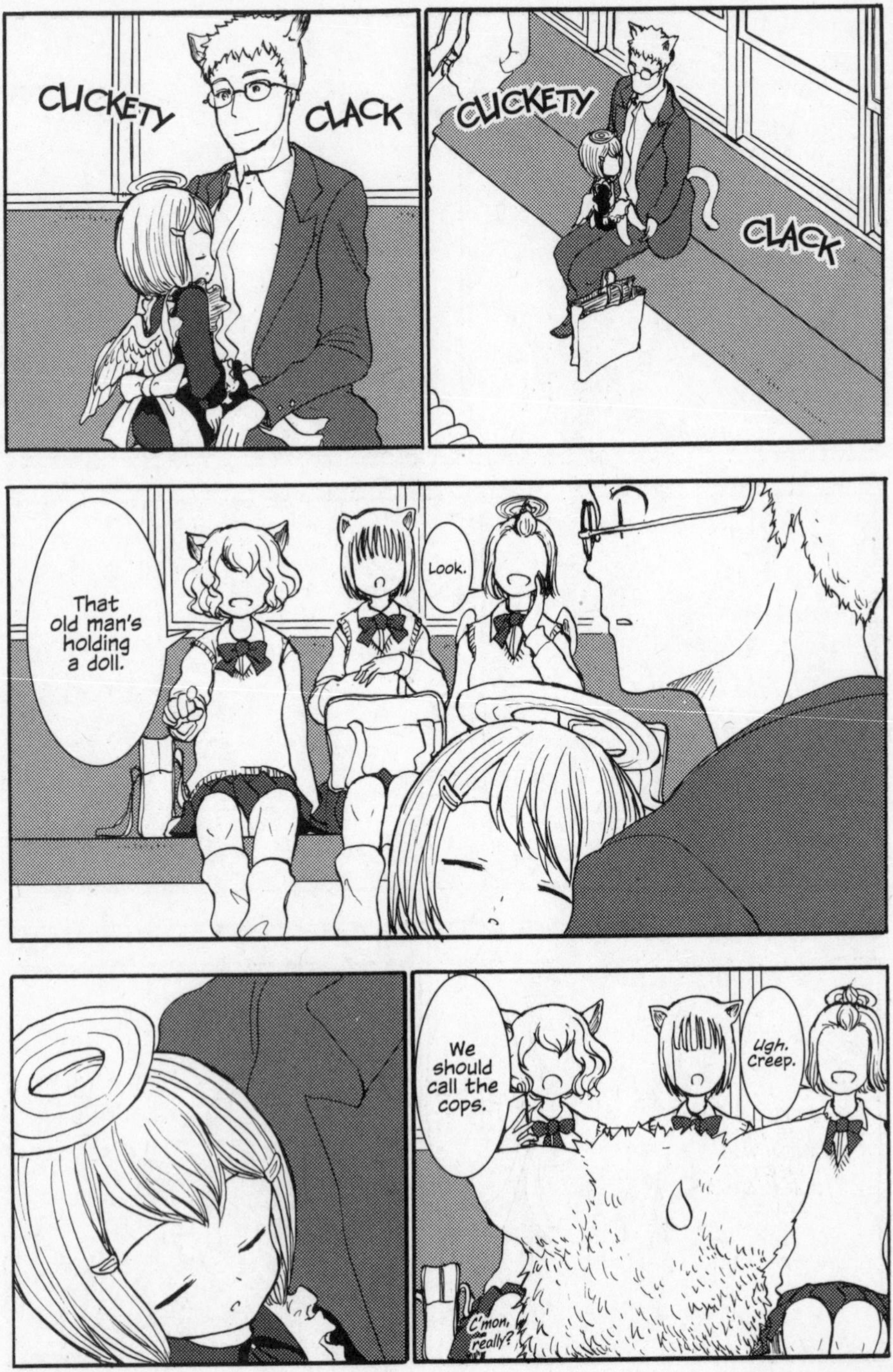
CLICKETY
CLACK
CLICKETY
CLACK
Look.
That old man's holding a doll.
Ugh. Creep.
We should call the cops.
C'mon, really?

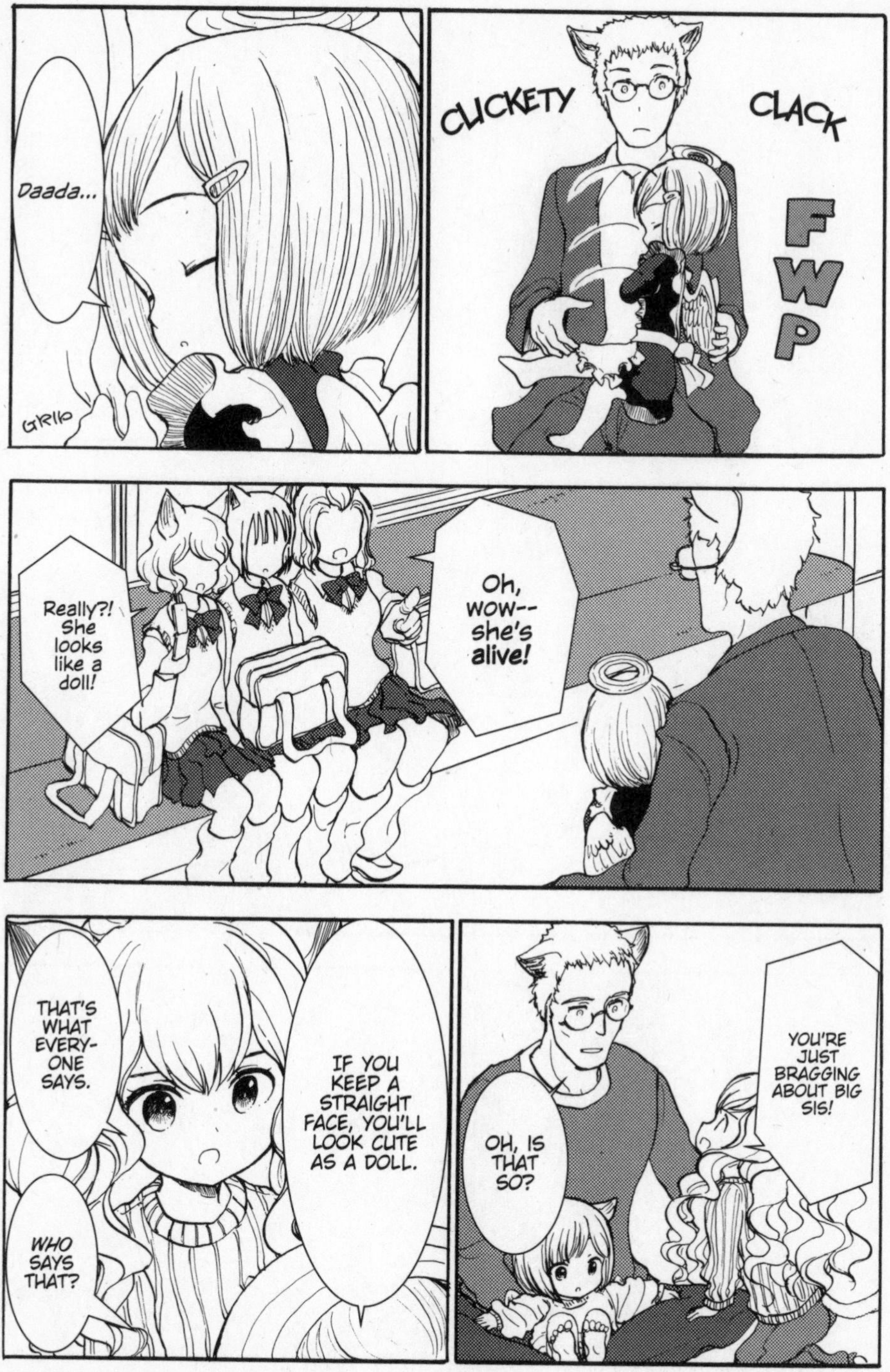
CLICKETY
CLACK
FWP
Daada...
GRIP
Oh, wow--she's alive!
Really?! She looks like a doll!
YOU'RE JUST BRAGGING ABOUT BIG SIS!
OH, IS THAT SO?
IF YOU KEEP A STRAIGHT FACE, YOU'LL LOOK CUTE AS A DOLL.
THAT'S WHAT EVERY-ONE SAYS.
WHO SAYS THAT?

A Centaur's Life

SPOTLIGHT ON MERFOLK:
< 10 > POSTWAR TO PRESENT

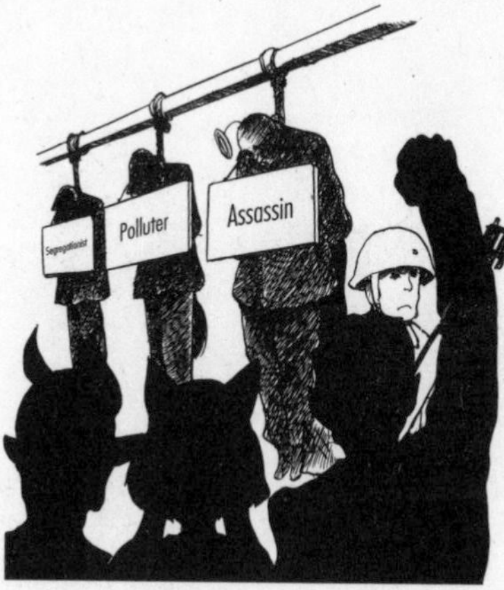
Segregationist
Polluter
Assassin

AFTER THE WAR, MOST MERFOLK MADE A MEAGER LIVING BY FISHING. THEY DID NOT GARNER MUCH PUBLIC ATTENTION UNTIL POLLUTION BECAME A MAJOR PROBLEM DURING THE POSTWAR PERIOD OF RAPID ECONOMIC GROWTH. TO PROTEST INDUSTRIAL WASTE DUMPING IN THEIR COMMUNITIES, MERFOLK ATTACKED FACTORIES AND SHIPS WITH ABANDONED TORPEDOES FROM THE WAR. THIS ALL-OUT CONFRONTATION FORCED THE GOVERNMENT TO CHOOSE BETWEEN ECONOMIC GROWTH AND RECONCILIATION BETWEEN ALL SPECIES. A DECISION BY THE PRIME MINISTER AT THE TIME RESULTED IN THE PUBLIC HANGINGS OF ALL EXECUTIVES, EXCEPT THE CHAIRMAN, AT TEITO STATION MARUNOUCHI FOR THE INTENTIONAL DUMPING OF HAZARDOUS WASTE THAT LED TO DEATHS AND ENVIRONMENTAL DESTRUCTION. AREAS WITH MERFOLK COMMUNITIES WERE ALSO ORDERED TO FOLLOW STRICTER ENVIRONMENTAL REGULATIONS. ALTHOUGH THIS CHOICE WAS INITIALLY VIEWED AS UNFAVORABLE FOR ECONOMIC GROWTH, OPINIONS CHANGED AS WORLDWIDE ENVIRONMENTAL AWARENESS INCREASED. IT ALSO HELPED TO RESTORE JAPAN'S REPUTATION, WHICH HAD BEEN TARNISHED BY ITS WAR OF AGGRESSION, AND LED TO THE CREATION OF THE WORLD'S LEADING ENVIRONMENTAL PROTECTION INDUSTRY. THIS DEMONSTRATES THAT ANY ATTEMPT AT PROSPERITY THAT INVOLVES HARMING PEOPLE WILL ALWAYS BACKFIRE AND FAIL. PEACEFUL COEXISTENCE IS THE ONLY PATH TO PROSPERITY, NO MATTER HOW DIFFICULT IT MAY SEEM.

IN SPITE OF DOWNSIDES LIKE POLLUTION, ONE SHOULD NOT DESPISE SCIENCE, NOR IGNORE THE USEFULNESS OF TECHNOLOGY. IN THE AGE OF TELEVISION, MANY MERFOLK WITH GOOD LOOKS AND SINGING VOICES WENT INTO SHOW BUSINESS. THE DEVELOPMENT OF TECHNOLOGY THAT ASSISTED IN THEIR TRAVEL BY LAND PROBABLY PLAYED A MAJOR PART IN THIS. SCIENCE AND TECHNOLOGY CAN SOLVE ETHICAL ISSUES; THEREFORE, IGNORING THEM IS AS DAMAGING AS RACISM. THE HISTORY OF THE MERFOLK TEACHES US THE IMPORTANCE OF CO-PROSPERITY.

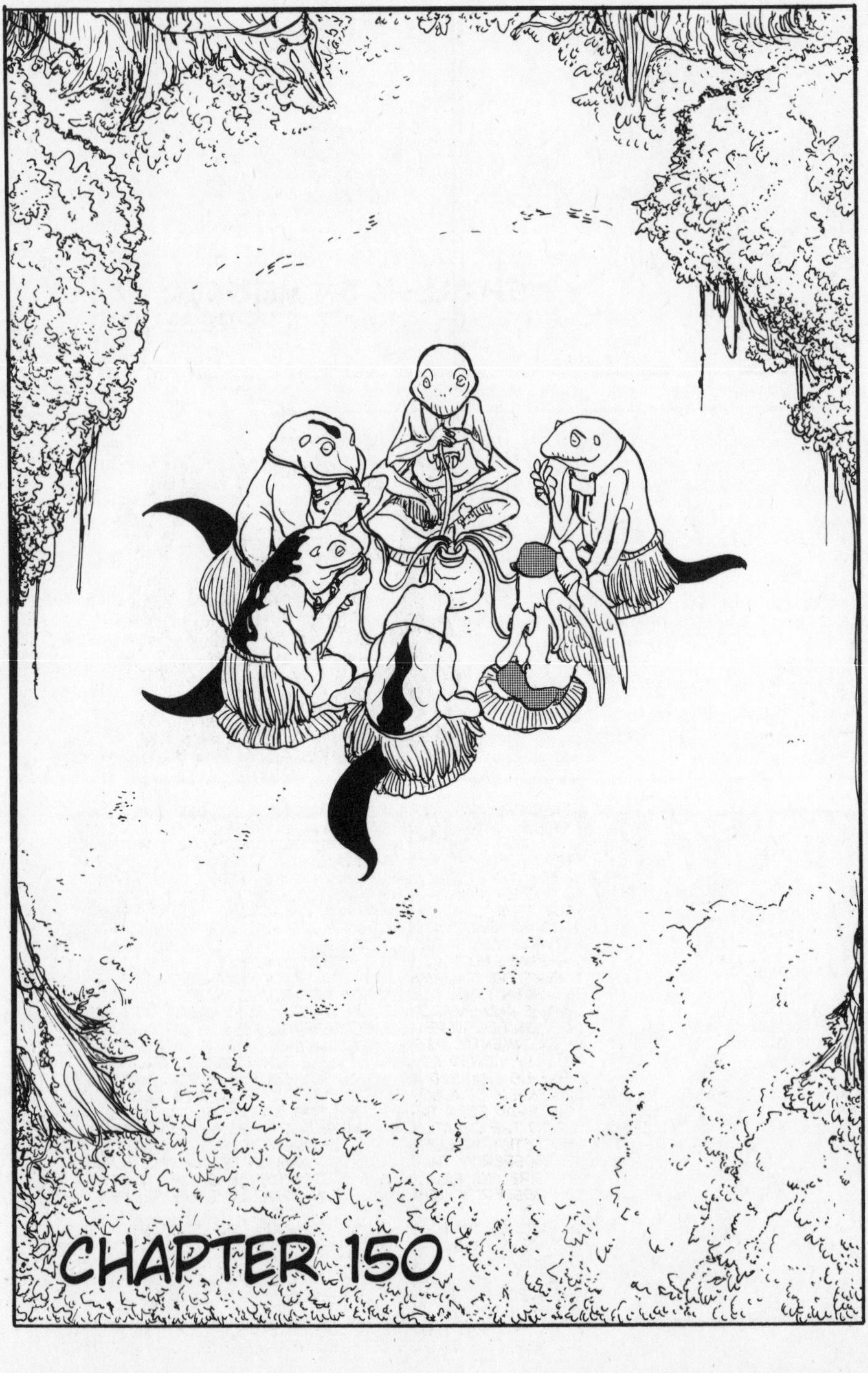
CHAPTER 150

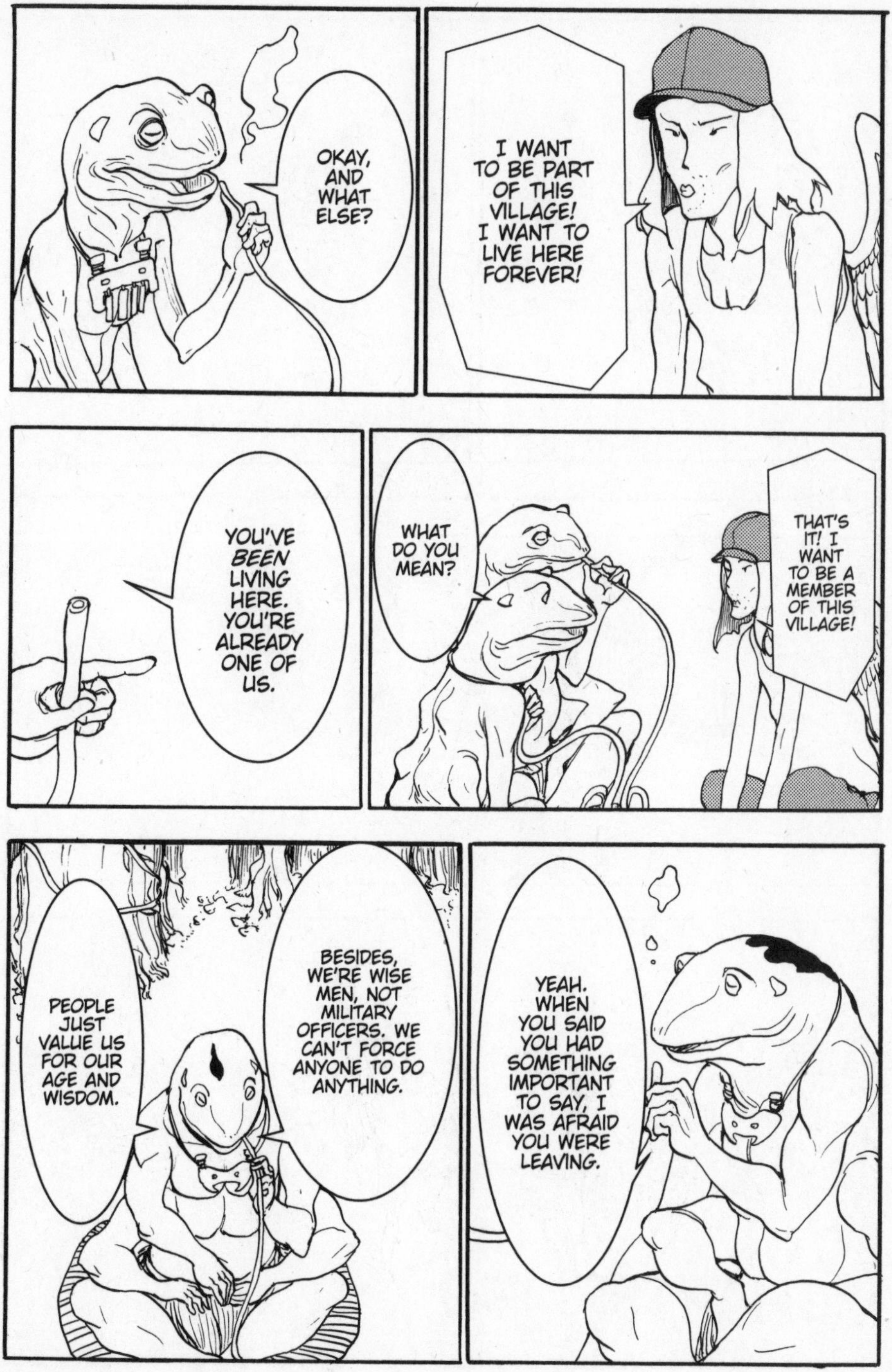
I WANT TO BE PART OF THIS VILLAGE! I WANT TO LIVE HERE FOREVER!
OKAY, AND WHAT ELSE?
THAT'S IT! I WANT TO BE A MEMBER OF THIS VILLAGE!
WHAT DO YOU MEAN?
YOU'VE *BEEN* LIVING HERE. YOU'RE ALREADY ONE OF US.
YEAH. WHEN YOU SAID YOU HAD SOMETHING IMPORTANT TO SAY, I WAS AFRAID YOU WERE LEAVING.
BESIDES, WE'RE WISE MEN, NOT MILITARY OFFICERS. WE CAN'T FORCE ANYONE TO DO ANYTHING.
PEOPLE JUST VALUE US FOR OUR AGE AND WISDOM.

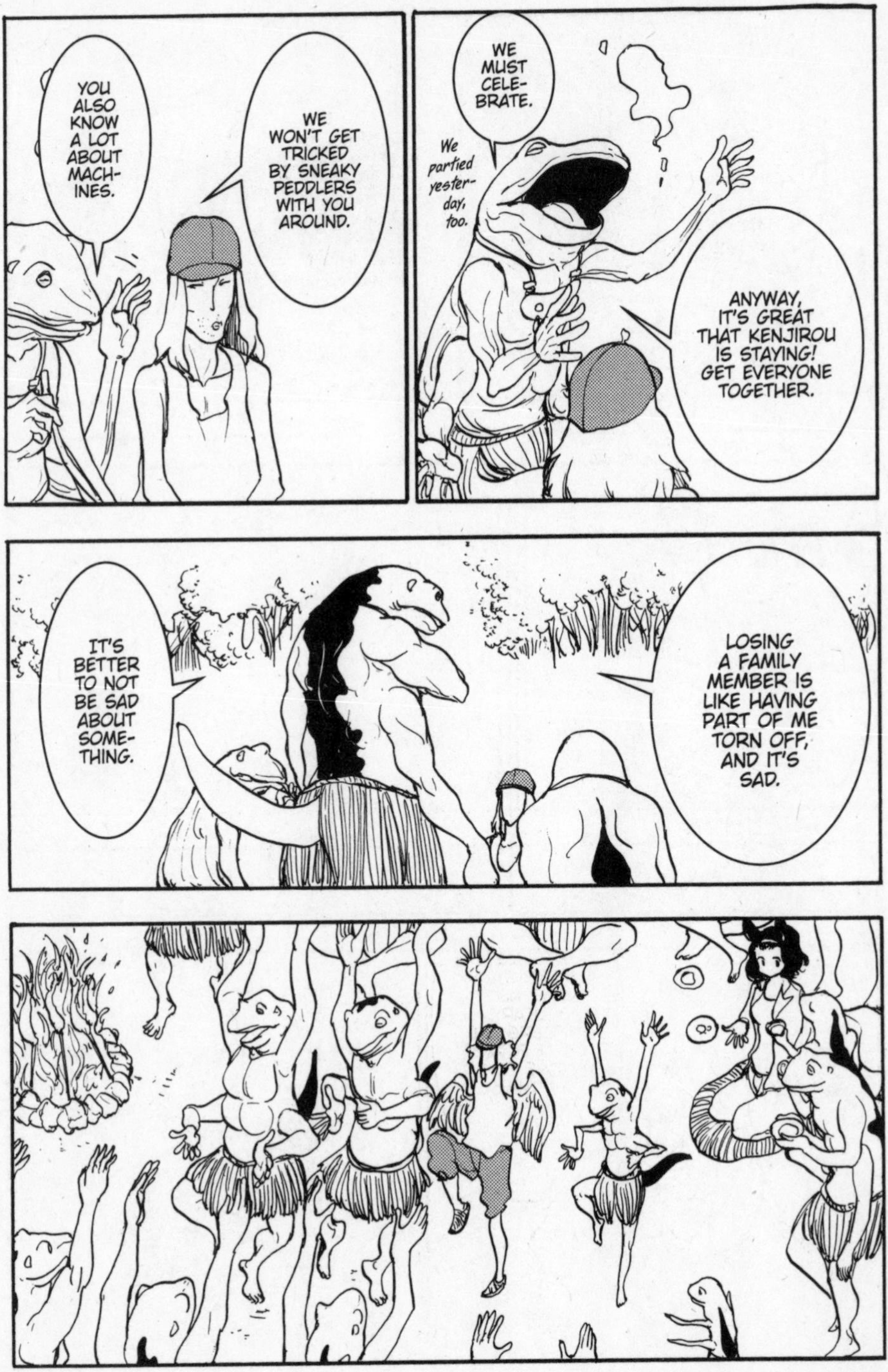
ANYWAY, IT'S GREAT THAT KENJIROU IS STAYING! GET EVERYONE TOGETHER.
WE MUST CELEBRATE.
We partied yesterday, too.
WE WON'T GET TRICKED BY SNEAKY PEDDLERS WITH YOU AROUND.
YOU ALSO KNOW A LOT ABOUT MACHINES.
LOSING A FAMILY MEMBER IS LIKE HAVING PART OF ME TORN OFF, AND IT'S SAD.
IT'S BETTER TO NOT BE SAD ABOUT SOMETHING.

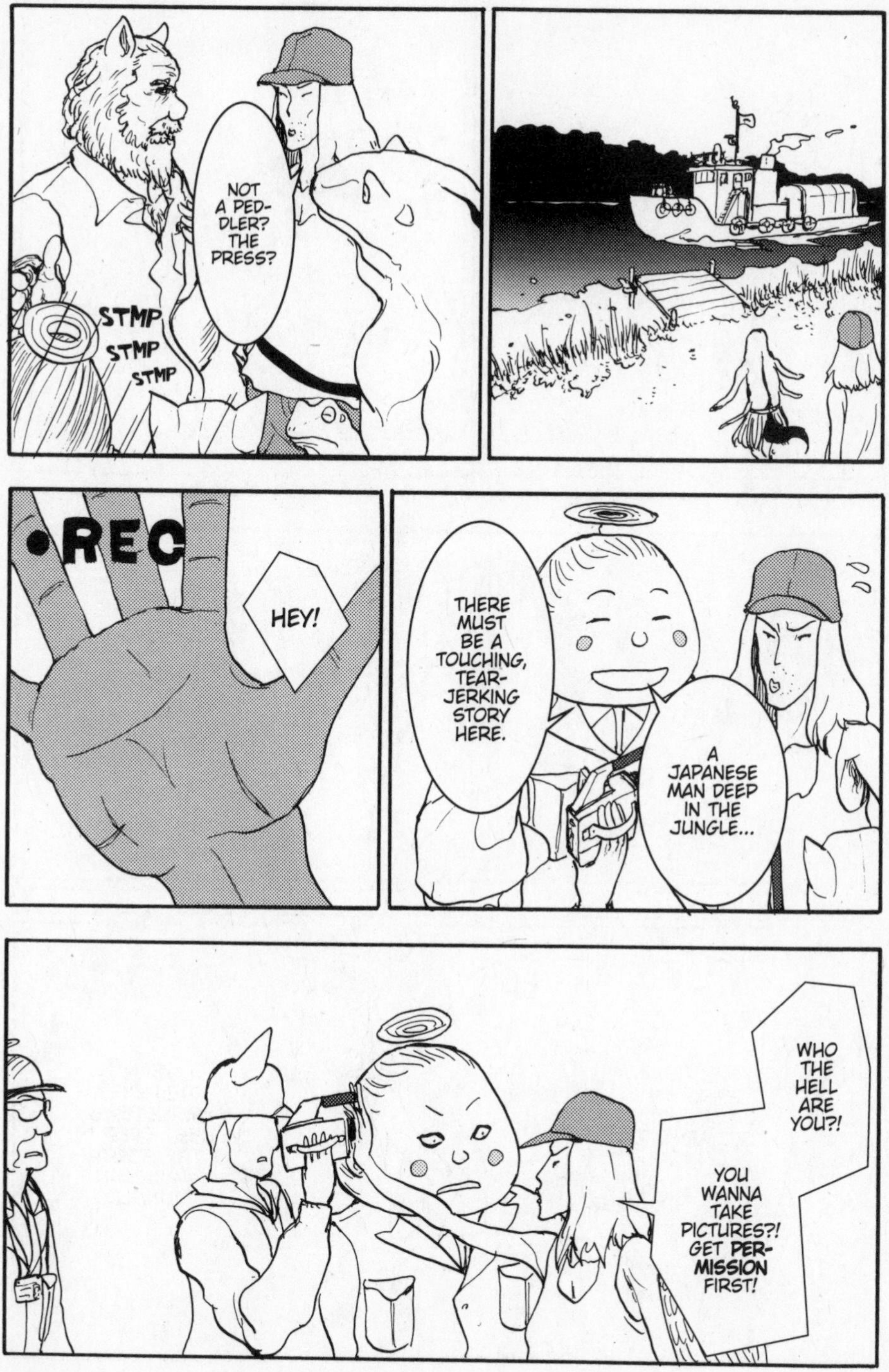
NOT A PEDDLER? THE PRESS?
STMP
STMP
STMP
THERE MUST BE A TOUCHING, TEAR-JERKING STORY HERE.
A JAPANESE MAN DEEP IN THE JUNGLE...
HEY!
•REC
WHO THE HELL ARE YOU?!
YOU WANNA TAKE PICTURES?! GET PERMISSION FIRST!

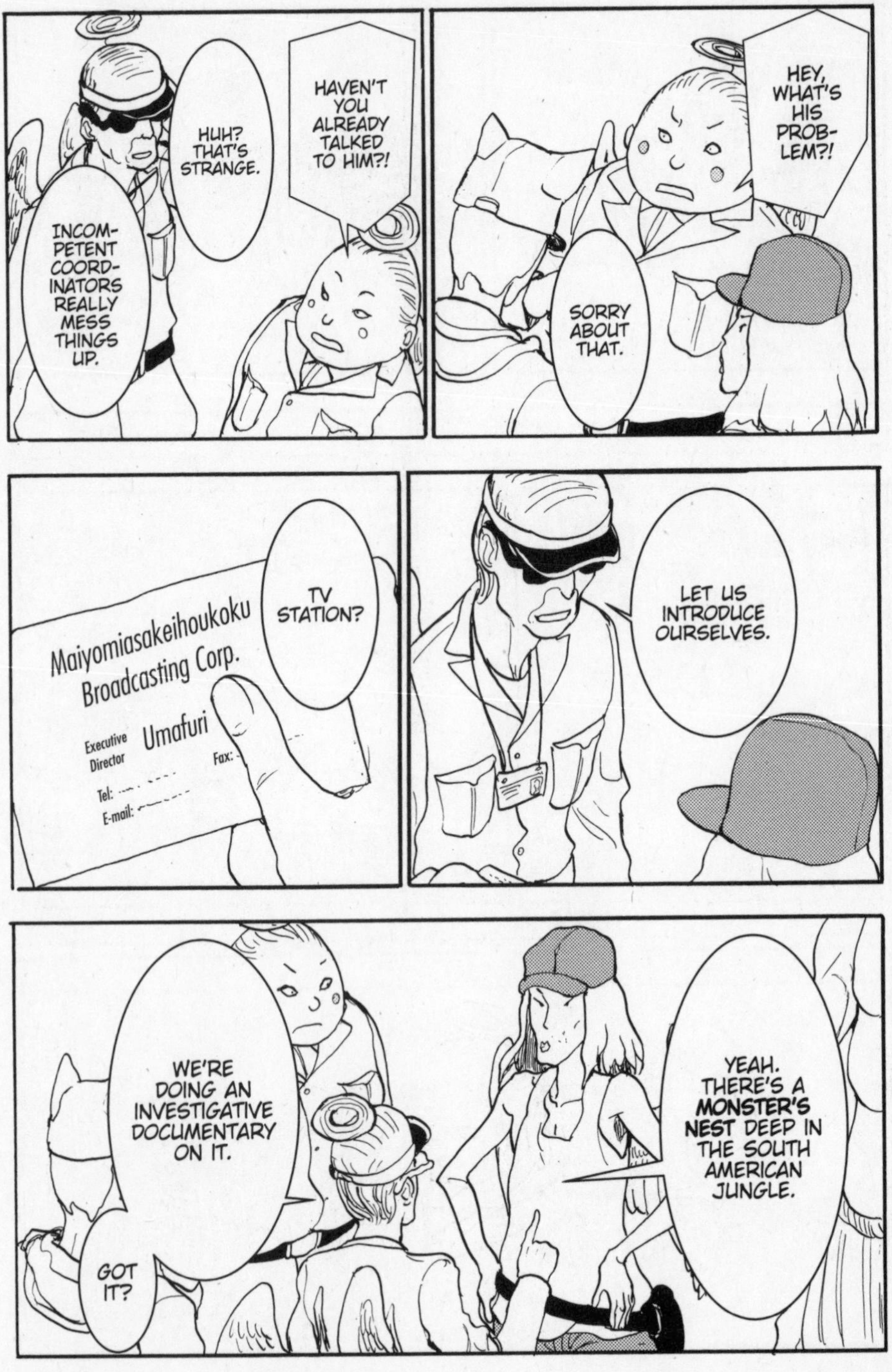
HEY, WHAT'S HIS PROBLEM?!
SORRY ABOUT THAT.
HAVEN'T YOU ALREADY TALKED TO HIM?!
HUH? THAT'S STRANGE.
INCOMPETENT COORDINATORS REALLY MESS THINGS UP.
LET US INTRODUCE OURSELVES.
TV STATION?
Maiyomiasakeihoukoku Broadcasting Corp.
Executive Director Umafuri
Tel:
Fax:
E-mail:
YEAH. THERE'S A **MONSTER'S NEST** DEEP IN THE SOUTH AMERICAN JUNGLE.
WE'RE DOING AN INVESTIGATIVE DOCUMENTARY ON IT.
GOT IT?

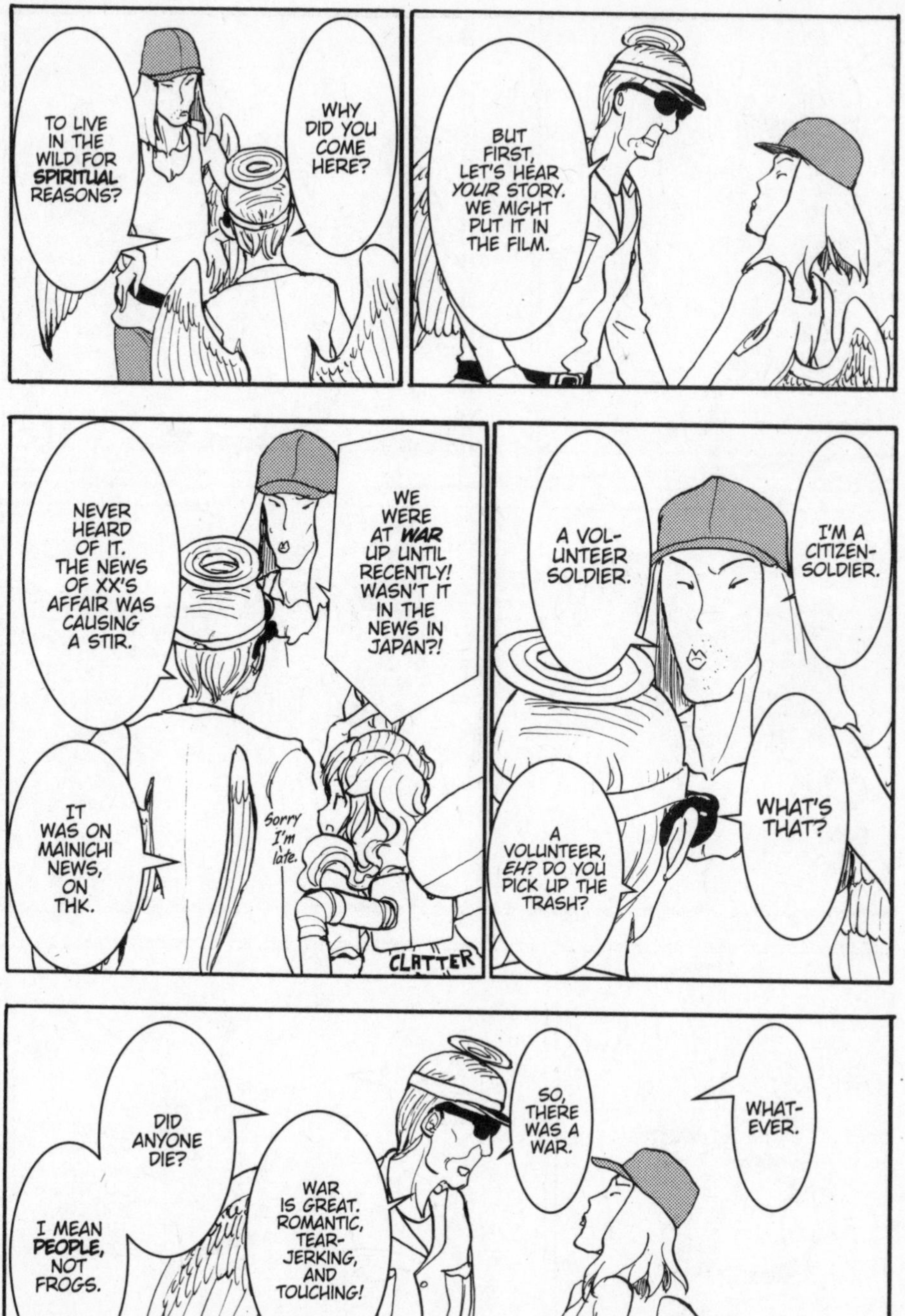
BUT FIRST, LET'S HEAR YOUR STORY. WE MIGHT PUT IT IN THE FILM.
WHY DID YOU COME HERE?
TO LIVE IN THE WILD FOR SPIRITUAL REASONS?
I'M A CITIZEN-SOLDIER.
A VOL-UNTEER SOLDIER.
WHAT'S THAT?
A VOLUNTEER, EH? DO YOU PICK UP THE TRASH?
WE WERE AT WAR UP UNTIL RECENTLY! WASN'T IT IN THE NEWS IN JAPAN?!
NEVER HEARD OF IT. THE NEWS OF XX'S AFFAIR WAS CAUSING A STIR.
Sorry I'm late.
CLATTER
IT WAS ON MAINICHI NEWS, ON THK.
WHAT-EVER.
SO, THERE WAS A WAR.
WAR IS GREAT. ROMANTIC, TEAR-JERKING, AND TOUCHING!
DID ANYONE DIE?
I MEAN PEOPLE, NOT FROGS.

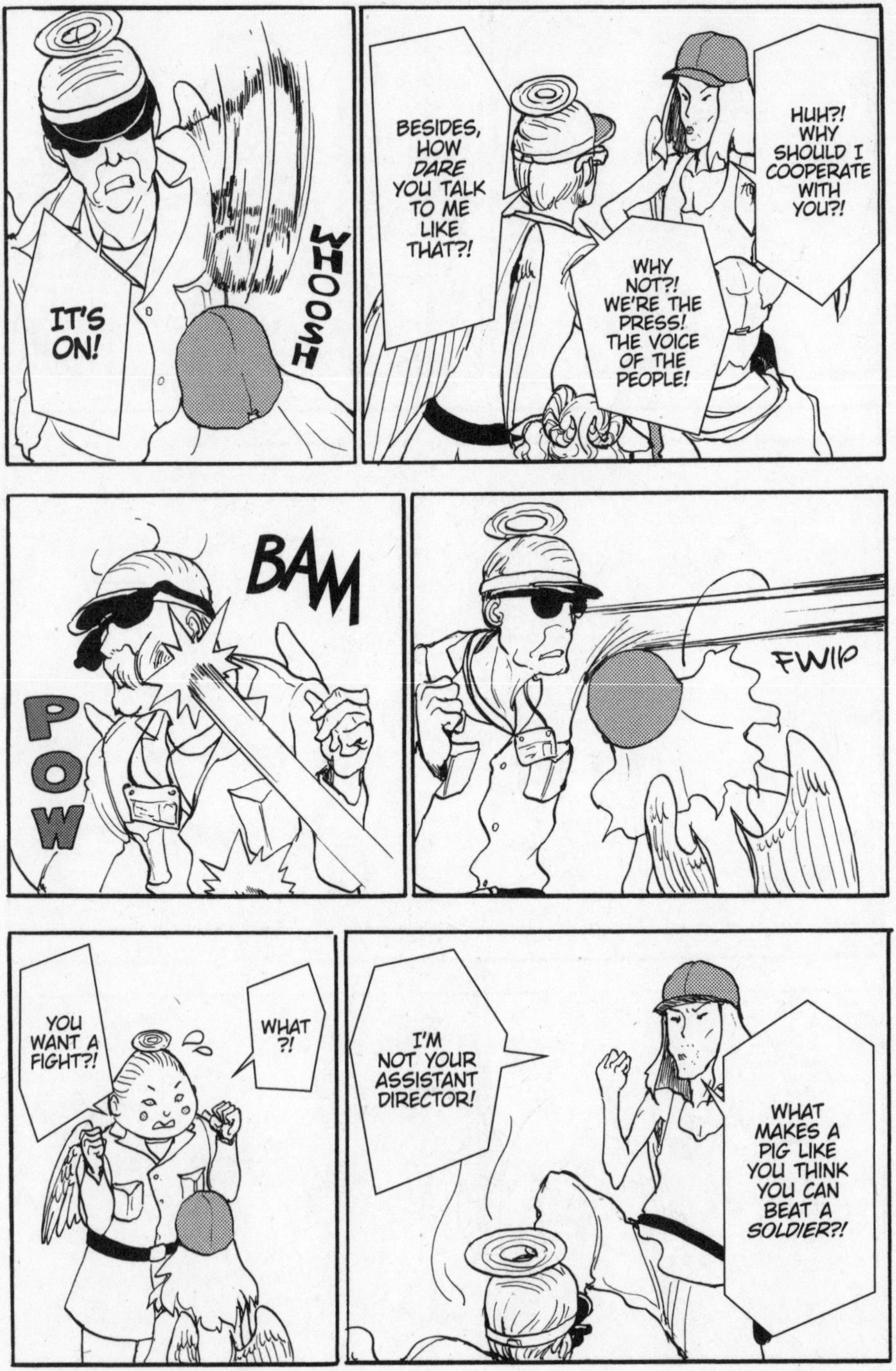
HUH?! WHY SHOULD I COOPERATE WITH YOU?!
BESIDES, HOW *DARE* YOU TALK TO ME LIKE THAT?!
WHY NOT?! WE'RE THE PRESS! THE VOICE OF THE PEOPLE!
WHOOSH
IT'S ON!
FWIP
BAM
POW
WHAT MAKES A PIG LIKE YOU THINK YOU CAN BEAT A *SOLDIER*?!
I'M NOT YOUR ASSISTANT DIRECTOR!
WHAT ?!
YOU WANT A FIGHT?!

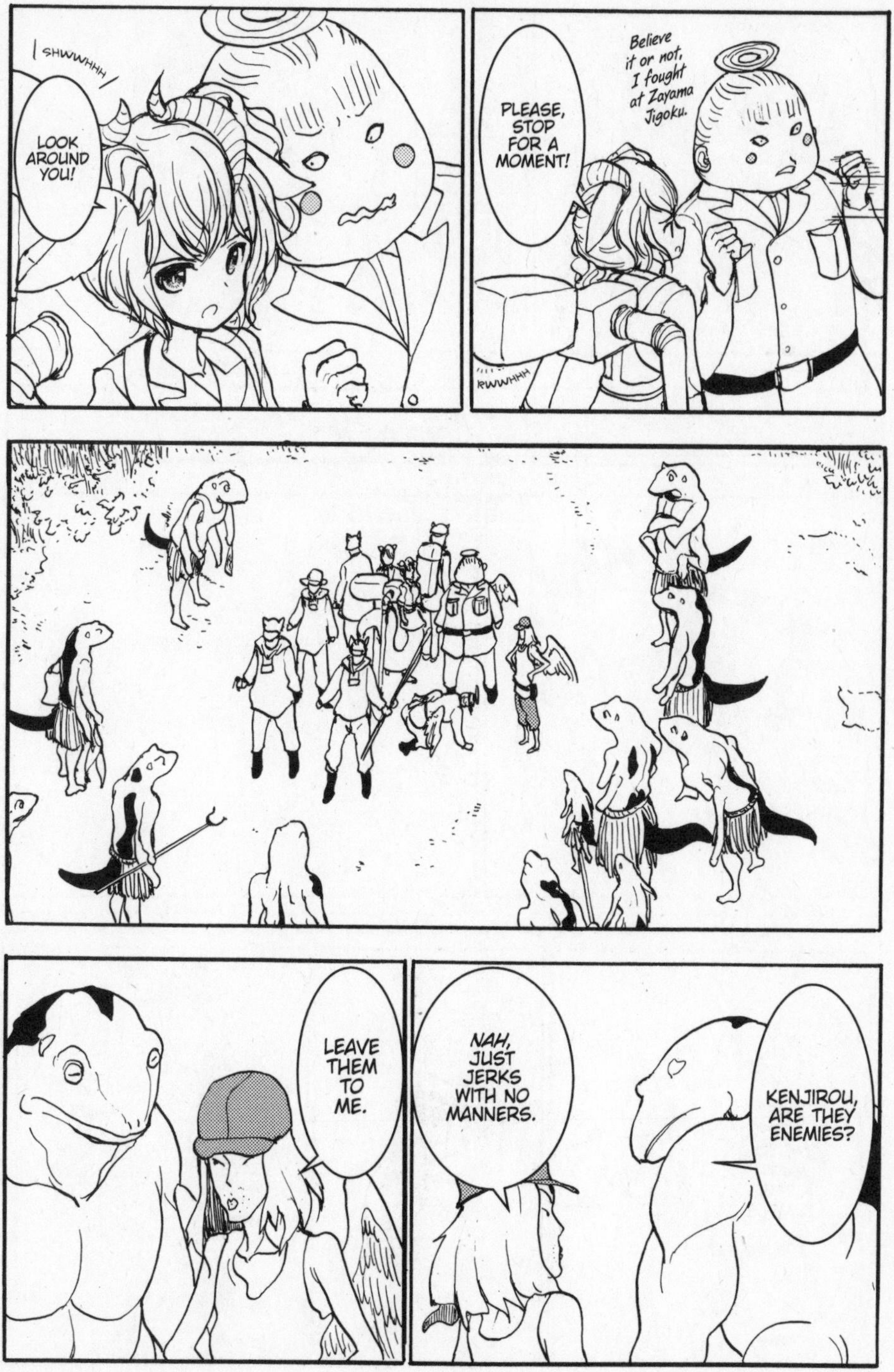
Believe it or not, I fought at Zayama Jigoku.
PLEASE, STOP FOR A MOMENT!
RWWHHH
SHWWHHH
LOOK AROUND YOU!
KENJIROU, ARE THEY ENEMIES?
NAH, JUST JERKS WITH NO MANNERS.
LEAVE THEM TO ME.

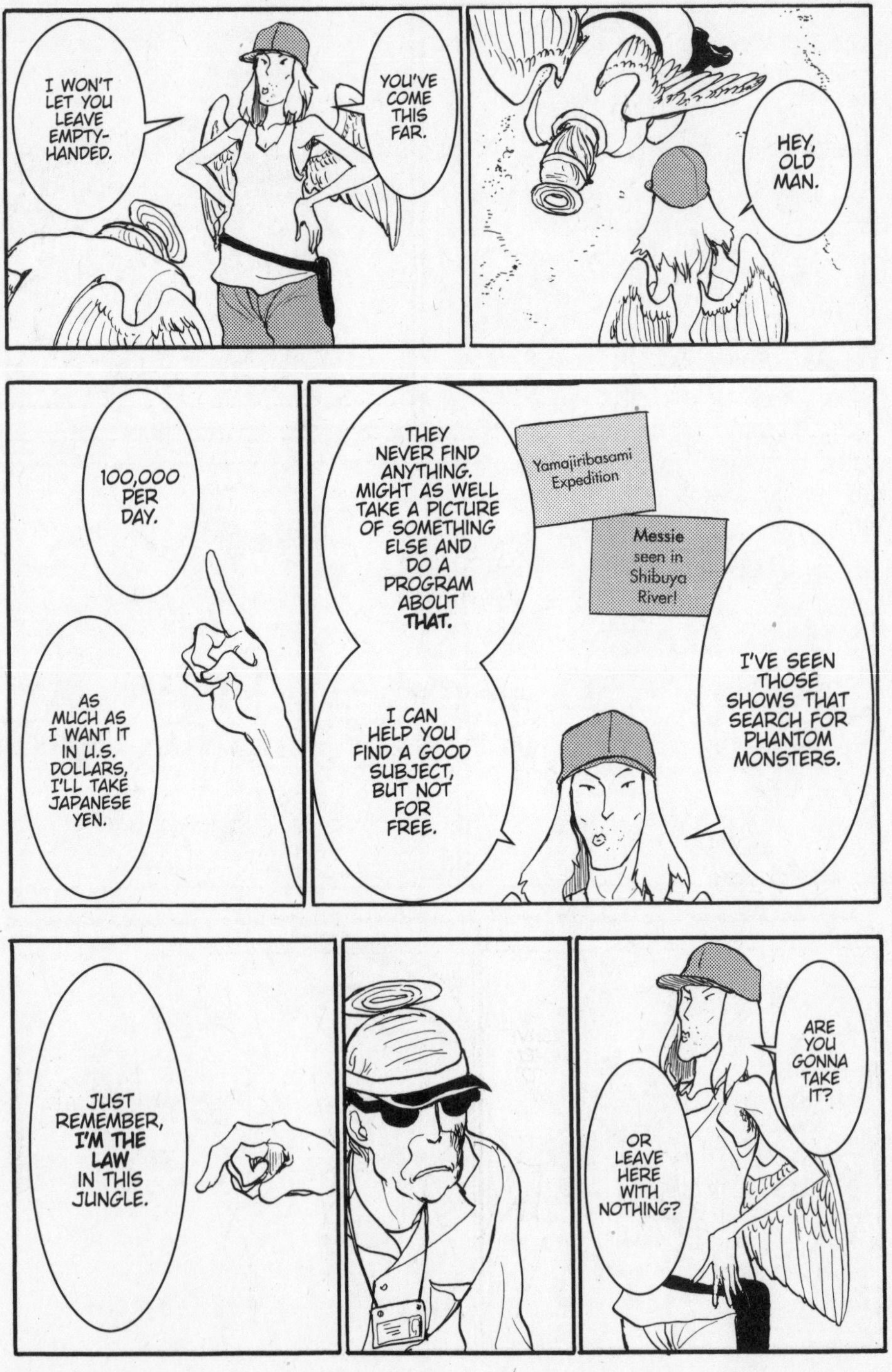

HEY, OLD MAN.
YOU'VE COME THIS FAR.
I WON'T LET YOU LEAVE EMPTY-HANDED.
I'VE SEEN THOSE SHOWS THAT SEARCH FOR PHANTOM MONSTERS.
Yamajiribasami Expedition
Messie seen in Shibuya River!
THEY NEVER FIND ANYTHING. MIGHT AS WELL TAKE A PICTURE OF SOMETHING ELSE AND DO A PROGRAM ABOUT **THAT.**
I CAN HELP YOU FIND A GOOD SUBJECT, BUT NOT FOR FREE.
100,000 PER DAY.
AS MUCH AS I WANT IT IN U.S. DOLLARS, I'LL TAKE JAPANESE YEN.
ARE YOU GONNA TAKE IT?
OR LEAVE HERE WITH NOTHING?
JUST REMEMBER, **I'M THE LAW** IN THIS JUNGLE.

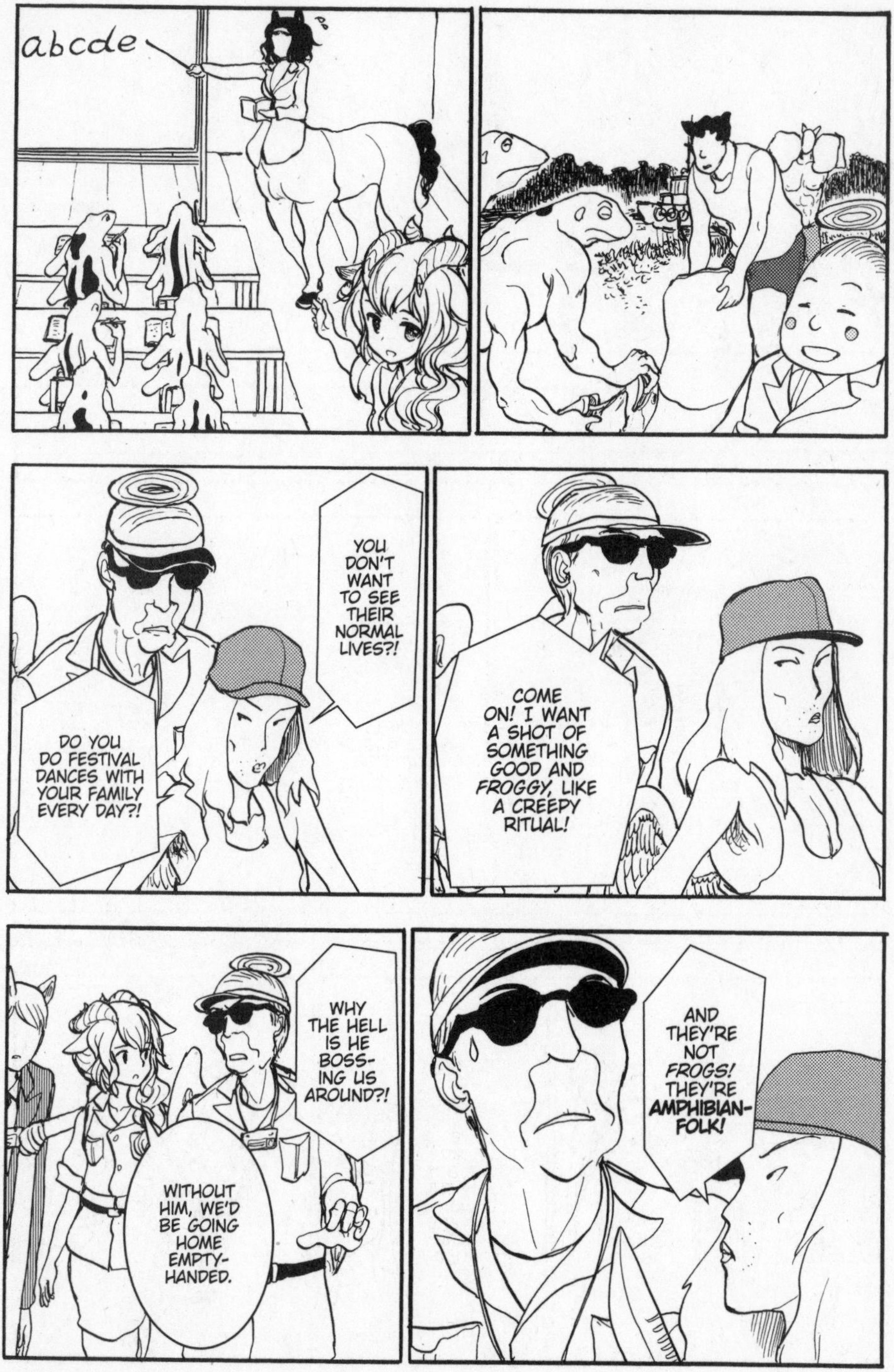
abcde
COME ON! I WANT A SHOT OF SOMETHING GOOD AND FROGGY, LIKE A CREEPY RITUAL!
YOU DON'T WANT TO SEE THEIR NORMAL LIVES?!
DO YOU DO FESTIVAL DANCES WITH YOUR FAMILY EVERY DAY?!
AND THEY'RE NOT FROGS! THEY'RE AMPHIBIAN-FOLK!
WHY THE HELL IS HE BOSSING US AROUND?!
WITHOUT HIM, WE'D BE GOING HOME EMPTY-HANDED.

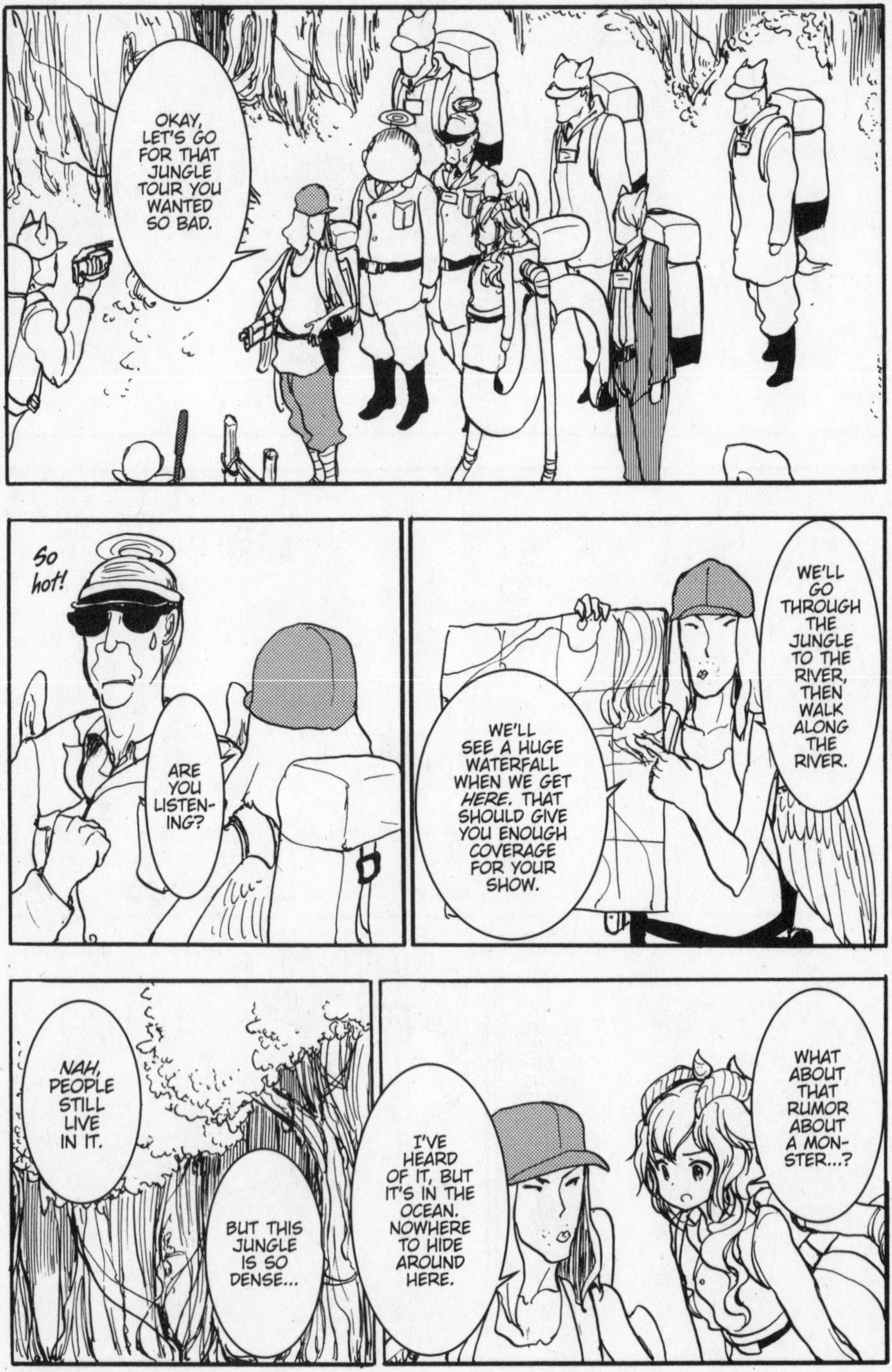
OKAY, LET'S GO FOR THAT JUNGLE TOUR YOU WANTED SO BAD.
WE'LL GO THROUGH THE JUNGLE TO THE RIVER, THEN WALK ALONG THE RIVER.
WE'LL SEE A HUGE WATERFALL WHEN WE GET *HERE*. THAT SHOULD GIVE YOU ENOUGH COVERAGE FOR YOUR SHOW.
So hot!
ARE YOU LISTEN-ING?
WHAT ABOUT THAT RUMOR ABOUT A MON-STER...?
I'VE HEARD OF IT, BUT IT'S IN THE OCEAN. NOWHERE TO HIDE AROUND HERE.
BUT THIS JUNGLE IS SO DENSE...
NAH, PEOPLE STILL LIVE IN IT.

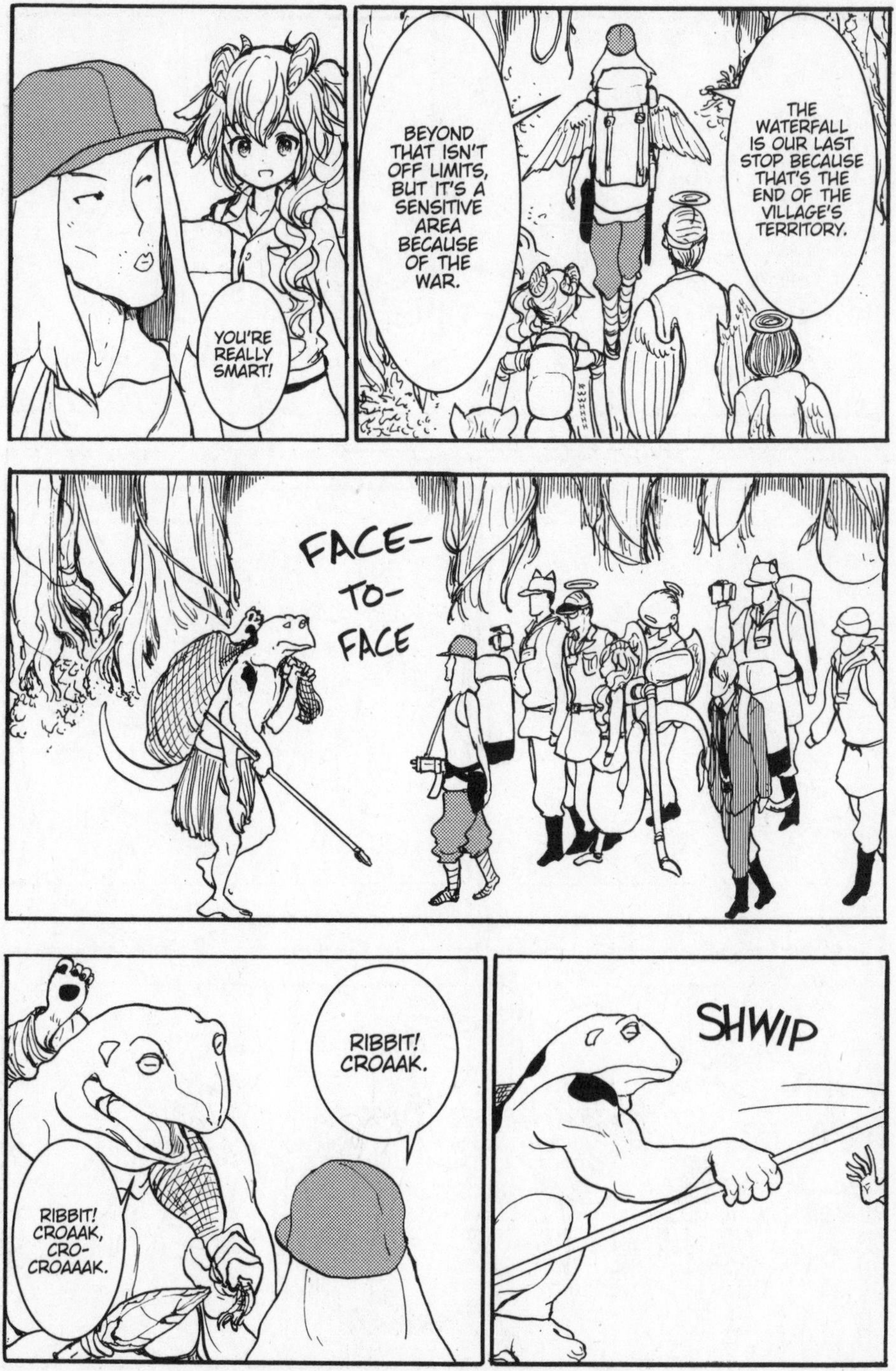
THE WATERFALL IS OUR LAST STOP BECAUSE THAT'S THE END OF THE VILLAGE'S TERRITORY.
BEYOND THAT ISN'T OFF LIMITS, BUT IT'S A SENSITIVE AREA BECAUSE OF THE WAR.
YOU'RE REALLY SMART!
FACE-TO-FACE
SHWIP
RIBBIT! CROAAK.
RIBBIT! CROAAK, CRO-CROAAAK.

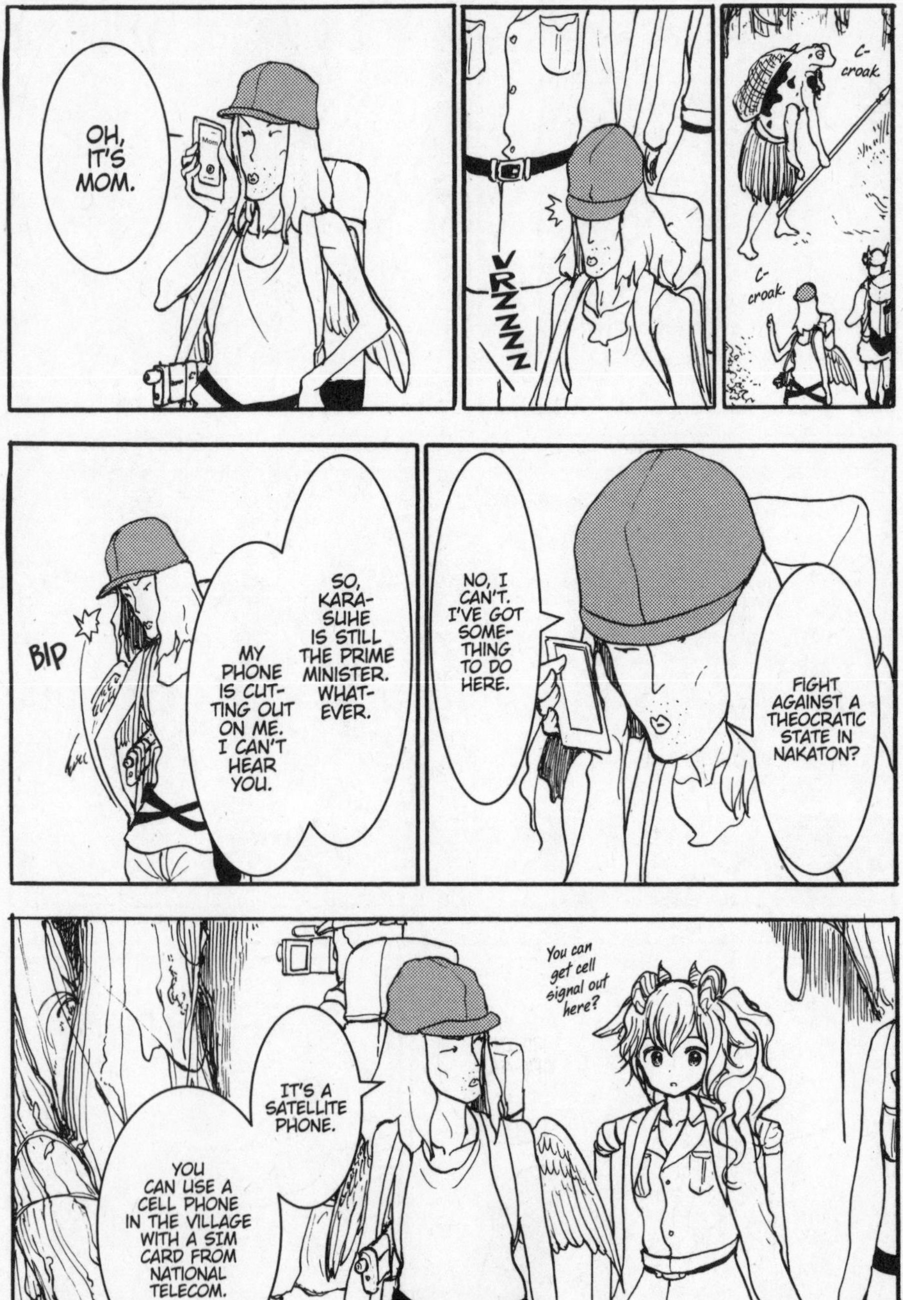
C-croak.
C-croak.
VRZZZZ
OH, IT'S MOM.
FIGHT AGAINST A THEOCRATIC STATE IN NAKATON?
NO, I CAN'T. I'VE GOT SOMETHING TO DO HERE.
SO, KARA-SUHE IS STILL THE PRIME MINISTER. WHAT-EVER.
MY PHONE IS CUTTING OUT ON ME. I CAN'T HEAR YOU.
BIP
You can get cell signal out here?
IT'S A SATELLITE PHONE.
YOU CAN USE A CELL PHONE IN THE VILLAGE WITH A SIM CARD FROM NATIONAL TELECOM.

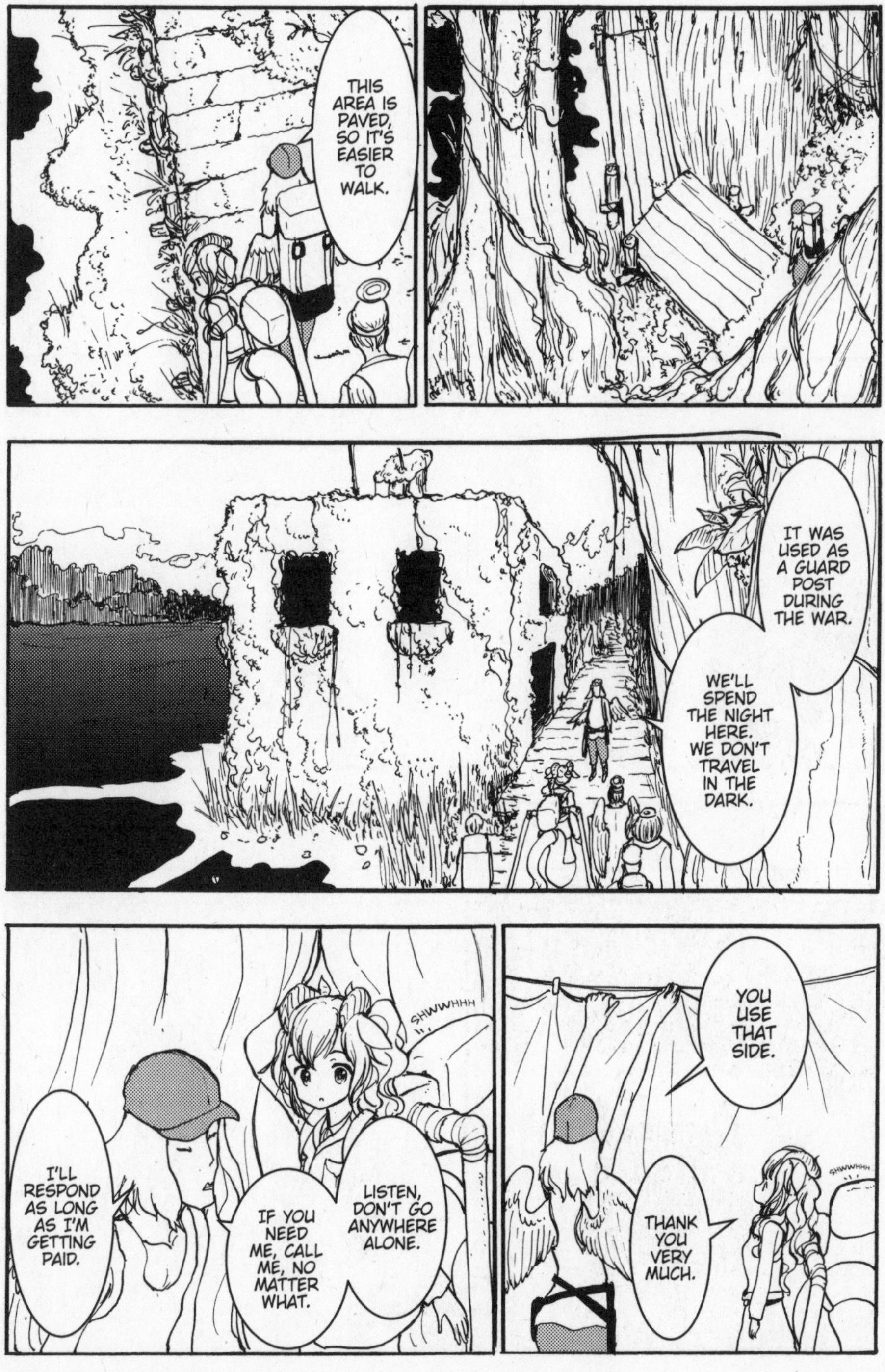
THIS AREA IS PAVED, SO IT'S EASIER TO WALK.
IT WAS USED AS A GUARD POST DURING THE WAR.
WE'LL SPEND THE NIGHT HERE. WE DON'T TRAVEL IN THE DARK.
YOU USE THAT SIDE.
SHWWHHH
THANK YOU VERY MUCH.
SHWWHHH
LISTEN, DON'T GO ANYWHERE ALONE.
IF YOU NEED ME, CALL ME, NO MATTER WHAT.
I'LL RESPOND AS LONG AS I'M GETTING PAID.

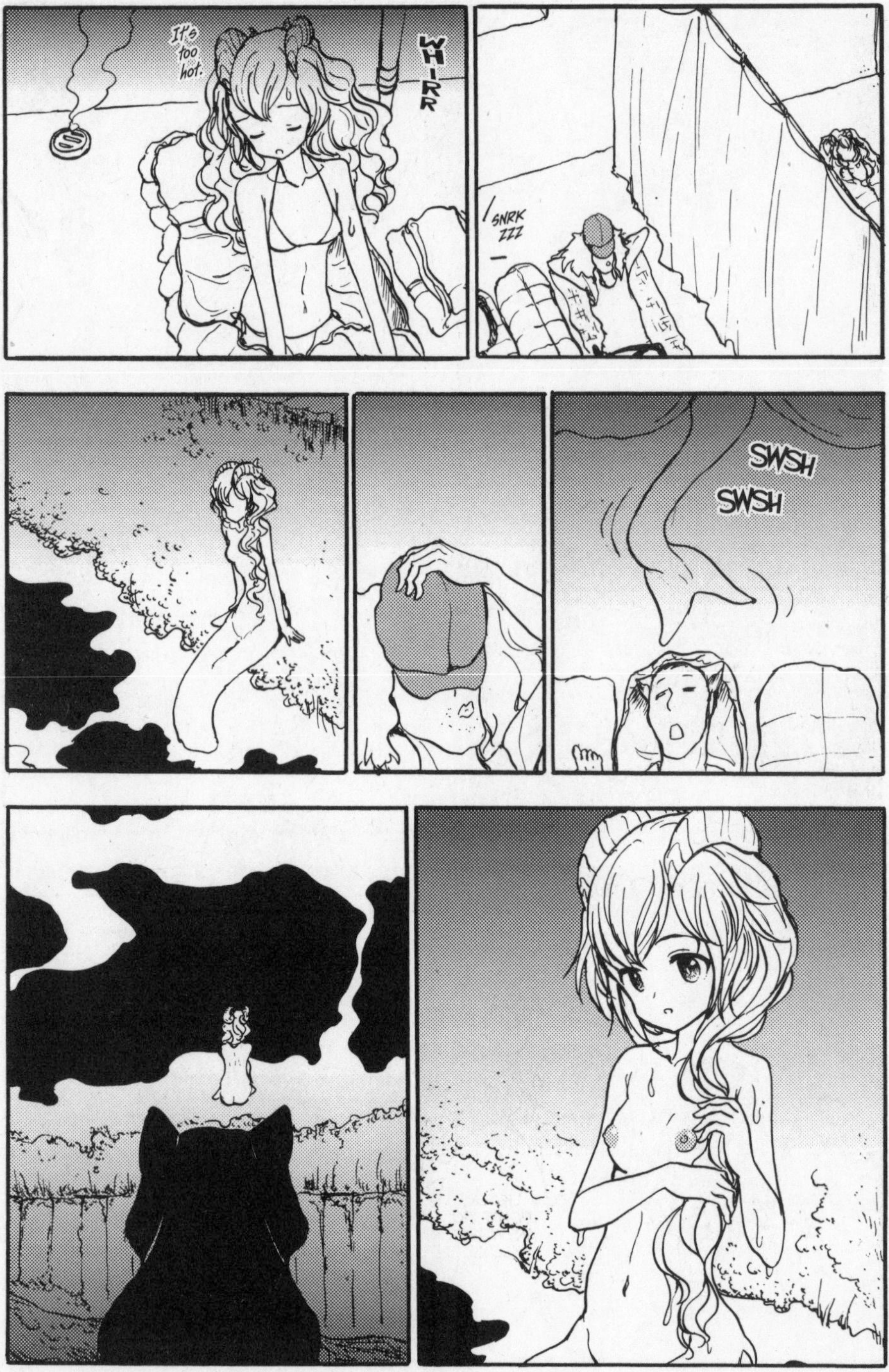
SNRK ZZZ
It's too hot.
WHIRR
SWSH
SWSH

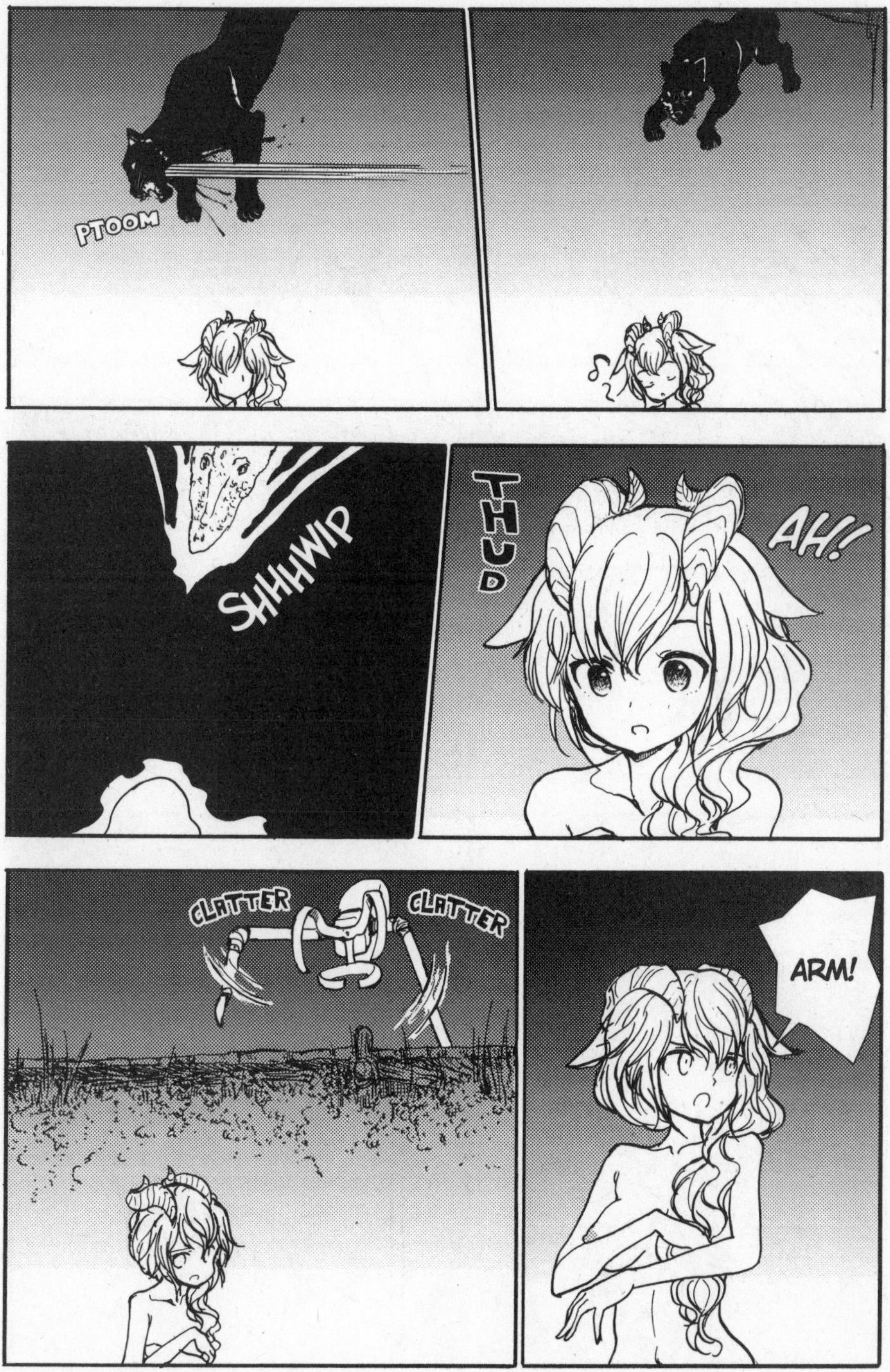
PTOOM
THUD
AH!
SHHWIP
ARM!
CLATTER
CLATTER

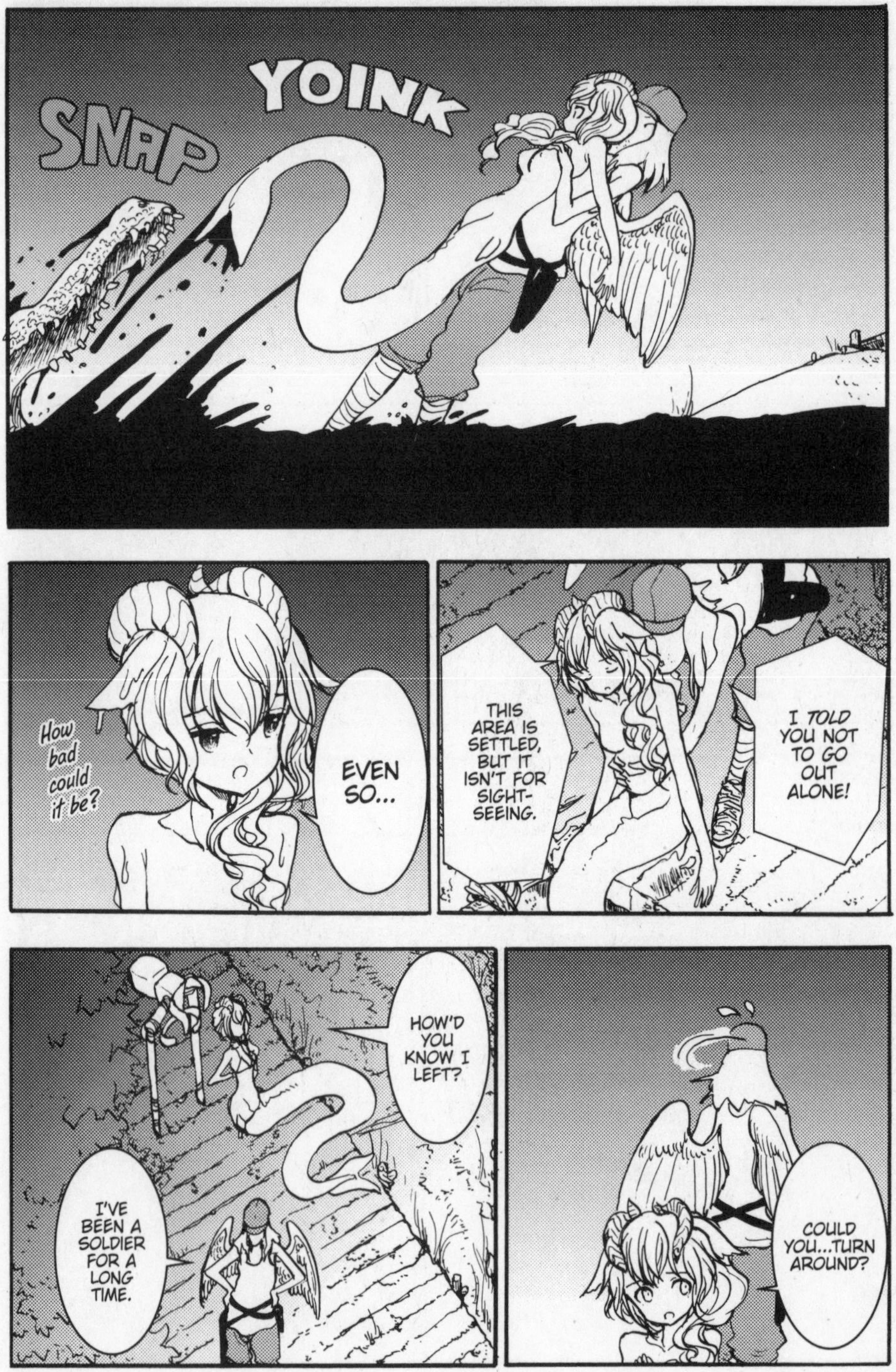
YOINK
SNAP
I TOLD YOU NOT TO GO OUT ALONE!
THIS AREA IS SETTLED, BUT IT ISN'T FOR SIGHT-SEEING.
EVEN SO...
How bad could it be?
COULD YOU...TURN AROUND?
HOW'D YOU KNOW I LEFT?
I'VE BEEN A SOLDIER FOR A LONG TIME.

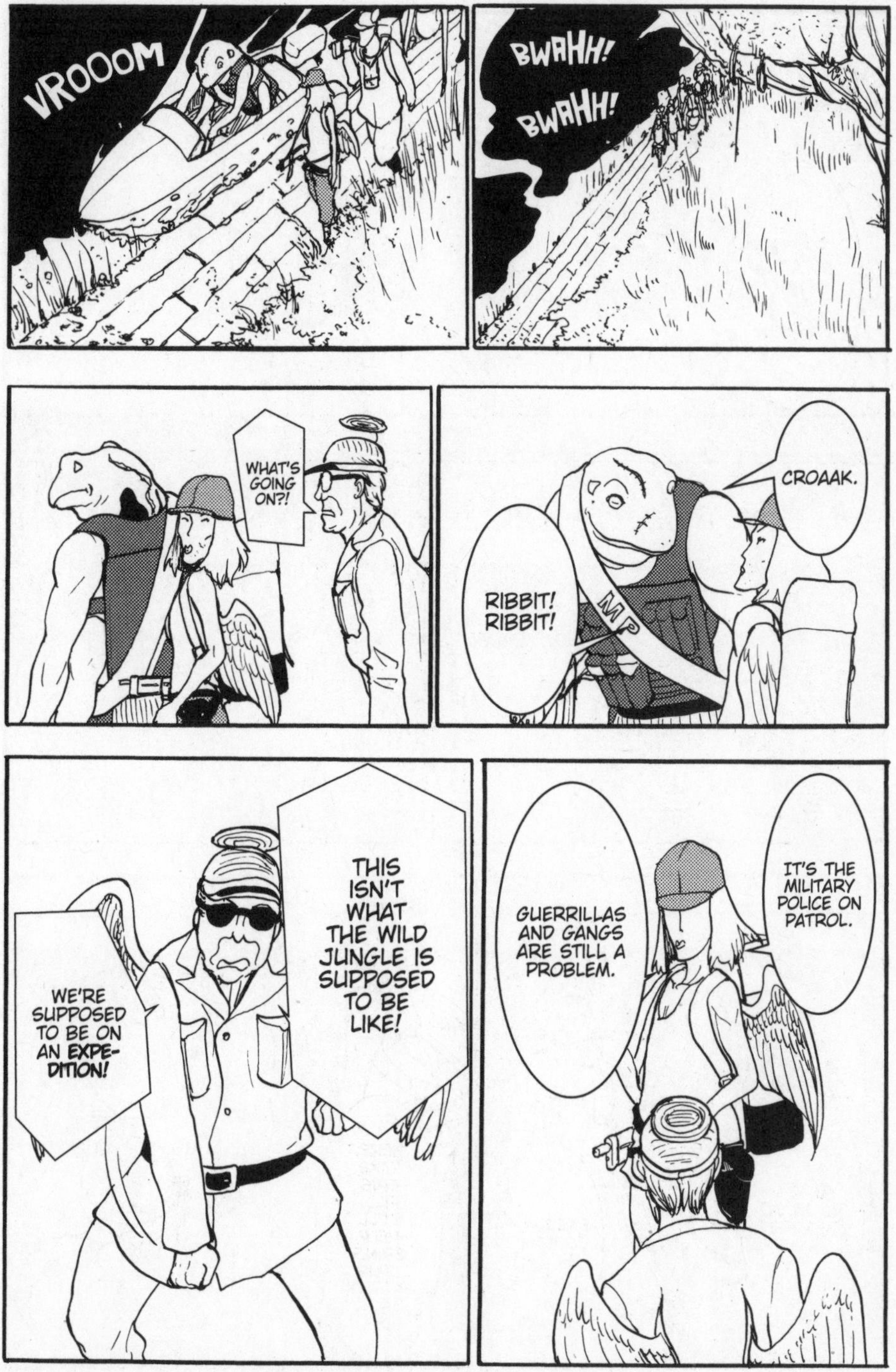
BWAHH!
BWAHH!
VROOOM
CROAAK.
RIBBIT! RIBBIT!
WHAT'S GOING ON?!
IT'S THE MILITARY POLICE ON PATROL.
GUERRILLAS AND GANGS ARE STILL A PROBLEM.
THIS ISN'T WHAT THE WILD JUNGLE IS SUPPOSED TO BE LIKE!
WE'RE SUPPOSED TO BE ON AN EXPEDITION!

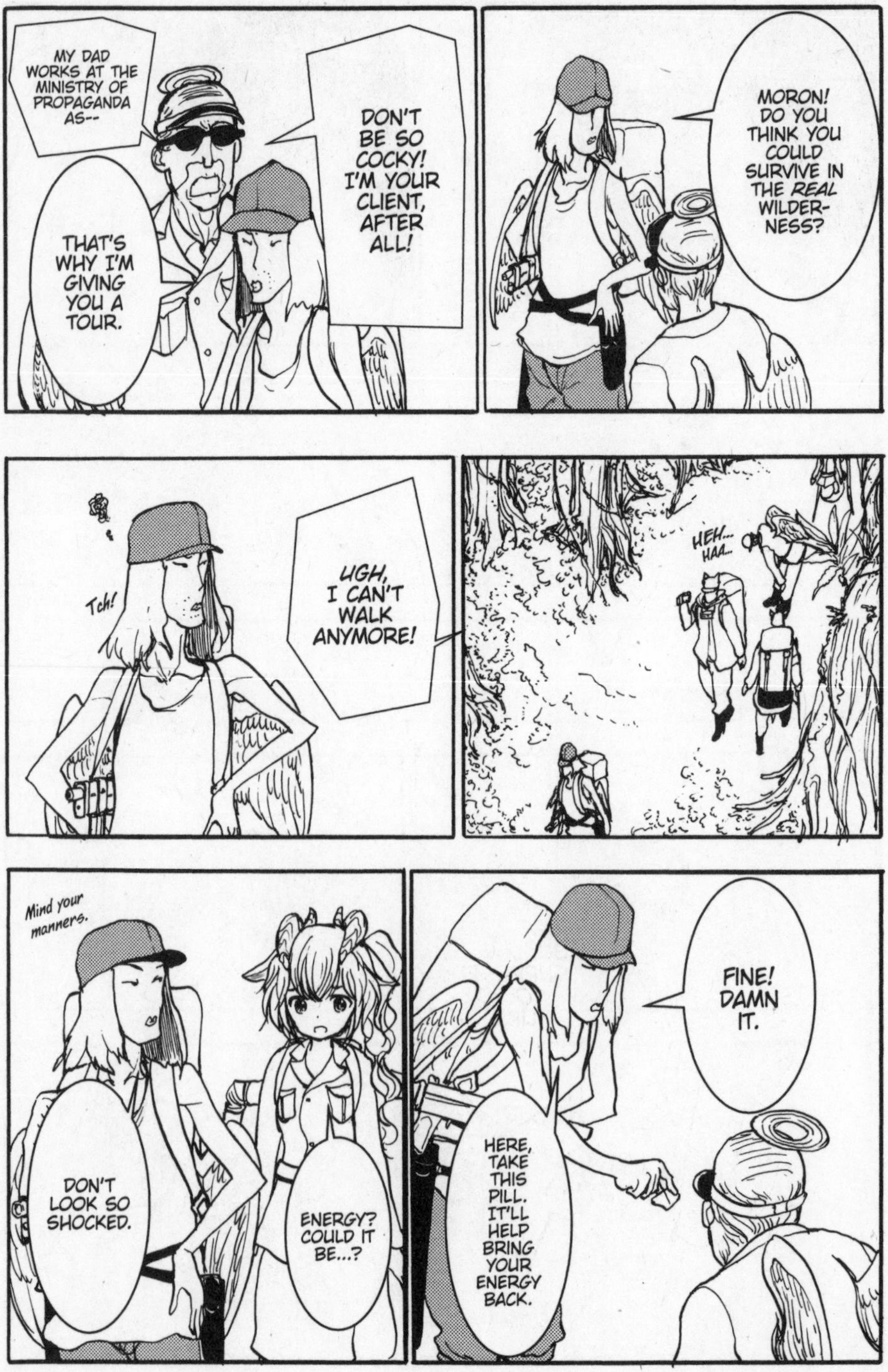
MORON! DO YOU THINK YOU COULD SURVIVE IN THE REAL WILDER-NESS?
DON'T BE SO COCKY! I'M YOUR CLIENT, AFTER ALL!
MY DAD WORKS AT THE MINISTRY OF PROPAGANDA AS--
THAT'S WHY I'M GIVING YOU A TOUR.
HEH... HAA...
UGH, I CAN'T WALK ANYMORE!
Tch!
FINE! DAMN IT.
HERE, TAKE THIS PILL. IT'LL HELP BRING YOUR ENERGY BACK.
ENERGY? COULD IT BE...?
Mind your manners.
DON'T LOOK SO SHOCKED.

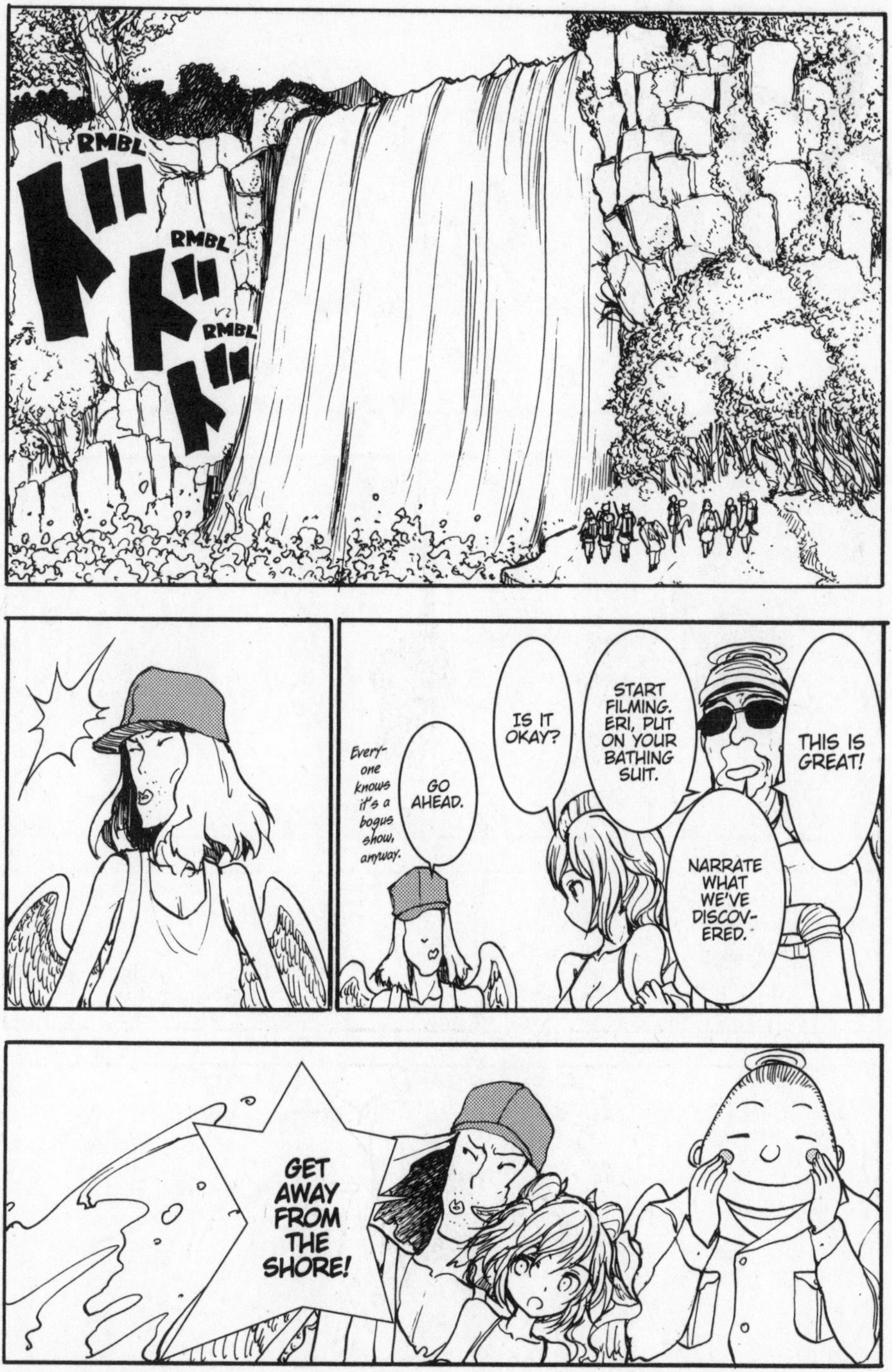
RMBL
RMBL
RMBL
THIS IS GREAT!
NARRATE WHAT WE'VE DISCOVERED.
START FILMING. ERI, PUT ON YOUR BATHING SUIT.
IS IT OKAY?
GO AHEAD.
Everyone knows it's a bogus show, anyway.
GET AWAY FROM THE SHORE!

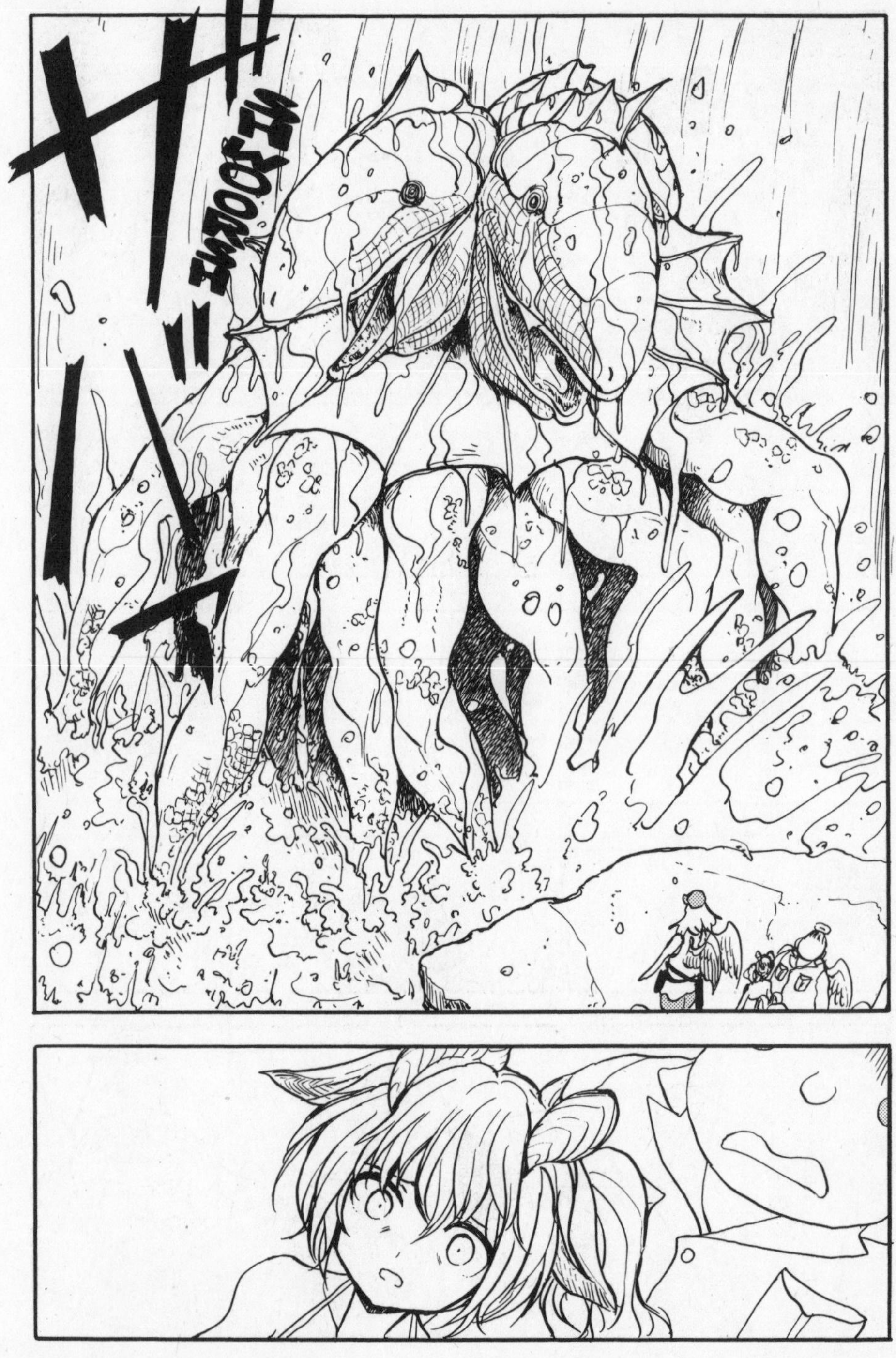
ザバァ
SPLOOSH

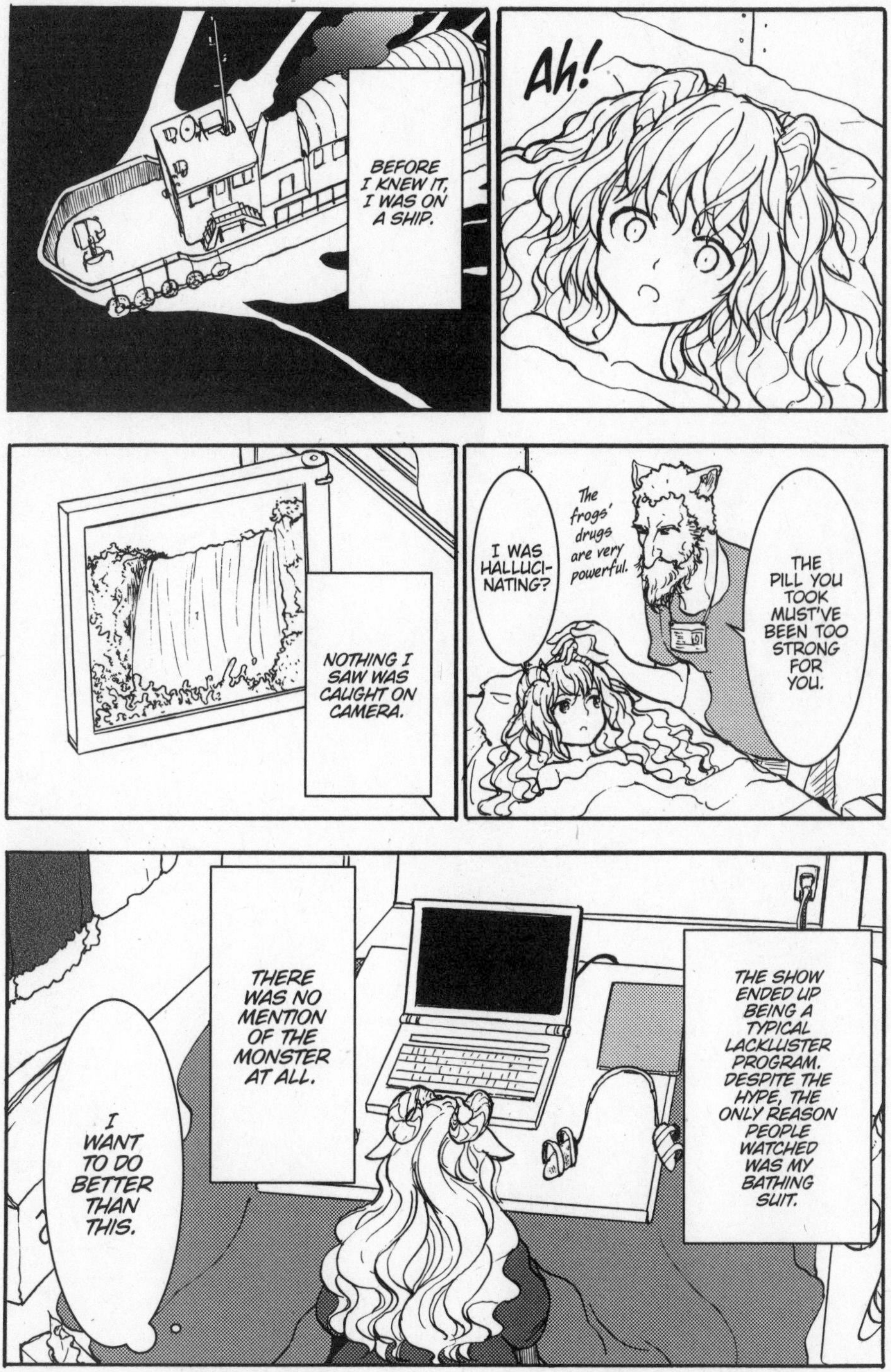
Ah!
BEFORE I KNEW IT, I WAS ON A SHIP.
THE PILL YOU TOOK MUST'VE BEEN TOO STRONG FOR YOU.
The frogs' drugs are very powerful.
I WAS HALLUCI-NATING?
NOTHING I SAW WAS CAUGHT ON CAMERA.
THE SHOW ENDED UP BEING A TYPICAL LACKLUSTER PROGRAM. DESPITE THE HYPE, THE ONLY REASON PEOPLE WATCHED WAS MY BATHING SUIT.
THERE WAS NO MENTION OF THE MONSTER AT ALL.
I WANT TO DO BETTER THAN THIS.

A Centaur's Life

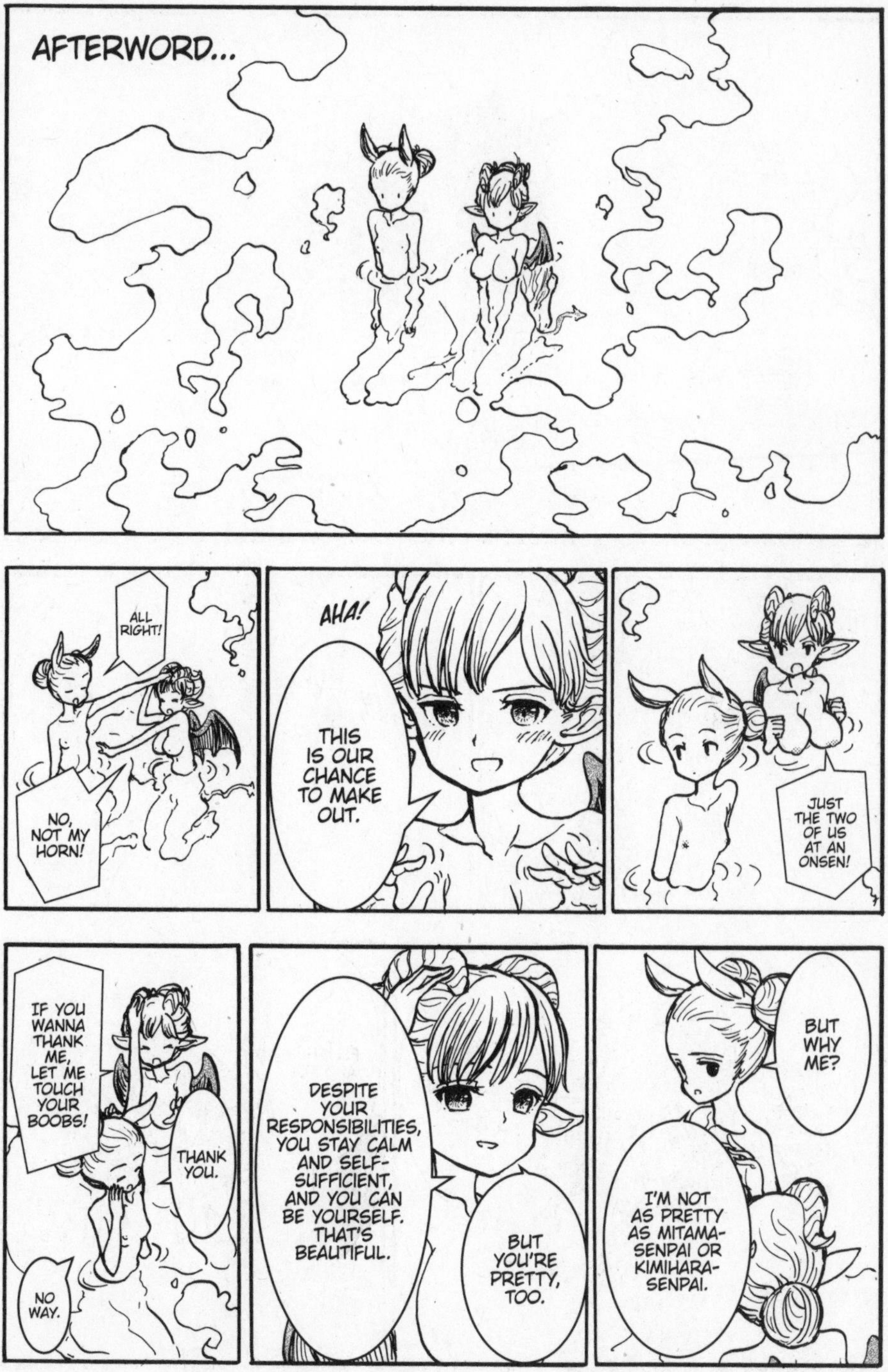
AFTERWORD...
JUST THE TWO OF US AT AN ONSEN!
AHA!
THIS IS OUR CHANCE TO MAKE OUT.
ALL RIGHT!
NO, NOT MY HORN!
BUT WHY ME?
I'M NOT AS PRETTY AS MITAMA-SENPAI OR KIMIHARA-SENPAI.
BUT YOU'RE PRETTY, TOO.
DESPITE YOUR RESPONSIBILITIES, YOU STAY CALM AND SELF-SUFFICIENT, AND YOU CAN BE YOURSELF. THAT'S BEAUTIFUL.
THANK YOU.
IF YOU WANNA THANK ME, LET ME TOUCH YOUR BOOBS!
NO WAY.

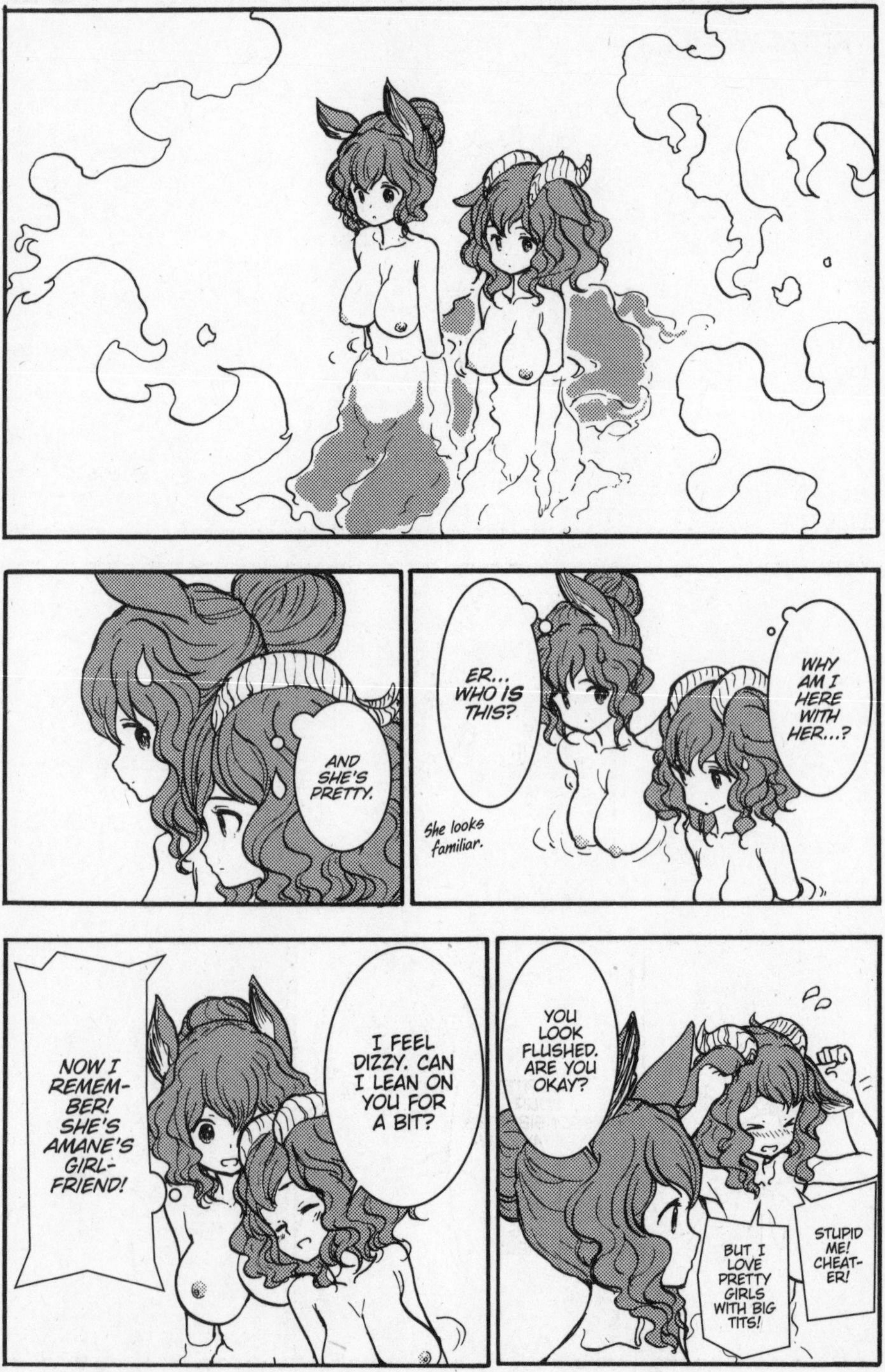
WHY AM I HERE WITH HER...?
ER... WHO IS THIS?
She looks familiar.
AND SHE'S PRETTY.
YOU LOOK FLUSHED. ARE YOU OKAY?
STUPID ME! CHEATER!
BUT I LOVE PRETTY GIRLS WITH BIG TITS!
I FEEL DIZZY. CAN I LEAN ON YOU FOR A BIT?
NOW I REMEMBER! SHE'S AMANE'S GIRLFRIEND!

A Centaur's Life

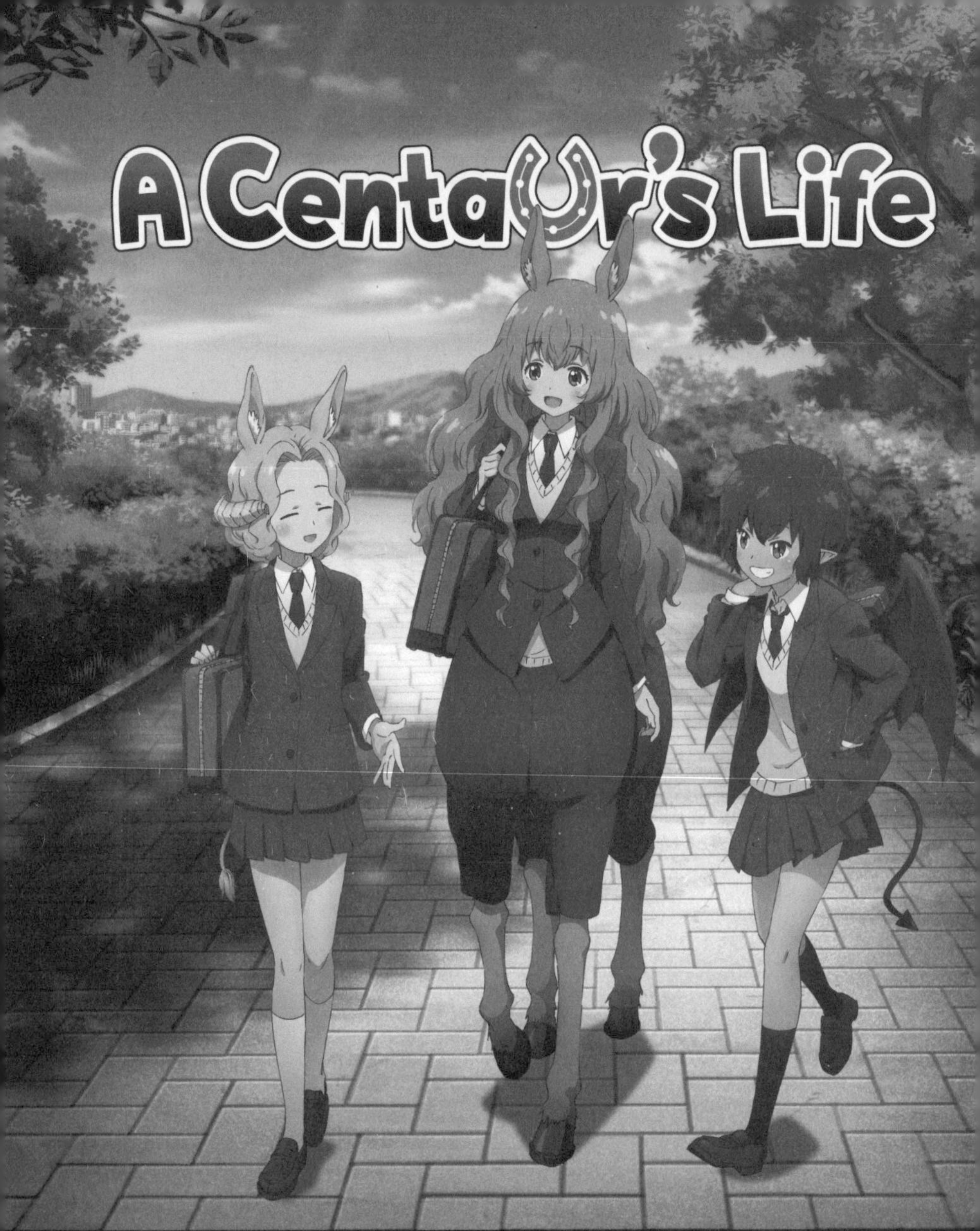
A Centaur's Life

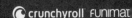

SEVEN SEAS ENTERTAINMENT PRESENTS

A Centaur's Life

story and art by KEI MURAYAMA

VOLUME 18

TRANSLATION
Elina Ishikawa

ADAPTATION
Holly Kolodziejczak

LETTERING AND RETOUCH
Jennifer Skarupa

LOGO DESIGN
Courtney Williams

COVER DESIGN
KC Fabellon

PROOFREADER
Danielle King

EDITOR
Shanti Whitesides

PREPRESS TECHNICIAN
Rhiannon Rasmussen-Silverstein

PRODUCTION MANAGER
Lissa Pattillo

MANAGING EDITOR
Julie Davis

ASSOCIATE PUBLISHER
Adam Arnold

PUBLISHER
Jason DeAngelis

CENTAUR NO NAYAMI VOLUME 18
© KEI MURAYAMA 2019
Originally published in Japan in 2019 by TOKUMA SHOTEN PUBLISHING
CO., LTD., Tokyo. English translation rights arranged with TOKUMA SHOTEN
PUBLISHING CO., LTD., Tokyo, through TOHAN CORPORATION, Tokyo.

Seven Seas press and purchase enquiries can be sent to Marketing Manager
Lianne Sentar at press@gomanga.com. Information regarding the distribution
and purchase of digital editions is available from Digital Manager CK Russell
at digital@gomanga.com.

Seven Seas and the Seven Seas logo are trademarks of
Seven Seas Entertainment. All rights reserved.

ISBN: 978-1-64505-471-9

Printed in Canada

First Printing: June 2020

10 9 8 7 6 5 4 3 2 1

FOLLOW US ONLINE: www.sevenseasentertainment.com

READING DIRECTIONS

This book reads from *right to left*, Japanese style.
If this is your first time reading manga, you start
reading from the top right panel on each page and
take it from there. If you get lost, just follow the
numbered diagram here. It may seem backwards at
first, but you'll get the hang of it! Have fun!!